To love, to honor . . .
To die.

The wife had made their house the shining centerpiece of her life and marriage. On March 6, 1996, everyone who knew her would have sworn that no place on earth could be safer than this idyllic home. Even the person stalking across the living area toward her as she raptly played the piano would have noticed the neatness of the room. Everything was in order. There was no clutter here.

She was a petite woman. Had she been larger or more athletic, the well-placed blow—from a foot-and-a-half length of two-inch pipe—would still have rendered her helpless. She recoiled from the force of the blow, her wound splattering a thin spray of blood on the ivory keys. More blows rained down on the back of her head. She fell to the floor. Even as she lay motionless, the attacker repeatedly pounded her.

The body was lying in front of the piano, blood oozing onto the carpet. The killer went to the kitchen. On the counter, a butcher block held a set of cutlery, including a razor-sharp carving knife . . .

When the story hit the daily paper, the headline voiced the anguish of many in Austin and the larger Texas evangelical community, where the victim and her work were widely known. The big red letters on the newspaper's front page screamed the question:

WHY?

Books by Clint Richmond

NONFICTION

The Good Wife:
The Shocking Betrayal and Brutal Murder
of a Godly Woman in Texas

*Red Star Rogue**

Willie Nelson

*Symphony of Spirits**

*False Prophets**

Selena!

Colorado:
Living and Working in the Rockies

Denver:
Mile High Center of Enterprise

**Written by Richmond in collaboration*
with other authors.

THE
GOOD WIFE

THE SHOCKING BETRAYAL
AND BRUTAL MURDER
OF A GODLY WOMAN IN TEXAS

CLINT RICHMOND

HARPER

An Imprint of HarperCollinsPublishers

The Good Wife is a journalistic account of the actual murder investigation of Roger Scaggs for the 1996 killing of Penny Scaggs in Austin, Texas. The events recounted in this book are true. The personalities, events, actions, and conversations in this book have been constructed using court documents, including trial transcripts, extensive interviews, letters, personal papers, research, and press accounts. Quoted testimony has been taken verbatim from court transcripts and other sworn statements.

HARPER

An Imprint of HarperCollins*Publishers*
195 Broadway
New York, NY, 10007

Copyright © 2007 by Clint Richmond
ISBN: 978-0-380-79743-1
ISBN-10: 0-380-79743-7

First Harper paperback printing: August 2007

HarperCollins® and Harper® are trademarks of HarperCollins Publishers.

Printed in the United States of America

Visit Harper paperbacks on the World Wide Web at
www.harpercollins.com

10 9 8 7 6 5 4

Acknowledgments

More than fourteen thousand people are murdered in the United States every year, most by someone who knows them. Yet few of these homicides seem to have a lasting impact on the communities where they occur. Fewer still draw national media attention.

The murder of Penny Scaggs in Austin, Texas, on March 6, 1996, and the trial of her husband Roger in late 1998, was an exception. This tragic incident profoundly affected the lives of many people in the community and gained national media coverage, because it happened to affluent people living in an upscale community that was supposedly insulated against such brutal crimes.

The victim devoted most of her adult life to teaching young Texas women how to apply biblical values to marriage. The accused killer was her husband—the patriarchal head of the household, a pillar of the church, and a highly respected corporate executive.

It was because this couple's seemingly perfect marriage and stellar lives touched so many that the crime made the headlines. And it was this notoriety that brought forth the depth of sworn testimony from friends, neighbors, fellow congregants, and family that made the reconstruction of the couple's lives possible in this book. Many of these witnesses, who had been friends or associates of both the Scaggses, testified at trial under obvious stress and emotional pain about the happy years, the unraveling of the "perfect marriage," and the tragic ending.

Beyond the details provided in the testimony, others who knew Penny and Roger shared with me their recollections about this family. Some of those interviewed have agreed to be identified; others did not wish to be named. I scrupulously honored their wishes to remain anonymous, and appreciate those unnamed in the text who shared experiences and insights. I also understand why some family members declined to be interviewed for this book and did not wish to relive those times. In such cases, only the public testimony of those family members was used, when it was material to the case.

The Austin Police Department arranged for interviews with investigators and provided records and assistance with technical information. Homicide detective Sgt. David Carter, in particular, offered valuable insights in a post-trial interview. The legal professionals involved in this case, including Judge Jon Wisser and the court's staff; prosecutors Buddy Meyer and Bryan Case and staff of the Travis County district attorney; and defense lawyers Roy Minton, Charles Burton, Randy Leavitt, Joe Turner, and Terry Kirk, were always willing to take time from busy schedules to explain fine points of the law or interpret complex forensic evidence. Likewise, medical examiner Roberto Bayardo was very helpful in our interview and in providing documentation about the case. Any misinterpretations I may have made in translating this technical information to the page, on either forensics or law, are mine.

A number of talented and professional reporters from local and national news media shared their investigative findings about the case. Their contributions to a better public understanding of this tragic story have been noted, with attribution to the individual reporters and their news organization.

As with most nonfiction books, many sets of eyes and hands were needed to bring the story to the readers.

Jim Hornfischer, of Hornfischer Literary Management, placed this story with Avon Books prior to its acquisition by News Corp. as an imprint of HarperCollins.

Senior editor Sarah Durand persevered through long delays preceding the trial and further delays during the several years of appeals. Her willingness to wait until the full story could be told and her excellent editorial suggestions made this a better book.

A special thanks to editorial assistant Emily Krump, who coordinated the project, publisher Liate Stehlik, and executive managing editor Anne Marie Spagnuolo; as well as the Harper team in marketing and sales, including marketing director Adrienne Di Pietro, and Kristine Macrides, Mike Spradlin, Carla Parker, and Brian Grogan.

Chapter 1

*Who can find a virtuous woman, for her price is far
above rubies. The heart of her husband doth safely trust
in her, so that he shall have no need of spoil.*

—PROVERBS 31:10-11

Music filled the spacious home in the upscale suburb of
Austin—a religious hymn, expertly played on a perfectly
tuned piano.

The sun was setting when the slender blond woman began
practicing the piece on the pale yellow, baby grand piano.
Her deftness at the keyboard was almost professional; but
she devoted her musical talent, as with many of her other
well-rehearsed skills, to serving others. In the case of her
music, it was a weekly recital, played for elderly residents of
a nearby nursing home. She spoke of her volunteer work as
"my ministry."

Playing for the old folks was the least of her ministrations. She was also a Sunday school teacher at an evangelical church and a mentor to young wives and soon-to-be
married women who wanted to create godly marriages and
perfect Christian homes. Though she was middle-aged, her
eager young domestic disciples considered her one of them.
She stayed youthful by keeping herself well groomed and
physically fit. She was not beautiful in the classical sense,

but radiated a bubbly personality and vitality that made her pertly attractive.

As she focused attention on her playing, there was no reason to be distracted by the occasional rattling of the windows from the gusting winds of a cold front moving into the area. These familiar noises, and the swelling chords of her own music, most likely muffled any sounds made carelessly by the stealthy figure approaching slowly from behind her. She was alone, she thought. After an early dinner, her husband had returned to the office to finish a project, due the next morning.

She was accustomed to his demanding work schedule, the long hours and frequent travel required by his steady climb up the corporate ladder to a chief executive position. After his years of diligent toil, supported by what their friends described as the "perfect marriage," the family seemed to have attained the American dream.

Their lives in the affluent, professional circles of Austin reflected that success. The wife had made their house the shining centerpiece of her life and marriage. On March 6, 1996, everyone who knew her would have sworn that no place on earth could be safer than this idyllic home.

Even the person stalking across the living area toward the woman raptly playing the piano would have noticed the neatness of the rooms. Everything was in order. There was no clutter here.

An observer would have thus found it almost preposterous to see that the intruder carried a foot-and-a-half length of two-inch industrial pipe. Such an odd piece of plumbing had no practical use anywhere on this property. Cap seals screwed on both ends made it look more like a component designed for bomb-making than for any household purpose.

The ugly gray pipe may have been out of place among the fine bric-a-brac decorating the room, but it had its purpose now.

The intruder came closer, towering above the woman seated low on the piano bench. The heavy pipe arched upward and then swung sharply into the right side of the woman's head. The powerful blow was delivered with such force that it fractured her jaw. It tore an earring loose, sending it flying, and severed the right earlobe holding the jewelry. As her right hand went up, she was slammed again.

She was a fairly petite woman, five feet six and a half inches tall, and weighed 120 pounds. But even had she been larger or more athletic, the well-placed blow would have rendered her helpless to fight back. She recoiled from the force of the attack, her wound splattering a thin spray of blood on the ivory keys. More blows rained down on the back of her head.

As she fell from the bench to the floor, the attacker repeatedly pounded her, some of the blows glancing off other parts of her body—her wrist, her thigh, her shoulder and foot. Though the woman lay motionless, the assailant continued to strike her. One blow smashed the base of her skull, causing a bit of bone to protrude through the scalp.

The body was lying in front of the piano, blood oozing into the carpet. The killer went to the kitchen. On the counter, a butcher block held a set of cutlery.

Armed with a carving knife, the assailant returned and poked the point of the knife twice into the flesh of her back, to see if any life could be stirred from the now still corpse. Then the killer rolled her over and began an even more frenzied attack, stabbing and slashing at her upper chest, neck, and throat. Her body took eight knife wounds, two so deep they went through her chest. Her throat was slashed.

After the assault, the killer walked back into the kitchen and washed off the pipe and the knife. Expensive jewelry—including a diamond necklace, a diamond tennis bracelet, and a two-karat diamond ring—was removed from the woman's body.

As she lay dead in the large living area, her belongings were ransacked. Jewelry boxes from the master bedroom were emptied into the sunken bathtub and strewn about the main bathroom. It was a hodgepodge of baubles. There was little of value, mostly costume jewelry and small souvenirs.

A black and green garbage bag was used to stow the few pieces of real jewelry, the pipe, the kitchen knife, and five surgical latex gloves.

The killer left under cover of darkness, as lights began to appear through the picture windows of the neighboring homes. A winter storm was now howling in full fury down the usually quiet, tree-lined street, with winds gusting to thirty miles an hour. No neighbor ventured out into the well-groomed yards in such a gathering chill. No one saw the intruder enter. No one saw the killer leave.

After the husband returned home to find the body, and the police had arrived, alarm spread quickly down the block. The savagery of the murder, the gross overkill, bore the hallmarks of a deranged maniac. Nothing like it had happened in recent memory in this almost crimeless suburban neighborhood.

*I*n the early days of Austin, unsolved murders abounded in this area south and west of the river, a place where renegades, moonshiners, and transient cedar-choppers had made their camps. Gradually, civilization came, with the demands for growth turning this wilderness area into a neighborhood of low-cost homes. Still, the settlers living in genteel poverty maintained a degree of harmony with the natural environment. It was only more recently that the lush, natural surroundings had been drastically altered to make way for rapid population expansion and economic progress.

Old-timers from the neighborhood whispered that nothing good would come of cutting down an enormous live oak tree that had become a local landmark. For generations the tree had been home to a ghostly female apparition, undoubtedly the victim of some forgotten violence. The gnarled old tree had weathered much during the century and a half it took to transform Austin from the sleepy capital of frontier

Texas to a modern mecca for international microchip and personal-computer makers. But like so much else that had made Austin quaint, the tree and its ghostly spirit fell before modernity's bulldozers when the vanguard of the great boom years arrived in the early 1980s with the high-technology revolution.

In the recent past, heirs of the early squatters, who had first claimed the home sites in this part of town more than a hundred years earlier, were gradually forced out of their comfortable but dilapidated neighborhood by nothing more sinister than soaring land values. The land immediately across the Colorado River from bustling downtown Austin had grown too valuable for the cluster of small whitewashed houses in the neighborhood surrounding the ancient tree. When the well-compensated owners left the area, and the giant oak tree was felled for a new road, its secrets disappeared, along with the oral histories of the area.

Many of those living near the tree at Old Walsh Tarlton Lane and Bee Caves Road could personally have attested to having seen the woman's ghost, on nights when the moon was full. The silvery figure was said to move slowly, coming up from Town Lake through the dense cedar thickets, to enter the giant oak as casually as a neighbor might cross the road to return home after a social visit. There were no reports that the forlorn spirit had ever threatened anyone in the neighborhood. She was just another of the benign souls whose complaints about "progress" were silent; or, if signaled at all, were etched on frowning brows rather than demonstrated in overt acts of protest or lawsuits that would eventually characterize Austin's antigrowth movements.

Those protests would come much later, after the first waves of techies and managers had taken possession of the emerging neighborhoods and then decided to pull up the ladder to keep others from overcrowding their newfound paradise.

Modernization, once set in motion, moved quickly to scour the scenic hills across the river from Austin, leaving them devoid of any historic marker. Only the stately homes of the old rich, situated in central Austin around the pink granite Texas Capitol Building and the sprawling University of Texas neighborhoods, stayed as reminders that there had even been an earlier time in Austin. Almost everything else could be dated A.D., for "after Dell," and the beginning of the computer era.

The choicest new home sites in the boom of the eighties were along the rims of the hills, looking down on the construction cranes busily altering the city skyline to accommodate the progress. The hilltop above the old ghost oak on Bee Cave Road was no exception.

At the very highest point was a two-level brick house on a new street called Winter Park Road. Street names in this exclusive subdivision had nothing to do with the rich history of Austin; in fact, quite the contrary. The spacious homes on large lots were clustered around winding roads named for Rocky Mountain ski resorts, even though it never snowed here. Some few environmentally aware developers tried, as much as financially practical, to keep the natural landscape of native oaks and cedars, as they bulldozed the home sites from the white chalk hills. This particular quarter-acre lot overlooked the emerging Austin skyline on the horizon, four miles to the northeast. If the vista was dimmed a bit during the day by the growing emissions from traffic jams, the night view was nothing short of spectacular.

While the subdivision was technically within the Austin city limits, it was surrounded by the prestigious Westlake community, buffered from lesser south Austin neighborhoods by the new six-lane highway Loop 1, also known as the MoPac Expressway. In that name, at least, some small history was preserved. MoPac is an acronym for Missouri-Pacific, the old railroad whose tracks run alongside the roadway.

The winding Colorado River, dammed many years earlier to form Lake Austin and Town Lake, was the other boundary of the new community. These small urban lakes were the last and lowest pair of a pearl-like string of waterways that were the legacy of Lyndon Baines Johnson and other powerful Texas politicians of the post-Depression era. The string of lakes, reaching all the way from Austin to the heart of the Edwards Plateau region west of the state capital, were collectively known as the Highland Lakes. Their strategic location was key to Austin's self-promoted image as the best place in America to live, play, and raise a family.

The upscale subdivisions referred to by Austinites simply as the "West Side" rose high in the foothills above and around the southwestern rim of the old city, founded in the early 1800s by enterprising American pioneers known as *impresarios*. They had come to Mexico's Tejas territory to settle on large land grants from the Mexican government. One of the greatest of these colonists was Stephen F. Austin, for whom the city was named. But these earliest pioneers, more practical than the boomers of the 1980s, had settled in the rich Colorado River valley and on arable blackland prairie, extending all the way from the hills of Austin to Matagorda Bay, 150 miles south, on the Gulf of Mexico.

The West Side, back then, was the beginning of Comanche country. Waves of mostly Anglo immigrants followed, until the sleepy little Texas state capital grew into a minor metropolis peopled by politicians, college professors and schoolteachers, retailers, business and association executives, and all the supporting craftsmen, clerks, and laborers it took to run a fair-sized city. Almost all of these first arrivals were satisfied to live down on the flatlands, where the city was laid out neatly along the river and the early railroads.

The families that relocated to the area in the 1980s might be described as the new rich; people who preferred the scenic, open environment of the Hill Country, and who could afford the view from the heights that looked down on the city skyline and the citizens living below. It was as if the developers had carved a special citadel from the beautiful highlands, with the river serving as a moat, to create a lifestyle sheltered from the emerging urban problems of crime and congestion.

The man-made serenity and security promised by that place were shattered one wintry evening in 1996 by a single violent event. The brutal murder that occurred there introduced fear for the first time to the families living nearby. Its lingering aftermath threatened to tarnish the image of Austin's high-tech business leadership, and tested the faith of many in Texas's evangelical Christian community.

Chapter 2

*She will do him good and not evil all the days of her life.
She seeketh wool, and flax, and worketh willingly with
her hands.*

—PROVERBS 31:12-13

*E*lizabeth Trower had been absorbed in pulling weeds
around the early summer flowers blooming in front of her
newly leased luxury duplex on Holly Hill Drive when a
shadow loomed over the small garden plot she was working.
Startled, she looked up to see what appeared to be a tall
blond woman standing between her and the late afternoon
sun.

"Hi, I'm your new neighbor," the woman said, introduc-
ing herself as Penny Scaggs, in a cheery voice with an almost familiar accent. "I live just across the street, there on
the corner." She motioned with her hand toward a stately
house on Winter Park Road.

Elizabeth rose from her knees, brushing the loose soil
from her hands. As she stood, she realized the woman was
not nearly as tall as she first appeared. She was no more
than five-foot-six or -seven, slim and attractive in a fresh-
scrubbed, permanently groomed kind of way.

After a few sentences of idle chat about the neighborhood,
the two women shared information on their respective fami-

lies. Penny said her husband was a vice president at a nearby tech company, which Elizabeth had never heard of, and that the couple had a twelve-year-old daughter. Elizabeth said she was a divorced single mother raising four children. She thought the other woman's brow furrowed a bit at the mention of divorce—but just for an instant. She went on to tell the friendly stranger that she worked in the administrative section in the Office of the Governor of Texas at the state capital, downtown.

It was their next exchange that was the catalyst for what was to be an enduring friendship.

"Where are you from?" Penny asked. "Seems like everyone I meet in Austin is originally from somewhere else."

"Well, I've lived all over the United States and traveled a lot," said Elizabeth. "I was born in California, but I was raised in Tulsa, Oklahoma."

The blond woman let out a squeal of delight. "Tulsa, Tulsa! That's where *I'm* from—originally. My husband and I have been traveling, too. We moved twelve times in the first thirteen years we were married. But Tulsa will always be home."

The women discovered they were fellow alumnae, having graduated from Central High School in Tulsa just two years apart. Penny excitedly told Elizabeth that she was going back for the twenty-five-year reunion of the class of '59 in a few weeks.

"I would have been a senior at Tulsa Central when you were a sophomore," Trower confirmed. She quickly learned that Penny Scaggs was originally Lou Anne Ehrle, one of four daughters of the owner of Ehrle's Party and Carnival Supplies store in downtown Tulsa.

"Of course, I knew it well," Trower said. "Whenever there was a birthday or sorority party, we all headed to Ehrle's for our decorations and favors. I bet I've been in there a hundred times."

Names of people, places, and events flowed rapidly, as the new neighbors and former Oklahomans compared memories both had left behind more than two decades before. Suddenly, Penny Scaggs glanced at her watch and let out another little shriek—this one of alarm.

"Oh, my, it's almost five o'clock. Roger will be coming home from work any minute. I've got to run and get things ready for my husband."

"Is this some special occasion?" Trower asked.

No, it was not, the now flustered woman replied, hurriedly saying her good-byes and glad-to-meet-you's before almost running across the street to her house. But before she broke away, she extracted a promise from Trower that the two would get together soon to talk about Tulsa.

The city of Tulsa, it would turn out, loomed large in the life of Penny Scaggs, as would her adopted new home of Austin, Texas. Indeed, in many ways her life story would be a reflection of these two, midsized, middle-American cities. But of the two, Tulsa was her true teacher, with its conservative, religious environment providing the values she espoused throughout her life.

A strong sense of place has an essential role in the development of the character and personality of most individuals. And the majority of Americans—be they native New Yorkers, Angelenos, Hoosiers, or Texans—carry the place where they grew up deep in the fiber of their being and as close as their skin, throughout all the days of their lives. The farmer-poet and philosopher Wendell Berry said, "With a sense of place, your identity is defined . . . Without a sense of place, what will fill the void?"

Austin and Tulsa, in the middle years of the twentieth century when Penny was growing up, were almost identical in size, with rapidly growing populations of almost 400,000 people. They were both situated on major rivers, Tulsa on the Arkansas and Austin on the Colorado. But there the similarities ended.

Tulsa's contribution to music was singer Anita Bryant, who graduated from a Tulsa high school and became Miss Oklahoma, just as Penny and Elizabeth were spending their teen years there. Anita Bryant's claim to fame and controversy was earned through her popularizing songs of old-time religion and Christian-right political crusades. At the time, Austin's contemporary diva was Janis Joplin, whose new rock music provided part of the soundtrack for the sexual revolution and generational wars that characterized America in the sixties.

Tulsa had a score of universities, colleges, and seminaries, almost all of which were established and run by Christian denominations. The Austin area had a score of advanced educational institutions, too; but most of the student population was enrolled in public colleges and tax-supported universities. Austin's most famous personality at the time was Willie Nelson, renegade songwriter and leader of the outlaw musicians who had fled the Nashville scene. Tulsa's was the Reverend Oral Roberts, faith healer and founder of American televangelism. Conservative radio commentator Paul Harvey went on the air for the first time in 1933, while still a student at Tulsa's Central High School.

For Penny Scaggs, the place that defined her would always be Tulsa, Oklahoma, although she and her husband had traveled widely around the world and lived in many American cities before settling down in Austin in 1984. Long after they moved into their new house in one of the most desirable cities in Texas, she often returned to visit her hometown, and spoke of it frequently as she made new friends.

*L*ou Anne Ehrle was born in a Tulsa hospital on November 3, 1941, the first child of Sylvester Louis (who went by S. L.) and Armitta (née Randle) Ehrle. The Ehrles had moved to Tulsa soon after their marriage in Childress, Texas, on May 10, 1939. When a nurse brought the baby to her waiting parents, she commented that the infant was as "bright and pretty as a new penny," and the nickname stuck. Forever after, a widening circle of relatives, friends, and acquaintances called her Penny, until most people outside her immediate family never even knew her real name. Throughout the years, the moniker given to the infant continued to reflect the vibrant, shining personality of the child, the young girl, and, ultimately, the woman she would become.

After Penny, three more daughters were born to the Ehrles in Tulsa. Sister Sharon arrived four and a half years later, followed by twins Marilyn and Carolyn in 1950. Their mother, affectionately known as Mittie, was forty when she had the twins; and Penny, as the eldest, naturally assumed a role as caretaker of the younger girls. Years after they had all left Tulsa for homes and careers in other places, she was still always ready to help her sisters whenever she was needed. The four girls were especially close, and even when thousands of miles apart, kept in almost weekly contact.

Penny's big-sister responsibilities did not prevent her from becoming socially involved in the Tulsa teen community, within the restrictions of the Southern Baptist traditions. The family was active in the First Baptist Church of Tulsa. Since most of the citizens of Tulsa were also Baptists, there were plenty of things for a teen to do in this midsize city in the fifties. The other lesser but still sizable Protestant congregations of Methodists and Presbyterians were considered a little loose morally, and some thought the Episcopalians downright hedonistic.

The Beatles had not yet invaded America, and, at least in Tulsa, Elvis and Buddy Holly singles were practically sold from under the counter by local record stores. Dancing was frowned upon, especially "slow" dancing, and movies were screened carefully before they were even brought to town. Necking or heavy petting was an absolute no-no, and girls who allowed the dating rules to be broken were usually found out and marked for the rest of their high school years. Teens lived under a strict code of conduct that mandated a shotgun wedding as the only remedy for a careless act in the backseat of a car at the drive-in theater. There were no exceptions and no abortions.

Dress codes were not a problem at Tulsa Central, since high-neck blouses, sweater sets, saddle shoes, and crinoline slips under long skirts were the fads of the day. Drinking alcohol was taboo among most of the student population, and the use of illicit drugs was still unheard of. Even boys smoking cigarettes behind the school gym was frowned upon by many of the Baptist girls, who had heard it preached that "smoking may not send you to hell, but it will make you smell like you've been there." Television was not yet a moral concern for middle-American parents, since everything aired locally would have earned today's G rating, anyway.

Still, there were plenty of things to keep a teenager busy. All told, there were thirty-nine student clubs and organizations involved in extracurricular activities other than varsity sports at Tulsa Central—everything from rifle teams to girls' clubs that were called sororities. Penny was a member of the Red Feathers, a team-spirit club that raised money for social events and boosted the sports teams known as the Central High Braves. She loved music and was dedicated to her organ lessons.

Because Papa Ehrle owned a well-established small business, the family was considered upper-middle class, and Penny's formative years were financially comfortable, though certainly not extravagant. Her childhood in the mom-and-apple-pie town of Tulsa during the booming post–World War II era could have been right out of an episode of *Father Knows Best*. A middle-class upbringing at that time might be considered dull or boring to some, but it was characterized by a naive innocence rarely instilled anywhere, before or since. This community wholesomeness was further enhanced by Tulsa's reputation as the unofficial capital of the Bible Belt. Most citizens considered it a great place and time to raise a family.

The era was, however, about to end in Tulsa and across the rest of hinterland America, with the advent of the 1960s. Penny also was about to leave the protective environment of small-town America and move out into a bigger, more troubled world, where her sheltered upbringing had not adequately prepared her to cope with the new realities.

*P*enny Ehrle graduated from Central High School in May 1959 and continued her education across town at the University of Tulsa. Soon after enrolling as a freshman at the four-thousand-student TU campus, she became actively involved in student activities and was invited to join the Delta Gamma sorority. At one school function, Penny met Roger Thomas Scaggs, a six-foot-one, good-looking upperclassman from Fort Worth, Texas. Roger, twenty, and Penny, eighteen, hit it off from their earliest dates and were soon going steady. Her sister Sharon remembered that for the next two years Penny's beau became something of a fixture around the Ehrle home in Tulsa. He was a junior majoring in management and marketing the year the couple began dating, and was enrolled in the university's Reserve Officer Training Corps. In his senior year, Roger was elected president of Alpha Tau Omega fraternity.

Roger was one of three brothers from a middle-class family that had long been associated with the Texas and Oklahoma oil industry. He was born in Tulsa on June 17, 1939, but reared in Fort Worth. His father was a mechanical engineer for Amoco Oil. His whole family—parents Dorothy and Wilburt, and younger brothers Phillip and Tom—still lived in Fort Worth, a four-hour drive away, when Roger began courting Penny.

Penny and Roger were married on April 4, 1961. Immediately after graduating summa cum laude from TU that spring, Roger went into the United States Air Force as a commissioned second lieutenant to serve his four-year ROTC obligation. Penny, having completed her sophomore year, left college to become a full-time wife, although she did hold various office jobs for short periods in the early years of their marriage.

In the Air Force, Roger became immersed in what was

probably the world's most sophisticated hands-on application of the rapidly growing field of high technology—computer sciences. Penny was by his side when he was sent to intensive computer training at a secret government facility near Roswell, New Mexico, where he was stationed as a second lieutenant from 1961 to 1963.

He was then assigned to a regular tour of duty at Tachikawa Air Force Base outside Tokyo, Japan, where he was promoted to first lieutenant and served until 1965. The sprawling military base was not only one of the busiest U.S. sites for strategic bombers in the Pacific, but also one of the largest Department of Defense computer centers in the world. Roger served as a logistics/computer specialist at the Air Force base. It was the site of frequent picketing by anti-American Japanese, with several violent demonstrations just outside the gates. For that reason, all but the most intrepid Americans assigned there stayed close to base during their tours of duty.

In Japan, Roger and Penny became friends with another young lieutenant and his wife. They met William and Nancy Snead in a neighborhood of officers' housing and started a close friendship that would last a lifetime. The Sneads got to know them as a happily married and ambitious young couple.

Though Roger was in the military with the command authority of an officer, he was an easygoing and fun-loving person.

"In all those years," Snead recalled, "I've never seen Roger angry."

"We were newlyweds together at the same time," Nancy Snead said. "We visited back and forth and we vacationed with them." She, too, remembered the Scaggses during their earliest years of married life as a fun and happy couple.

Bill Snead, who was from Georgetown, Texas, a county seat forty miles north of Austin, had always planned to return home when his hitch was up, to take over the family-owned crushed-stone business. But Roger and Penny had many more miles to travel before finally settling down. The Sneads would renew their acquaintance with the Scaggses years later.

After Roger completed his military obligation, he and Penny returned to the United States. Roger held jobs in computer technology with IBM and Haggar Clothing in Dallas from 1965 to 1969, when he joined a small computer company, URS Systems, Inc. The company, which did government and military contract work, assigned him to a position at Fort Hood, Texas.

While living in nearby Killeen, the Scaggses met Joe Edwards and his wife Sidney, who also remained lifetime friends. The depth of that friendship would be tested and proved many years later, through the darkest of Roger's days.

Roger's job with URS Systems led to a government contract post in Vietnam, where the U.S. was getting more deeply mired in a hopeless war. Roger's work was apparently safe enough, since Penny went with him to one of the burgeoning U.S. logistical bases near Saigon. During that period, Roger built his credentials and reputation in the computer field, working with some of the leading American companies in the industry.

But no matter how far the young couple traveled, Penny never lost touch with her family.

"Penny was a wonderful correspondent," said sister Sharon. "She wrote once or twice a week and wanted to know everything that was going on in the family."

Once Penny and Roger were stateside again, this close contact continued even as they moved from city to city to accommodate Roger's career. He worked in several high-tech jobs before settling into a position as systems engineering specialist in Ross Perot's Electronic Data Systems Corporation. After he joined EDS in November 1971, he and Penny moved to Plano, Texas, a high-tech center on the northern outskirts of Dallas where the company was headquartered. But the couple still traveled extensively for EDS.

On an assignment in Topeka, Kansas, in 1972, they adopted an infant daughter shortly after the baby was born on August 25. They named their daughter Sarah. The family soon moved to Yorktown in Westchester County, New York, where they stayed almost three years before returning to Plano.

Wherever she lived, Penny was never far removed from her sisters and parents by phone, mail—including tape-recorded messages—and frequent trips home.

"She always wanted to be home for Christmas for sure, and any other events whenever possible," Sharon recalled. "May was a big month for family get-togethers: Mother's Day, Mother's birthday, and our parents' anniversary. November was another month for visiting, because there were other birthdays clustered then. We were a very close, very open and sharing family."

There was one constant in Penny's marriage that all her sisters noticed. She would never come for a visit without Roger, unless she had made elaborate arrangements to take care of him in her absence. "She was an extremely loving, caring, doting wife," sister Sharon recalled. "If Roger wasn't along on her visits or traveling somewhere else himself, she made sure everything he would need in her absence was provided at their home before leaving."

Since Penny seldom worked outside the home, the household responsibilities were solely hers, and her day-to-day routine was designed to support Roger's work schedule and needs.

Perot's pioneering computer service company was less than ten years old when Roger was recruited. And "recruited" was the right term for the bright young men who went to work for EDS in those days, because a person had to be asked to join that elite crew. Perot called these recruits his "eagles" and defined them as "high fliers." The motto of EDS during those early years was: "Eagles don't flock—you have to find them one at a time."

Most of the supersalesmen and computer wizards at EDS

were ex-servicemen, many of them recent combat veterans with experience in Vietnam. The workforce operated much like a large military unit, running not so much on strict discipline as on a gung-ho esprit de corps. The company, which was built around a niche of the booming computer industry that had been ignored by the giants like IBM, went public on the New York Stock Exchange in 1971, the year Roger joined. The piece of the business that Perot and his eagles focused on was computer service, the 20 percent of the computer market that involved people who knew how to make the technology work. Nearly every medium-sized and large company in America wanted to computerize, and there was an acute shortage of experts who knew how to use these marvelous machines. EDS simply provided the teams to the companies that were buying the main frames.

"It became more and more obvious to me—people were buying the hardware, but they didn't know how to use it," Ross Perot told Crayton Harrison of the *Dallas Morning News* in an interview four decades after the successful launch of his multibillion-dollar company. "What they really wanted were systems that worked."

Perot's second secret to success was the people he hired. "We looked for people who couldn't live with themselves if they weren't winning. We just did not want anybody [who was] indifferent."

The EDS staff operated like a cohesive unit or family, people who "worked tirelessly together as a team." The team included not only the men and few women working at EDS, but their spouses, children, and dependent parents, as well. Most employees shared generously in stock ownership of the company, and their personal and private needs were also considered part of the company's embrace. Roger worked directly with Perot on one such "fringe benefit" in 1979, when he was tapped to organize a junket to Miami for 150 key EDS employees to attend Super Bowl XIII between the Dallas Cowboys and the Pittsburgh Steelers.

"I'll tell you the secret to what made the company successful," Perot confided. "It all came down to the spirit of the people within the company. We built a company with huge spirit."

In 1978, while Roger Scaggs was a manager at EDS, the Iranian Revolution caught up several EDS executives and their families in Tehran. Though the company moved mountains to have the families and most of the employees evacuated, two executives who were operating health-care computer systems for the former Shah's government were arrested by radical Islamists in the new regime. When it was clear that the U.S. State Department would be unable to free the men, Perot swung into action. He mobilized key members of his EDS staff and hired a retired Green Beret colonel to form a rescue team. Their mission was to go into revolution-torn Iran, break his men out of prison, and take them, over land, out of Iran into Turkey. Perot himself was waiting at the Turkish border for the courageous corporate rescue team.

To accomplish this feat, EDS had shut down its worldwide operations and put every available human resource at the headquarters in Plano into a support role for the mission. Roger Scaggs's logistical training in the military, as well as his management experience at the Plano headquarters, were called on during a planning phase of the bold operation. Perot asked him if he could provide high-frequency communications from Dallas to Iran and Turkey. Roger said he could create such a command center if needed, but the covert mission was accomplished without it. Years later, Roger never hesitated to let people know he had been a Perot man.

From the moment he joined EDS, Roger was very much a part of this new corporate environment. Of course, there was a quid pro quo for membership in this exclusive "club." EDS expected nothing less than a hundred percent from its employees and their families in exchange for the many perks, including a generous offer of participation in the EDS stock plan. That expectation of personal and family commitment had a downside, too. As with many jobs in the burgeoning new field of computer technology, the long hours, frequent travel on short notice, and being on 'round-the-clock call could be wearing on a family.

Whether it was because of Roger's demanding job or for some other reason, Penny would later tell friends that their marriage had hit a rocky patch. Without going into too much detail, she said marital discord and frequent verbal confrontations had threatened the relationship. The sexually permissive sixties and the complex workplace transitions of the seventies had wreaked havoc on American culture. Divorce rates were soaring, the traditional institution of marriage was challenged, and the Scaggs marriage fell prey to the stresses.

During this troubled period, Penny Scaggs met a woman who would have a profound and lasting impact on her life and marriage. Author, family counselor, and lecturer Linda Dillow lived in nearby Richardson, Texas, just a dozen miles down the highway from the Scaggs home in Plano. Penny was introduced to Dillow and attended one of her workshops on creating a Christian marriage. She became a devoted student and enthusiastic early adherent in a small but growing reactionary movement to restore traditional American marriage to its Old Testament roots. Conspicuous in the language of the cause was putting "obey" back in the wedding vows, in an era when many young women were clamoring for more equality in the workplace and the home.

Without any formal announcement to friends or family, Lou Anne Ehrle Scaggs set out on what she described as "my ministry"—a journey that was to occupy the rest of her life, and possibly even become a contributing factor in her untimely death.

Chapter 3

She is like the merchants' ships; she bringeth her food from afar. She riseth also while it is yet night, and giveth meat to her household, and a portion to her maidens.

—PROVERBS 31:14-15

The victory celebrations at EDS headquarters in late February 1979 for the breathtaking rescue of their fellow employees from Iran had hardly concluded when a local success of quite another sort was unfolding a short distance away, on the outskirts of Plano. This event was centered on a location that would become internationally famous as "Southfork Ranch" and a fictional family that would soon be a household name—the Ewing family of Dallas.

Dallas, a nighttime television soap opera starring Larry Hagman as the Texas business tycoon J. R. Ewing, was an instant hit, setting all kinds of ratings records. The show was lauded as the most successful serial drama in television history. Its central themes of corporate greed, marital promiscuity, and dysfunctional family seemed to resonate with a vast majority of TV viewers, who each week tuned in to watch in fascination as the Ewing family careened from one moral crisis to another. The fictitious drama presented a glamorized version of the real-life, topsy-turvy decade that was roiling the traditional family values of America.

The new television genre piqued the interest of the Scaggses and their friends and coworkers solely because of the Plano connection. Many of the scenes of Ewing family outings and work around Southfork Ranch were filmed at a mansion on a few acres just at the edge of town.

While the television drama might have made for good conversation, Penny's personal reality was accelerating in a diametrically opposite direction. Rather than passively watching the weekly dramatization of the Ewing brothers' fictitious, failing relationships, Penny was concerned with actively saving a real marriage—her own.

The road map for her new life course was Linda Dillow's best-selling self-help book, *Creative Counterpart,* first published in 1977. The teachings of Dillow and her disciples were a direct response to what they saw as the family-destroying fallout of the women's liberation movement of the sixties and seventies. The book's foreword challenged Christian women to fight back for traditional marriages and homemaking, based on biblical mandates.

Citing the recent "salvos from the women's rights crusade," the opening pages of the book warned, "We have been jarred from our complacency by spasms of ink-slinging feminists picking up their standards and marching . . ."

Thus, while a CBS production crew was filming one of the most popular and titillating television dramas yet to be brought into the American living room, Penny Scaggs and a small group of housewives were a short distance down the road, absorbed in devout Bible study to learn how they could turn the tide.

As an instructor, Linda Dillow was not strident or militant, like many of the antifeminist, anti-abortion crusaders who would soon rise up as vanguard for the politicized Christian Right backlash against the cultural changes taking place in America. She was a soft-spoken, inspirational lecturer who used her own marriage and child-rearing experiences as testament to the success a wife could expect from a biblical marriage. She was the wife of Joseph (Jody) Dillow, who would become president of the international educational ministry, BEE World—Biblical Education by Extension World—headquartered near Colorado Springs. The mission of BEE World is to train lay leaders and ministers working in predominately Islamic, Buddhist, or Hindu states where Christianity or Protestantism is usually unwelcome, and sometimes even persecuted. Like Penny and Roger, Linda and Jody had met and married while in college.

Linda Dillow's confidence-building, nonpreachy style won Penny to the cause. The Dillow teaching method meshed perfectly with Penny's cheerful, bubbly personality. Soon, she decided to do more than take home the lessons of building a Christian marriage, which she vowed to make central to her own relationship.

Penny heard the calling in *Creative Counterpart*, where Dillow wrote: "I asked God to use me in the lives of women—to teach, to train, to share the good news of eternal life in Jesus Christ." Penny wanted to bring the biblical message of the joys of living as a godly wife to other women in her circle of executive spouses. After further study, she became a teaching disciple in 1982, and began hosting classes in her Plano home.

In the meantime, Roger Scaggs had been offered the opportunity to get in on the ground floor with a strong ownership position in a start-up, management service company that appeared to have significant financial potential. This forced him to make a difficult decision. He would have to sever relations with the highly successful EDS and take a risk that the new company would be equally as career-enhancing.

Ross Perot took umbrage at any of his eagles leaving the nest to join the competition. Even though Perot himself had left IBM and taken his unique piece of the market with him to start EDS in 1961, he expected a more or less lifetime commitment from his employees and their families.

"It was almost as if Perot took it as a personal insult that someone should want to work elsewhere," wrote Ken Follett, whose 1983 best-seller, *On Wings of Eagles*, chronicled Perot's dramatic rescue of the EDS employees from Iran.

Leaving the EDS family was more like getting a divorce than changing jobs. There were reports of Perot wanting to remove employees' names from achievement plaques in company displays when the awardees left the corporate fold to take jobs with competitors.

Nevertheless, Roger dared incur Perot's wrath by making the drastic career move on August 25, 1980. He quit EDS and joined American Physicians Service Group, a fledgling company providing malpractice insurance management and financial services to doctors and the medical industry. APS was headquartered in Dallas at the time, but within a few years would move its corporate headquarters to the high-tech Texas boomtown of Austin, two hundred miles to the south. In those early years with APS, Roger earned rapid advancement up the executive ranks as he assumed wider responsibilities within the organization.

Roger welcomed the chance to leave the hassle of the congested and overpopulated Dallas–Fort Worth area for the more bucolic environs of Austin. The move offered him the ego-massaging opportunity to be a bigger fish in a smaller pond, as opposed to competing with the emerging technology titans in Dallas.

Whether Penny shared his enthusiasm for a move that would take her hundreds of miles farther from her younger sisters and aging parents in Tulsa is unknown. She would also be leaving her new ministry to women in the Plano area. And they would be uprooting daughter Sarah, who was then nearly twelve, separating her from friends she had known throughout her school years.

But having recently embraced a biblical interpretation of the obedient wife, Penny felt that such decisions were left up to the head of the household—the husband. So the Scaggs family moved to Austin in 1984 to start a new life.

In the mid-1980s home buyers coming into Austin's scenic hills west and south of the old town were mostly young and upwardly mobile. They included newly tenured academics from the universities, medical and legal professionals who had only recently hung up their shingles, retired military officers, and youngish executives from Austin's burgeoning high-technology industry. Roger and Penny Scaggs were typical of these newcomers.

The Hill Country subdivision they chose to live in was called Bee Cave Woods, where they ultimately made an offer on a hilltop house on Winter Park Road.

The neighborhood was located within the southwest city limits of Austin. More important, it was served by the most prestigious public school system in Central Texas, the Eanes Independent School District. If that suburban school system had largely escaped the earlier throes of racial integration in Texas, it was primarily because the average price of a home in the district at that time was over $280,000, which was extraordinarily high for the Austin area. However, equivalent homes in other high-tech centers like California's Silicon Valley were already selling for a million dollars, and people relocating enjoyed a bonanza when it came to Texas real-estate values.

There was another factor drawing the upper-middle-class newcomers to the area. Crime of any kind was nonexistent in these neighborhoods. As violent crime rates climbed with the population growth in Austin, the tony foothill subdivisions south and west of the city remained havens of security. Austin police and officers from the nearby suburb of West Lake Hills regularly patrolled the winding streets without having to respond to anything more serious than minor vandalism perpetrated by sometimes overindulged and bored Eanes teenagers.

If Austin was the town in which many Texans aspired to live, the neighborhood the Scaggses chose was the one most Austinites wished they could afford. Roger and Penny Scaggs *could* afford it. By then he was a member of APS se-

nior management, with the commensurate salary and benefits.

His company's new Austin headquarters were also located in the Hill Country, just five miles from the house they
decided to buy. Roger would easily be able to drive home for
lunch every day.

That part of the Hill Country was where the modern, new
campuslike high-tech parks were being constructed. In what
was half jokingly called "Silicon Gulch," a young Michael
Dell had barely moved his pacesetting personal-computer
company from a garage near the University of Texas into the
first of what was to become scores of clean manufacturing
plants.

Roger Scaggs was ranked among the innovators in applying computer technology to real-life, marketable products
and services, and was rapidly advancing within APS. A residence befitting the stature of the successful executive was
important to his image. The Scaggses closed the deal on the
house on Winter Park Road on June 8, 1984. Roger, Penny,
and Sarah moved in shortly afterward, and began to enjoy
what seemed to family, friends, and associates the ideal
American lifestyle. The imposing, two-story, 3,625-square-
foot-house was not a mansion, but was considered large at
that time. The circle drive to the portal-framed entryway
gave the house a stately appearance from the street. All the
homes along Winter Park Road and the crisscrossing
streets—Copper Mountain, Steamboat Springs, Crested
Butte—were, similarly, custom-built.

If the house gave Roger the prestige address to match his
position, it meant far more to Penny. It provided the foundation on which she built everything of value in her life. Under
her devoted ministrations, it became the sterling example of
the perfect, if somewhat materialistic, modern Christian
home.

As Penny set about turning the mere mortar and bricks
into a showcase of her beliefs and dreams, certainly the last

thing on her mind was some arcane ghost prowling the winding streets. It's doubtful she and Roger were even aware that, in the old days, there were reported sightings of a ghostly woman just at the bottom of their hill. Realtors, in general, don't mention tales of haunted places when extolling the features of their developments; and every trace of topography—historical or mythical—had been quickly plowed under and paved over, without so much as a pencil mark on a plat map. Even had the Scaggses heard the story before they moved in, they surely would have scoffed at such superstition. It was not until two years later that community historian Dorothy M. Depwe and writer Linda Vance reintroduced the specter in their book *Eanes: Portrait of a Community*. It is unlikely that Penny and Roger's busy neighbors, who were newcomers, too, had ever heard tell the ghostly tale.

The movers had barely unloaded their van before Penny set out to convert her new house into a model home. Roger may have been the head of the house, but Penny was in charge of the home, and she decorated it throughout in her favorite pale blue hues.

Despite the fact that Roger was drawing a good executive salary by Austin standards, Penny believed an important virtue of a good wife was frugality with household expenses. She drove all the way across Austin to the north side of town to stock up on supplies and groceries at Sam's Club, the giant discount warehouse. Within no time she had the house in order and ready for her husband and daughter to resume their normal lives. Her neighbors were amazed at how quickly she had unpacked all the boxes and put everything in place, as if a major move had never happened.

The American dream home was complete, right down to a dog for Sarah, a border collie named Duke, romping in the large, fenced-in backyard. With five bedrooms and four baths, the house provided each family member plenty of personal space. Roger took one bedroom for his home office, and Penny converted another to her arts-and-crafts room. Roger also had a well-outfitted workshop in the oversized garage.

On the first floor, an impressive den with a cathedral ceiling and brick fireplace served as the main living area. A two-story wall of windows looked out on a large redwood deck with built-in hot tub. The deck ran the entire length of the back of the house. When Penny was playing her piano, the sound carried from the den throughout the open floor plan, filling the house with music. She would build her life around that room.

Her second most important center of activity was the huge gourmet kitchen, complete with modern, built-in appliances and a twelve-foot utility island. The kitchen abutted the den. There was a formal dining room and a small, formal living room or reception area off the foyer. For privacy, the large master bedroom with adjoining master bath was also located downstairs.

A distinctive U-shaped staircase led from the ceramic-tiled foyer to the second floor, where the other four bedrooms were located. Another large room upstairs, equipped with television and stereo, was designed as a family media and recreation center.

Penny embellished the decor of the house with creative flower arrangements and small plaques inscribed with inspirational messages and quotes from the Bible. An expert calligrapher, she hand-lettered and painted the plaques, which she posted on cabinets and hung in various places around the house. She created a decorative calendar for the kitchen that offered, for each month, a different Bible verse on the Christian home and family. And she put the custom kitchen to good use, preparing almost all the family meals from scratch, with gourmet dinners and home-baked breads and pastries.

Her home was her sanctuary and she devoted herself to making it a perfect haven for her husband and daughter.

Diana and Arthur Coleman, who lived directly across the street from Roger and Penny, got to know the newcomers immediately after they moved to the area. The Colemans had recently moved there themselves. The two women soon bonded, and their husbands were friendly as well, "particularly in the early years," according to Arthur. A self-described "New York Jewish kid, who had never read a page of the New Testament," he converted to Christianity in late 1986. Afterward, he and Roger began attending the same Bible study fellowship, and drove there together almost every week. Arthur believed Penny had been instrumental in his conversion, more than he could ever know. "My guess is she prayed incessantly for it," he said.

"Penny viewed their house in a special way," Diana Coleman recalled. "She always felt God gave them the house to teach her courses [the Christian wife classes]. It had the large room at the center of the house that was big enough to accommodate a number of people for the classes."

The Scaggses quickly took steps to assimilate into their new community. Through his company, Roger applied for a family membership to the Barton Creek Country Club, and Penny found the family a permanent church home. Roger, Penny, and Sarah joined the congregation of the fastest-growing Baptist church in the Austin area. For Penny, who had been raised a Southern Baptist in Tulsa, it was a return to the flock. Roger had been raised in a more moderate Methodist denomination.

The Riverbend Church, founded in 1979 by Dr. Gerald Mann, had about 1,600 members when the Scaggses joined in 1984. Dr. Mann, the charismatic and controversial chaplain of the Texas Legislature, had presided over a split in the congregation at the University Baptist Church in a dispute over membership admission standards. When he left to form the new church, he took a good number of members from the old church with him. His new church had been given a large tract of valuable lakefront property by two developers, and used the proceeds from the sale of that land to build the first sanctuary at a scenic site on Lake Austin, a half mile south of the Heart of Texas Highway. The waterfront site had a breathtaking view of the Austin hills. Within a few years the congregation had swelled to more than eight thousand members.

But in the 1980s, when Roger and Penny were members and taught a couples' Sunday school class, the church was in rapid growth that required an almost continuous building program. Roger often complained to friends that the church was constantly pressing its members to make ever larger contributions to the building fund.

Dr. Mann, already a nationally known television personality and author of religious publications, later would gain added fame as a minister who counseled President Bill Clinton in the White House, after he confessed to the Monica Lewinsky affair.

While Roger and Penny were active in the Austin church, the Southern Baptists were involved in a doctrinal controversy over the role of the wife in the church and home. Unlike most mainstream Protestant denominations at the time, many Southern Baptist congregations held strongly to the belief that "a woman should submit herself graciously to her husband's leadership." This interpretation of the covenants also mandated the less controversial adjunct that "the husband should provide for, protect, and lead his family." Ultimately, the subservient-wife dogma would cause a major rift in the Southern Baptist church in Texas, with more than half the congregations rejecting this strict interpretation of the wife's role. The Texas General Convention removed its churches from its historic fellowship with the more than two-million-member national organization, the Southern Baptist Convention. The Riverbend Church remained in the hard-line Southern Baptist group.

*T*here was no doubt where Penny stood on the issue of the subservient wife. She had already been teaching new brides and soon-to-be-married young women that the godly wife must be obedient to her husband. She resumed her teaching ministry shortly after the family settled in Austin. The house itself became a prop for her teachings. She used her kitchen for demonstrations, as well as a place to serve refreshments after each session. The classes were taught in the big den, which could comfortably accommodate twenty or more attendees.

Diana Coleman was one of the first Austin wives to take a course from Penny.

"We were already very good friends," said Diana. "I was forty-one, with a baby due in six weeks. Penny had a lot of empathy for an older woman with young children, and she wanted to be helpful, to be involved in other people's lives. Her class was based on passages from Chapter 31 of Proverbs, which describes the attributes of a biblical wife. The course she taught was the way she lived her own life."

Penny did not charge for the classes, and sold her students copies of *Creative Counterpart* at a discounted price. She taught each class directly from one of the chapters of Dillow's book, which was the centerpiece of the course. The sessions were two hours long, once a week, for nine weeks.

Penny taught that women should establish a life goal of being all God wants them to be as a person, wife, and mother. They would reach that goal by pursuing six defined priorities. Priority number one was God. The other priorities, in descending order of importance, were Husband, Children, Home, Yourself, and Outside the Home. This last category encompassed everything else, including job, school, community activities, etc.

She showed her students how to make a "priority planner" that broke down their weekly and daily schedules into specific activities, appointments, and goals. The chart also covered such details as menus for every meal, grocery shopping lists, and other household chores.

After devotion to God, the most important thing in life, Penny told her classes, was a wife's relationship with her husband. That relationship was based on a marital plan called the three A's, wherein the wife gave the husband Acceptance, Admiration, and Authority. The husband was to receive a hundred percent of the wife's efforts in a "lifelong process" built on complete trust of and obedience to her husband. "We must trust and obey," Dillow writes. "That is our 100 percent."

The book title *Creative Counterpart*—which was also what Penny's students called her courses—refers to the role of the wife in marriage. Dillow wrote, "God's plan for marital happiness involves a spiritual head and a creative counterpart." The book further defines creative counterpart as "a helpmate, a complement to her husband. She not only allows him to be the leader but also encourages him to take the leadership role by reverencing him and being submissive to him. She has chosen to be submissive because God has commanded it and because she is convinced that only *completion* will result in a vital, fulfilling marriage.

"She is submissive but she strives to be capable, intelligent, industrious, organized, efficient, warm, tender, gracious—all virtues we saw in the beautiful blueprint in Proverbs 31."

The message of the course was apparently deeply impressed upon many of the students. Years after they attended the sessions, they could readily recall much of the teaching.

"Penny taught that if the wife faithfully applied the three A's, there would almost inevitably be a positive change in the home," Diana said. "You submit to your husband, and if he is allowed to be the man of the house, it will be a harmonious home. She handed out small calligraphy pieces she had made, reminding those in her class that a wife should honor her husband." Diana added that, from her observations as a close friend over the years, Penny practiced in her home life what she preached in her classes.

*I*n addition to the Dillow book, Penny used the New International Version of the Holy Bible in the classes, as well as religious tracts and pamphlets, and printed sermons and monographs. She also often referenced the curiously titled book *Sex Begins in the Kitchen*, by Dr. Kevin Leman.

The title notwithstanding, this self-help book was more about creating a husband-wife partnership in the family than about making love in the kitchen. Addressing the subject of sex in the larger context of a reciprocally satisfying relationship, Dr. Leman writes: "A good marital relationship is based on pleasing each other, being sensitive and tuned-in to each other's emotional as well as sexual needs." According to the author, if the wife made the initial overtures to create a home where the husband felt in charge after a hard day of being battered in the workplace, he would reciprocate by willingly assuming more household chores and child-rearing responsibilities.

While this type of loving and equal partnership was potentially a side benefit of wifely submission, Penny's teachings made it clear that such an outcome was neither guaranteed nor reason for a wife's rebellion if the husband chose not to respond in kind.

Penny taught that the wife's duty of submission also extended to the sexual relationship. But one of the two-hour sessions was devoted to exploring ways a woman could be "creative" in the bedroom, and how to be a willing sexual partner rather than merely a submissive one.

Appearance was important, she taught. The wife should make herself as glamorous as possible when she was going to be around her husband. She should stop whatever she was doing early enough in the day to prepare herself physically for his homecoming. He should always be greeted at the door by an enthusiastic mate, freshly bathed, well-coiffed and manicured, and dressed attractively. In the home, the wife was to play a large role in planning intimate, romantic times when just the two of them were together. Whenever the husband desired his wife, she should be available, even if she was not interested in sex at the moment. Penny was quick to remind the wives in her class that their husbands were constantly confronted in the workplace by well-groomed, attractive women, some of whom might be intent on tempting the men in their office.

Risa Pardue was a student at the University of Texas in 1984 when her roommate introduced Penny to her as a mentor for young women. Risa was dating her future husband at the time. She and Penny formed a close friendship that was to last for years.

"Penny became like an aunt to me," she said. "I took her course twice, once when I was dating my future husband and again after I was married. Over the years, I stayed in close touch with Penny through our church."

Risa Pardue recalled felling uncomfortable at one of the sessions when the chapter on sexual relationships was being presented. The class was in the den, and Roger Scaggs was in the adjoining room.

"It seemed awkward that he was nearby when Penny was discussing how important it was for women to make themselves available to their husbands and not take that part of the marriage for granted," she said. "Sometimes a wife can get real busy with children and other details and neglect that aspect of the marriage. Penny made the joke that if you *act* enthusiastic you will *be* enthusiastic. Roger was sitting within earshot, and it made me cringe. It seemed a bit perfunctory, like the only reason for having sex was being dutiful, as opposed to being passionate or spontaneous."

Another of Penny's students, Delaney Clement, said that the nine-part course was very thorough, covering almost every topic a wife would need to create a new Christian home or make over a troubled marital relationship.

Everything was taught from the woman's perspective. The underlying theme was that the woman had to change, since a man could not be expected to change. Penny used a variety of sources—parables, Bible verses, and modern-day examples from real lives—all leading to the ultimate conclusion that it was the wife's responsibility and job to make the marriage work.

"The instructions were targeted at how to be a godly wife; that marriage required unconditional commitment to the husband, who might be an imperfect man," recalled Clement. "The husband should be number one in the wife's life [after God]."

Penny told her class that if the husband called home from work and the wife was on the phone, she should conclude her conversation immediately and take the husband's call. She practiced this in her own relationship. A longtime acquaintance remembered numerous times when their phone conversations had been interrupted by a call-waiting signal. Penny would immediately end the conversation with "That's probably Roger," and hang up.

Though the study sessions were serious, they were conducted in the relaxed atmosphere of a Tupperware party. The women, primarily young wives and newlyweds who had learned of the seminars from announcements in their churches, sat in a circle in Penny's large den. Usually, the sessions were scheduled from seven to nine in the evening. Penny held a few of the classes in church auditoriums during working hours, but most were in her home.

Student Patty Edling recalled that most of the wives were just starting their families far from their parents and "needed a mom to support us.

"We wanted to support our families through God, to learn how to make a better home," she said.

Theresa Neal, another class participant, said that after the prayers and the lesson of the day, the group usually had refreshments and socialized for a good amount of time, roaming around the big house, into the immaculate kitchen or to use one of the downstairs bathrooms. On one occasion, Penny brought out a large jewelry case to show the women how she had customized the box with plastic inserts to make it easier to find things quickly.

During the social periods, Roger, who was usually home for the evening by the time the sessions concluded, frequently mixed with the attendees for refreshments. The women described him as a friendly and sociable host, who sometimes shared a humorous story about his day at the office with the group.

The classes consumed a large part of Penny's life, and she was personally devoted to her students. Most became life-long friends, and she kept up with them for years after they completed the course. She shared births, deaths, and child-rearing experiences with them as if they were members of an extended family. And they were on her mailing list for the detailed and elaborately decorated annual newsletters she mailed out around Christmas to relatives, friends, and associates.

To her friends, it seemed that Penny was always either in the process of teaching a seminar, studying for another class, or preparing materials. Even with this busy schedule, each Thursday afternoon she diligently drove to a north Austin nursing home to play piano for the aging residents.

Penny conducted the classes in Christian homemaking for at least twelve years in Plano and Austin, as she continued to refine the course and expand the materials she used and distributed to her students. In Austin, she averaged five classes a year, with fifteen to twenty-five women each; which meant she taught nearly a thousand young brides-to-be, married women, and some older wives trying to rejuvenate failing marriages. On at least one occasion she accepted an invitation to conduct a seminar in her old hometown of Plano, and returned there to give a compressed series of workshops. In addition, her teachings about the Christian home extended to the weekly Sunday school classes she and Roger held for married couples at their church.

Penny Scaggs's influence as a teacher of Christian family values spread throughout Central Texas, and her reputation as a living example of the perfect Christian wife was known far beyond her immediate neighborhood and church community.

Chapter 4

She considereth a field, and buyeth it: with the fruit of her hands she planteth a vineyard. She girdeth her loins with strength, and strengtheneth her arms.

—PROVERBS 31:16-17

*P*enny Scaggs's dedication to making the home a duty-free-zone for her husband provided Roger the support he needed to devote his energy and talents to the pursuit of success for himself as a corporate executive and for the business interests he managed at American Physicians Service Group, Inc.

Roger, who had joined APS in Dallas in 1980, was soon made a corporate vice president. The company had a number of subsidiary operations, offering a wide range of financial services to physicians and the health-care provider industry, including clinics, medical schools, and physician networks. The financial services included billing systems, brokerage and investments, and the management and placement of malpractice insurance.

APS was well-positioned in the rapidly growing business of providing medical professionals with insurance and systems management. The booming new opportunity was called the computer service industry, and when Roger entered it at the bottom, it was far from the $500 billion annual industry it has become.

He was named senior vice president for corporate development in February 1985, about eight months after the move to Austin. He served in that position for three years, with primary responsibility for expanding the company's product and service lines.

The enterprising young men who made up the bulk of Texas computer professionals were different from the Silicon Valley tech wizards who invented the wonderful new systems. The Texans were more nerdy than geeky. They wore white shirts and ties. They were the practical guys, the ones who figured out how to apply the new technology the Californians invented—how to make money squeezing out mind-boggling applications for the gee-whiz gadgetry and programs invented in San Francisco, San Jose, and Mountain View.

Roger was one of the brightest of this new breed of buttoned-down, short-haired techies. With APS, he had the opportunity to focus his university training, military computer experience, and years with one of America's most innovative high-tech companies on the development of a new line of computer applications.

The original company was founded in 1975 when a group of doctors organized to address the medical malpractice insurance crisis. The officers and owners took the company public in 1983, listing it on the Nasdaq stock exchange. As an insider at the time, Roger acquired substantial shares of common stock and was gifted large blocks of stock options.

Ultimately, APS Group, the parent company, spun off three major operating subsidiaries. APS Financial, Inc. was an investment company handling stock and bond trades and other financial instruments for its clients. Facilities Management, Inc. was an insurance company that wrote malpractice policies for doctors and medical facilities. APS Systems was the computer systems management service, which Roger was instrumental in developing.

In the early 1980s the company acquired a prime piece of property in the booming high-tech corridor circling southwest Austin along the scenic new Capital of Texas Highway. This was a divided, four-lane, controlled-access loop that connected Interstate Highway 35 on the south with U.S. Highway 183 on the northwest. When the company moved its headquarters to Austin in 1984, two prominent Texas political figures—former speaker of the House Ben Barnes and former Governor John Connally—joined its board of directors.

The new property included a modern office building called Capital View Center, at 1301 Capital of Texas Highway. The building housed three levels of office suites above an underground parking garage. APS took Suite C, consisting of the entire top floor, for its national and international headquarters. The space on the two lower floors was leased out to other companies through the APS property management office. While serving as company vice president, Roger also managed the real estate office for a brief time after moving to Austin.

However, his ultimate contribution to the company was the creation and management of a lucrative new line of high-tech business services. About four years after the Austin move, he was named president of APS Systems, Inc. and served as its chief operating officer. The products and services sold through this subsidiary were similar to the computerized operating systems pioneered by Ross Perot's organization twenty years before, but upgraded with the latest in technological advances.

The move to Austin had been good for Roger's career. In addition to his other responsibilities, he was promoted to senior vice president for data processing of the parent company in 1988. Roger had taken full advantage of the opportunities the fledgling company offered. He had grown in both rank and responsibility as APS prospered with the rapidly booming high-tech market, serving national and international clients from its Austin business hub.

During the late 1980s and early 1990s, *Fortune* magazine frequently ranked Austin among the ten best business locations in the country, several times as number one. Its commerce-friendly climate, low cost of living, and high quality of life were cited as the city's chief attributes.

"You can feel the growth here," a corporate executive who had moved his company from the Silicon Valley to Austin, told the magazine. "We're doubling [business] every year."

One article in the prestigious business journal concluded, "Austin's reputation as the breeding ground for high-tech entrepreneurs will be assured. And as long as you can listen to great live music and chow down on cheap enchiladas, the old-timers won't complain much."

This phenomenal business growth was true for APS, too, and Roger, as a senior executive, played an important role in the company's early expansion in Austin. His work demanded more and more of his time at the office and away from Penny and his comfortable new home. After developing major technical services for the company, Roger began traveling coast to coast to market them.

His niche in the company was assured because of his unique computer knowledge and skills. He may not have been the "indispensable man," but he was one of the most valuable rainmakers in the corporation. As such, he had been named a member of the board of directors during the period of the company's most rapid growth in the mid-1980s.

Roger's large glassed-in corner office reflected the importance of the position he held. It offered unobstructed views of the skyline of downtown Austin to the north and the Hill Country to the west. Looking straight down from his windows, the view was less attractive. At street level was a large outdoor parking lot for visitors and lower-ranking employees. At the far end of the lot, in an alleyway behind the building, there were two industrial-size trash Dumpsters. But the lofty view, befitting a former Ross Perot "eagle" and a real comer in Austin's booming high-tech industry, was the long one—above the parked cars, Dumpsters, and treetops, to the most distant panoramas. Throughout the eighties, Roger Scaggs's horizons must have seemed limitless.

APS Systems, the subsidiary he headed, sold complete computer systems and operating software, designed to each major client's specific criteria. While some of the components were standardized, the particular system had to be tailored to each new client's operation, and frequently updated as needs changed. The products Roger's unit designed and sold featured an automated practice-management and billing system. The users and potential customers were large, multiphysician medical clinics, medical schools, physician hospital organizations, HMOs, and other health-care provider networks. In quick order, Roger brought in a number of large clients, including the Yale School of Medicine with its five-hundred-doctor teaching hospital, and the Nebraska Clinicians Group of the University of Nebraska Medical Center at Omaha, with three hundred doctors. The North Mississippi Health Services system, headquartered at Tupelo, was another important client. That medical operation was the largest rural health system in America, with fourteen major clinics and hospitals in Mississippi. In addition, APS Systems sold to and serviced dozens of other smaller clients operating health-care facilities across the country.

The company's proprietary software, which Roger helped create, performed a wide variety of valuable services. The system offered the client a one-source computer database that integrated patient and physician financial, demographic, and medical information. It generated patient scheduling, patient recalls, and special reports. It also prepared billing statements and forms for filing insurance claims. The system could be linked, for automatic claim-filing, to medical insurance companies, Medicaid, and Medicare. APS Systems software was run on Hewlett-Packard hardware, which APS also sold to their clients.

In the extremely competitive, fast-paced, high-tech field, Roger's accomplishments earned the recognition of his corporate bosses and the board of directors. His professionalism and low-key management style won the admiration of his peers and the respect of the employees who worked for him. He supervised a staff of thirty-five highly trained technical specialists and sales and service representatives.

Patty Adams, a marketing vice president at APS, worked directly with Roger Scaggs. She said that he had a good reputation around the country as one of the most technically competent in the industry. "He was always up front with his staff, mostly quiet and nonconfrontational. He never got upset."

Ken Shifrin, who was chief executive officer of the parent company, had been promoted to that position in 1989, after serving as its chief financial officer. Roger, as president of the subsidiary, reported directly to him. The two men had developed a close business relationship when they held positions of equal rank, and their friendship continued after Shifrin became president of APS Group and Roger's boss. They worked down the hall from each other during this vital growth phase of the company.

Shifrin said Roger was a thoughtful boss. "He always did everything possible for his employees. He cared for them. Whenever there was an opportunity, he worked to get them promotions."

Roger frequently talked about his daughter Sarah and wife Penny with his coworkers. Penny was also well known and liked by the officers and employees at the company. She always attended company-sponsored employee events with him.

"Roger talked about Penny and Sarah a lot on the job," the corporate president recalled. "He loved them very much."

As those early years in Austin passed, the job demands on Roger's time and energy were not the only external forces competing for his family's attention. Even when he did manage to get time away from his hectic work schedule, he did not always want to spend it at the perfect home Penny had created.

An avid sailor, Roger described one of his favorite vacations as a charter trip in the Caribbean Sea he and Penny took aboard an old sailing schooner earlier in their marriage. Later he took up sailing on one of the Highland Lakes near Austin. After becoming proficient as an inland-water sailor, he eventually purchased part interest in a twenty-seven-foot Catalina yacht for $6,000. It featured full cabin accommodations with two double and two single berths. The boat was kept at a commercial marina on Lake Travis, a fifty-minute drive from his home and office. The closest major lake in the string of recreational lakes that runs west from Austin into the heart of the Hill Country, Lake Travis was ideal for weekend pleasure trips, with beautiful canyons winding along the sixty-four miles of its length. The lake was four miles across at its widest point, and offered extraordinary boating conditions year-round.

Roger also owned a hundred-acre farm near Coleman, Texas, 165 miles northwest of Austin, for use as a private hunting reserve and weekend retreat. A trailer-type cabin was located on the property, making it suitable for overnight stays without the discomfort of camping out. During quail, dove, and turkey seasons, which lasted most of the fall and winter months, Roger took every opportunity to spend weekends at the ranch.

The problem with these outdoor activities Roger so avidly pursued was that Penny did not care much for them. She complained that the harsh Texas sun and dry, parching winds were too damaging for her fair skin and northern European features. So she seldom went along, opting instead to remain at home to pursue her arts and crafts or church activities with friends. Sarah, now in her teens, frequently accompanied her father on both his trips to the lake and weekends at the small ranch. Roger also hosted coworkers and other friends for brief sailboat outings on Lake Travis.

Another outside assault on the tranquil haven Penny tried

to create in the safety of the home on Winter Park became far more problematic. The public schooling of daughter Sarah brought an unwelcome influence into their tightly knit Christian home.

*T*he Eanes Independent School District was not only one of the best-funded public school systems in Texas, but was also reputed to offer the best educational and social environment. Like the neighborhood they served, there was little or no crime reported within the Eanes schools. The thirty-two-square-mile EISD, which abutted Austin on the southwest, was the primary governmental entity that bound the area into a common community. Its natural landscape consisted of high cedar- and oak-covered hills and mesas, and was traversed by the meandering Colorado River. These Hill Country vistas commanded the highest real estate prices in Central Texas.

The neighborhood where Penny and Roger bought their home was the only part of the Eanes school district actually located within the Austin city limits. The other municipalities in the area were hamlets, with a few convenience stores and service stations built at county crossroads. At the time, the only other real town in the area was West Lake Hills, which was little more than a shopping strip incorporated into a village. It offered a few upscale stores and a supermarket.

As desirable as it was, the Scaggses' neighborhood was by no means the most posh in the district. Nearby multimillion-dollar homes, located in luxury developments like Rob Roy Estates and Davenport Ranch, sprawled across the mesa tops behind gated communities guarded by private security firms. Most of these exclusive communities were located in an unincorporated part of Travis County.

A few pockets of lower-priced housing remained along the river that marked one boundary of the area. These neighborhoods of $100,000 houses were considered Westside "slums" by some of the locals.

Many of Austin's most notable personalities owned mansions in the westernmost part of the Eanes school district. Several members of the immediate family of the late President Lyndon Baines Johnson had homes there, as did Governor Ann Richards and such nationally recognized celebrities as actress Sandra Bullock, author Bud Shrake, artist John Guerin, former presidential security advisor Walter Rostow, and syndicated columnist Liz Carpenter. The stunning panoramas from the hilltop homes were top-drawer; but for most of the 25,000 residents, it was the schools that made the families stretch to buy one of the ten thousand pricey homes in the district.

"Almost everyone who moved to the West Side did so because of the quality of the Eanes school district," according to Ed Allen, editor of the award-winning community weekly newspaper, the *Westlake Picayune*.

Roger and Penny enrolled Sarah in junior high school when they moved to Austin, and she matriculated into high school as a freshman when she was fifteen.

Westlake High School was the flagship of the school district. The large public high school was the educational and sports pride of the community. Its influential outreach was the glue that held the affluent community together.

The school's motto was simply: "It's all good!"

But in 1987, when Sarah Scaggs entered high school as a freshman, it was not "all good" at the much ballyhooed Eanes campus. Despite its reputation, when it came to social problems, Westlake High was not much different from the thousands of other junior and senior high schools in the Texas public school system. Rebellious teen subcultures, whether centered around heavy metal music, the dark atmosphere of the goth aesthetic, or experimentation with drugs, were just as much a challenge to parents and educators in the wealthy school district as they were in urban high schools in less affluent communities.

Apparently, Sarah's strict upbringing had not made her immune to the siren call of one of these subcultures, which expressed its rebellion through provocative dress and music. When she adopted a preference for all-black clothing and began turning up after school wearing dark lipstick and nail polish, Penny was appalled.

"She preferred me to have bows in my hair and [that I] hang out with the preppy little kids," Sarah said later, in an interview with an Austin reporter.

Sarah began violating her 11:00 P.M. weekend curfew, coming home later and later, with no explanation as to where she had been. Penny refused to accept that a child raised from infancy to be a good Christian could fall under the influence of an aberrant youth movement without the intervention of some outside evil force. She believed in a living Satan, and that possession by the devil could cause a person to go astray. As one friend said of Penny's concept of an incarnate evil spirit, "She believed that Satan was as real as the mailman."

Roger and Penny tried every form of restriction to keep Sarah from her new friends and remove the negative influences they believed would wreck their daughter's life. The more they tried, the more Sarah, abetted by her friends, rebelled against the strict discipline.

Whether Sarah's sudden involvement with what Penny considered the "dark side" was adolescent rebellion against religion and the strict home Penny kept, or simply a typical teenager's response to the magnetic pull of peers, will never be known. A family friend whom Penny called on for advice during this time because of similar experiences dealing with a teenager years earlier said that Penny and Roger were not willing to let the problem with Sarah work itself out. Penny wanted her wayward daughter removed from the evil influences in the public school immediately. Although Roger seemed a little more tolerant of his teenage daughter's rebelliousness, he finally went along.

"My mother could be very controlling of both me and my

father," Sarah admitted to the *Austin Chronicle*. "If either one of us did something that she didn't like, she had her ways of either subtly, or not so subtly, making you feel [awful] until you did it her way."

Whatever the genesis of the problem with Sarah, Penny and Roger soon settled on a drastic solution for it. Sarah had been raised her entire life in the nurturing arms of a fundamentalist faith in a Christian home and Christian church. That belief system could also be unforgiving of youthful deviation from the strict rules set forth in the Bible.

In Sarah's case, the remedy came fast and harsh. Penny found a no-nonsense school for girls, which was operated by a Christian fundamentalist sect and located in a small piney-woods town in far northeast Texas. The school was on a farm more than three hundred miles from Austin. In addition to their studies, the girls were required to labor on the land, raising crops as part of their reeducation program. A tearful but still defiant Sarah was consigned to the isolated Christian school for the remainder of her high school years. It provided a harsh, daily twelve-hour regime of work, prayer, and worship, in addition to the continuation of high school studies.

Part of the Scaggs family adoption experience was featured in a textbook entitled *Children of Adoption and Their Parents* by Kathleen Silber and Patricia Martinez Dorner, published by Corona Publishing Company in 1990. The Scaggs family was identified in the monograph simply as "Penny, Rog, and Sarah."

Pointing out that Sarah had been adopted as an infant, the case study said that she had not exhibited early distress pertaining to adoption, but began having related problems when she was fifteen. She wanted to know where she came from, who she looked like. According to the study, these problems manifested themselves in rebellion toward her adoptive parents and the strictness of her upbringing.

The story covered the parents' attempts to get help. "They . . . sought counseling and other forms of assistance in their local community. Feeling a need to remove her from her peers in an effort to break the cycle, they sent her to a residential religious facility."

The teenage daughter lived at the rural church school for the next three years, with only infrequent visits by her parents allowed. At one point in her program the school suggested that the Scaggses locate Sarah's birth mother and reintroduce them. Sarah herself was interested in knowing her biological mother. The focus of the book that related the Scaggs story was an exploration of the pros and cons of reintroducing adopted children to birth families. In this case, it was apparently deemed advisable. The family invited Sarah's birth mother, Kathy, to Sarah's high school graduation, and she accompanied Penny and Roger to the ceremony.

After completing high school at the church farm, Sarah returned to Austin and her home on Winter Park Road. If Penny was hoping the three years of "tough love" at the religious school had turned the teenager into a dutiful biblical daughter, she would soon be disappointed. Sarah had emerged from the rigorous regime and strict discipline meted out at the church farm a stronger young woman, determined, if nothing else, to live her own life.

The Scaggs parents had a plan worked out for Sarah's return, which included enrolling her in Concordia University, a Lutheran, church-sponsored institution whose motto was, "We develop Christian leaders." Concordia is consistently ranked among the "Best Comprehensive Colleges" in America by *U.S. News & World Report* in their annual evaluation of colleges and universities. The school operates an extensive undergraduate and graduate program from a twenty-acre campus near downtown Austin and charges one of the highest tuitions of any college system in Texas.

During the summer following Sarah's high school graduation, the Scaggses joined Penny's sisters and their families for a vacation at a resort condominium near Breckenridge, Colorado. The families planned to spend a weeklong holiday together with their children at the retreat, which was owned by one of Penny's sisters. They drove together, in a caravan of cars, from Dallas to the Rocky Mountains. Sarah, fresh from the rigorous training at the religious school, accompanied her parents on the trip.

There were thirteen spouses and children in the vacation party. Sarah slept on a cot in a loft bedroom in the trilevel apartment. Despite the crowding, the families seemed to get along fairly well, amicably sharing the space and scheduling the use of bath facilities, cooking, washing dishes, laundry, and house-cleaning.

Toward the end of the week an incident occurred that was so out of character for the Scaggs couple that Penny's sisters were shocked by it.

Some of the women were doing laundry, in preparation for leaving in the next day or two. Twin sisters Carolyn Pittenger and Marilyn Muecke were on the landing between two bedrooms when an argument ensued.

"Roger became very upset that Penny had not packed a towel in his suitcase that he wanted," Carolyn recalled. "Penny packed for him most of the time, and had apparently failed to bring the towel. He became very upset . . . and began to talk very loud. By his body language, you could tell he was mad. He continued to tell her he wanted that towel. He said she *knew* he wanted that towel—why had she not packed it? Penny was trying to explain that circumstances arose . . ."

Marilyn was standing on one side and Carolyn on the other. But when Roger's verbal attack escalated, the twins, sensing he was at the point of striking Penny, instinctively stepped between them. If he were going to hit Penny, he would have to go through them. Roger immediately turned his anger on the younger sisters. He shouted that it was none of their business and warned them to keep out of it. Penny, aware that others could hear them, was clearly embarrassed by the scene. She insisted it was just a little misunderstanding and assured her siblings that everything was going to be fine.

Then Penny and Roger went into the bedroom they were sharing. Although they closed the door, it was a loft with one side partially open to the downstairs living area, and their argument could easily be heard outside the room. Everyone else in the condo had stopped their activities and were listening in surprise at the rising anger in Roger's voice.

The twins went to the door and waited anxiously outside as the fight worsened. Roger's voice was getting louder, stronger.

Carolyn told her sister that she thought they should go in. But Marilyn was reluctant. "Roger said it was none of our business," she argued.

"This is my condominium," said Carolyn, "and I'll go anyplace I want to." With that, they burst into the room. Carolyn yelled at Roger that it was over, that it had gone far enough.

By then the twins' husbands had also come upstairs and appeared in the doorway. With that, the argument finally stopped.

"Roger visibly shook to get control of himself, but he backed down," said Carolyn.

The atmosphere was frosty around the condominium for the rest of that day. The next day, Penny, Roger, and Sarah left, and returned to Austin.

The ugly incident left a lasting memory with Penny's sisters, and years later would be vividly recalled. Marilyn said she had never witnessed such a confrontation between Penny and Roger, although there had been a few minor spats in front of the family before. The sisters also agreed that they never saw them fight like that again.

Shortly after the Colorado vacation, Roger bought his wife a Kawai baby grand piano. Penny was thrilled. The piano became the centerpiece of the den, drawing attention, not only for its imposing profile, but also for its unusual color. Instead of the traditional satin or high-gloss ebony, this baby grand was finished in a canary yellow hue.

For years Penny had owned and played a standard upright, which she moved with her from Plano. Even though she had become an accomplished amateur pianist, she did not have a piano in her childhood home or during the early years of marriage when she and Roger changed job locations frequently. As a child she had taken lessons on an organ, and attained her musical mastery of the piano pretty much on her own.

The beautiful new baby grand became her pride and joy, and her friends believed it was her most prized possession. Penny spent hundreds of hours practicing, and cheerfully played for anyone who would sit still for a hymn or a tune.

Chapter 5

> *She perceiveth that her merchandise is good: her candle goeth not out by night. She layeth her hands to the spindle, and her hands hold the distaff.*
>
> —PROVERBS 31:18-19.

Not long after Sarah returned home from the girls' school, Roger and Penny Scaggs took a somewhat drastic step in an important area of their lives. They decided to leave the congregation of nearby Riverbend Church, where they had regularly worshipped for almost ten years, and move to another congregation, all the way across town. They joined the First Evangelical Free Church of Austin, with its sanctuary and classroom complex at Red River and Forty-fifth Streets in north Austin. Reverend Rob Harrell was the senior pastor of the church.

It was not just a change of church fellowship, but also a change to a religious denomination with which neither Penny nor Roger had ever been affiliated. Roger had been raised a Methodist, and Penny in the traditional Baptist communion. The new church was associated with the Evangelical Free Church of America, formed in 1950 by the merger of two church bodies: the Swedish Evangelical Free Church and the Norwegian-Danish Evangelical Free Church Association. Unlike the tightly controlled Baptist denominational conferences, the Evangelical Church was a loosely knit affiliation of autonomous churches, which pretty much governed themselves and practiced the faith as they saw fit. These churches traced their histories to Scandinavian immigrant communities in America at the turn of the century. The Austin church had been formed from original churches at the Decker and Elroy colonies founded by Swedish settlers at about that time. However, when Penny and Roger joined the congregation, any ties to a specific nationality had long been severed, and the church served a broad general membership.

The edifice of their new place of worship was far less grand than the one they had left. Riverbend Church conducted its main assemblies in a beautiful, modern tabernacle-style building on a sprawling nature preserve, with views of the Colorado River and surrounding Hill Country. First Evangelical held its services in an aging, traditional sanctuary in a somewhat rundown residential area of narrow streets and heavy traffic. The church, in the most densely populated neighborhood in Austin, had an eclectic congregation, ranging from a large group of elderly, longtime members to transient young students from the nearby University of Texas.

Their friends did not know why Roger and Penny stopped attending Riverbend, though they were aware that Roger had often complained about the building committee constantly passing the collection plate for larger and larger contributions.

The couple apparently did not make the move because of any major differences in church dogma or beliefs. The basic tenets of the evangelicals were similar to the fundamentalist beliefs held by the Southern Baptists with whom the Scaggses were formerly associated. Both denominations believe the Holy Bible to be the unerring and literal word of God; and that God, Jesus, and the Holy Spirit make up the divine trinity. Both believe that man was created in the image of God but fell into sin. Both believe that humankind can only be redeemed by faith in the atonement offered by Jesus and acceptance of Christ as Lord and Savior. Both believe in Heaven and Hell in the afterlife. Even though it has the word "evangelical" in its name, the First Evangelical Free Church is still considered one of the mainstream denominations of American Protestantism. The Austin church defines the word evangelical as a "commitment to the proclamation of the gospel and the authority of the Scriptures as being inerrant in the original autographs and the only safe and sufficient guide to faith and practice."

One of the notable differences in the First Evangelical Free Church the Scaggses chose over their former Baptist affiliation is the concept of the independence of the local church. As the word "free" indicates, the local churches retain the right to follow their own consciences on major issues of the day, rather than adhering to the rigid dictates of a central organization or synod. As a result, the Austin church had not been caught up in or divided by such controversies as acceptance of gay members, women in the ministry, pro-life versus pro-choice, or even the role of women in the workplace and the home. The First Evangelical Church practiced strict political neutrality. While encouraging voter registration and participation of its members in elections, the leadership did not advocate for one political party or another, as increasingly was the practice of the Southern Baptist leadership.

First Evangelical readily accepted Penny's teachings on how to make a godly home, and actively encouraged young women to attend her seminars. In contrast, her teachings had been barely tolerated at Riverbend, where some in the leadership considered her classes outside the structured program of the church.

At their new church, Penny and Roger began teaching a Sunday school class for young adults and became heavily involved in the activities of the congregation and the social lives of its members. They were soon held in high regard by their fellow evangelicals, and Roger was asked to join the church's ten-man board of elders, the lay fathers of the congregation. Penny, as always, acquired a large circle of close female friends, and many younger women from the church and the university enrolled in her Christian-wife seminars.

It was during this period of transition that Roger's mother, Dorothy, was diagnosed with cancer. His father had passed away in 1982, leaving his mother a relatively young widow in her early sixties. Dorothy Scaggs had moved from Fort Worth to Austin in the late 1980s and taken an apartment to be closer to her oldest son, Roger.

When she became ill, Roger insisted that his mother be brought into their home, presumably so Penny could administer her medicine and general care around the clock. After all, he argued, they had plenty of room for another person, with spare bedrooms and baths that were rarely used.

Penny was adamantly opposed. It was one of the few times she was known to have defied her husband's decision on an issue of major importance to the family. Though she would rush off to care for an ailing relative in her own family, or even to help a sister pack for a move, Penny in this instance told one friend that she was simply not trained for, nor physically up to, the rigors of caring for a seriously ill elderly person.

The incident apparently caused considerable and long-lasting friction in her marriage. Roger finally relented and placed his mother in an expensive nursing home in the nearby hills. Penny was perfectly willing to make frequent trips to the elder-care center to visit Dorothy, and personally saw to the delivery of a favorite rocking chair and shawl to make her more comfortable.

After his mother passed away in April 1991, friends recalled that they saw Roger less frequently in the neighborhood or working in his yard. In casual encounters, he seemed cooler, more distant. One very close friend and neighbor noted that he did not seem as easygoing and outwardly friendly as he had always been before.

The death of a close relative reminds others in the family

of their own mortality, and it can often lead them to set their own metaphorical house in order. Following Dorothy Scaggs's death, and thirty-one years after her marriage to Roger, Penny asked her brother-in-law, Bill Pittenger, a Dallas attorney, to prepare a formal will for her. The official Last Will and Testament of Lou Anne Scaggs left everything of value in her estate to her husband, Roger T. Scaggs. Although the section on property did mention jewelry, she gave no special instructions for some of her more personal items, which included her collections of porcelain dolls and figurines. Penny displayed most of the dolls, dressed in frilly Victorian fashions, in lighted glass cases that lined the upstairs hallways. The figurines she placed in nooks and crannies around the home, as pleasant surprises for anyone browsing around the immaculately kept house.

Likewise, the eleven-page will left no clue as to Penny's personal preference for the kind of funeral she wanted or instructions for her burial. It did provide one stipulation that some might find unusual, and which seemed to suggest that Penny was still not comfortable with Sarah's life choices. Not surprisingly the document stated that in the event her husband Roger did not survive her, daughter Sarah was to be the sole beneficiary of the estate. However, the inheritance was to be held in trust until Sarah reached the age of forty-five, with partial release of assets when she attained the ages of twenty-five and thirty-five. One of Roger's younger brothers was named administrator of Sarah's trust.

"Travel broadens the mind," the old adage goes, and Roger and Penny traveled extensively throughout their marriage. Since leaving Tulsa as a nineteen-year-old bride, Penny had accompanied Roger, for pleasure as well as his job, around the United States and to a number of foreign countries.

No doubt these extensive travels and long sojourns overseas did broaden Penny's horizons, even if the exotic cultures she encountered did not cause her to waver in her strongly held core beliefs. Her focus remained steadfastly on the concept of her fundamentalist Christian home.

In Penny's teachings and annual family newsletters, she described the landscapes and topography of the places they visited. These trips took her outside the narrow confines of the home and local church pew to view the world, in particular nature's grandeur, as the handiwork of the Creator in whom she believed so fervently. In many of her letters and annual Christmas messages, she described the most impressive sights in biblical terms and drew inspiration from them.

On a road trip through Holland, Germany, and Austria in the spring of 1992, Penny's focus seemed to be on the natural beauty of old Europe, rather than on any man-made landmarks or historical places. Penny, who loved flowers and tended plants and gardens in temperate Austin almost year-round, was most impressed by the magnificent displays of color created by the more than seven million tulips at Holland's Keukenhof Park. She wrote of the "colorful Dutch tulips, the scenic German countryside, and the majesty of the snow-capped Alps" of Austria. These were the same type of sights—nature and landscapes—that she often wrote home about when she traveled around the States. There was no mention of the art museums or historic cathedrals that were the living memorials to western civilization.

On this spring motor trip, the Scaggses were accompanied by longtime friends Robert and Phyllis Culp. Culp had retired to Georgetown, just north of Austin, after years of heading the APS financial services operation. He said the two-week tour was trouble-free, and that Penny and Roger seemed like the perfect couple on a happy vacation.

Roger and Penny had traveled widely on vacations, having visited Hong Kong, the Philippines, Singapore, Malaysia, France, and Belgium earlier in their marriage, in addition to the foreign countries where his work and military service took them. They would eventually visit every state in the Union, as well.

* * *

*N*ew family problems greeted Penny when she returned home from Europe. For one thing, Sarah had decided to leave the Lutheran university and continue her education at Austin Community College.

Another decision Sarah made at that time brought Penny to the edge of distraction. Despite Penny's dedication to creating a perfect Christian home for her family, and her daughter's three years of fundamentalist training at the church farm, Sarah had no desire to follow in her mother's footsteps. To express her frustration, Penny might well have turned from her oft-quoted Bible verses to a fitting lament from Shakespeare's *King Lear*: "How sharper than a serpent's tooth it is to have a thankless child!"

Penny confided in one of her closest friends that she was at her wits' end when she learned her daughter was taking a job as a waitress at an Austin strip club and restaurant. To make matters worse, Sarah was dating one of the bartenders, Cory Munson. Penny was not consoled by the fact that the new boyfriend was also a fellow student, who was working part-time there to pay his way through college.

While Sarah's choice to leave the Christian atmosphere of the Lutheran university for the secular, urban junior college was disappointing, the close friend said the daughter's choice of employment was emotionally devastating for Penny. She did everything she could to hide the fact from her other friends, fellow church members, and family.

The place where Sarah waitressed was one of Austin's earliest and best-known "gentlemen's clubs." It featured topless exotic dancers and adult comedy at a time when strip clubs were just beginning to garner negative public attention in the Texas capital. The strip clubs set off a raging controversy between the owners and customers on one side, and the preachers and city fathers on the other. Some of the clubs installed giant-screen TVs that featured all the major professional and collegiate athletic events and offered full-service restaurants as well. But opponents focused their wrath on the exotic dancing that, they claimed, was the main draw for the mostly male clientele.

When these establishements first appeared on the scene, most Texas towns and small cities still did not permit hard liquor to be sold in bars and nightclubs. Anyone wanting a mixed drink had to brown-bag it. Many of the new gentlemen's clubs circumvented the state's dry laws by using the same private-organization exception that rich Texans had used for years to operate open bars in their exclusive country clubs.

The local crusades to curtail this rapidly spreading, new form of male entertainment were led by the churches, so Penny had plenty of good company in her objections to these establishments.

Certainly to her, serving men alcohol in a club that featured exotic dancers was an unacceptable job for anyone, let alone her college-age daughter. Her reaction to Sarah's latest demonstration of independence was swift and final. Penny delivered an ultimatum: Either find another job or move out of the house on Winter Park. Sarah opted for banishment and quickly found a place of her own. Her new apartment was in the Hyde Park area of north Austin, close to the college she now attended and the club where she worked. A furious mother did not help with the move. A more accepting father did. Roger quietly provided Sarah with financial assistance to make the transition, apparently hoping Penny would come to terms with the fact that their daughter was now a grown woman who would be making her own decisions in the future.

In her newsletter, which Penny wrote and sent at each year's end to hundreds of friends, family, and former students, she did not mention her daughter's job, and addressed the college choice tersely: "Sarah is continuing her college studies and working on a degree in psychology."

Concerning Roger's work, the newsletter mentioned that

he made frequent trips to the East Coast and Seattle. The East Coast trips were mostly to New Haven, where Roger was firming up one of APS Systems' largest contracts, with Yale University Medical Center.

The newsletter also noted that Sarah's birth mother, Kathy, and half sister, two-year-old Kerra, had come to Austin for a visit. "What a joy and pleasure to expand our friendship with them, as well as show them around Austin," Penny wrote.

The rest of Penny's year seemed to improve after an autumn trip with Roger to the Northwest. The combined business/vacation trip allowed time for them to tour Yellowstone National Park in Wyoming and Glacier National Park in Montana. The fifty slow-moving glaciers and two hundred lakes in Glacier National Park did not seem to capture Penny's attention. But the geyser displays at Yellowstone drew rave reviews and provided the inspirational theme for her 1992 family newsletter.

As usual, the newsletter featured a snapshot of Roger and Penny, which that year showed the couple standing in the Upper Geyser Basin of the park. Penny was moved to draw an analogy between the reliability of Old Faithful and God's love.

The phrase "Great is thy faithfulness" from the Lamentations of Jeremiah was the theme of her newsletter that year. Regardless of the trials that might beset a person, God's faithfulness would ultimately prevail.

"We were truly in awe of God's creative genius as we toured the Big Sky Country of Montana and Wyoming," she wrote. "Just as Old Faithful Geyser in Yellowstone continues to predictably spew forth steam and hot water year in and year out, we know too that God's loving kindness never ceases. His compassions never fail. They are new every morning."

She reported in the newsletter that she conducted her seminars throughout 1992. "God continues to bless the Bible Study I teach to women, which is based on Proverbs 31,

Being a Godly Woman," she wrote. Describing Roger's activities, the newsletter noted that, other than his job, he spent his time sailing on Lake Travis and hunting turkey and dove on the Coleman, Texas, ranch.

Chapter 6

*She stretcheth out her hand to the poor; yea, she reacheth
forth her hands to the needy. She is not afraid of the
snow for her household: for all her household are clothed
with scarlet.*

—PROVERBS 31:20-21

Work demands intensified for Roger as APS expanded its
product lines and his own division grew rapidly, adding both
new clients and new services for existing customers. In
1993, as president of APS Systems Inc., he negotiated a major strategic development and marketing alliance with
American International Healthcare, Inc.

"This new relationship will enable the two companies to
offer a sophisticated medical practice management application combined with a powerful managed care system," he
told business writers at a news conference announcing the
consortium. "The resulting product will be the industry's
most comprehensive and complete. The partnership is very
important because no single company in our industry has
the expertise necessary to respond to today's challenging requirements."

Indeed, the systems that Roger had created and marketed
through APS were groundbreaking for the health-care in-

dustry, which was facing critical problems of spiraling costs on all fronts, particularly in the area of medical liability insurance. The parent company, APS Group, was having a record-breaking year as a whole, with a greater than 60 percent increase in revenues in 1995.

APS Group had also expanded its operations from its Austin headquarters and opened major new offices in San Antonio, Dallas, Houston, and Little Rock, Arkansas. In addition, the company was undertaking international operations in Mexico. The company's stock was soaring.

Base salaries for executives at APS were generally at the low end of the scale for similar jobs in the area. However, they compared favorably with Austin's average family income, and were higher than professional salaries in state government and the universities. As is the practice in most of the corporate world, the top APS executives did enjoy extra income potential through bonus incentives established by the board for reaching certain benchmarks, and could also receive stock options.

According to the company's annual report in 1995, when he was president of APS Systems, Roger was paid a salary of $105,333, and bonuses amounting to about $46,000. The report stated the income was paid to him as a vice president of the parent company, and showed no additional income for being president of the subsidiary.

However, Austin's low cost of living and well-priced upscale housing meant that Roger's income could provide a more than comfortable lifestyle for his family.

As a senior executive of a rapidly growing organization, he was expected to be available to the company 24/7. His job increasingly demanded travel, and when he was in town, his hours at the office stretched into every evening and some weekends. Penny, who had anticipated traveling with Roger more often now that their daughter was grown, was disappointed that she was actually invited on fewer trips than they had shared earlier in his career. She complained to friends, only half in jest, that she had created the perfect home for a husband, and now there was no husband around to enjoy it.

Penny's sisters had all married and moved to various suburbs around Dallas, so she was not too far from them. Her aging parents had moved to Richardson, Texas, to be closer to their younger daughters. In February, Penny received an urgent call to drive immediately to Dallas, where her father had been hospitalized with a minor stroke. She rushed to his bedside and made frequent trips back to the Dallas area over the next few months, to help her sisters and mother take care of her father during his convalescence.

In July, Penny was invited to accompany Roger on one of the now rare business trips she took with him. The trip to the nation's capital included a reunion with an old friend and her family. Dao Thu, who had worked with Roger in his civilian job in Vietnam during the war in the early 1970s, had finally been able to secure an exit visa and leave Saigon (by then renamed Hanoi City) the year before. The Vietnamese family had settled in Washington, D.C.

Penny continued teaching her seminars, and Roger remained actively involved in volunteer leadership at the First Evangelical Free Church. In spite of his busy schedule, Roger found time to teach a men's Bible study course at the church on Monday evenings. The title of his course was "The Measure of a Man." Penny wrote in the family newsletter that Roger was teaching a course on "being a godly man in today's hectic world." She said his class was the male version of her seminar on teaching women to be godly wives.

In her newsletter that year she provided her interpretation of a cautionary warning from the Bible: ". . . be careful how you walk (live) not as unwise, witless men and women, but as wise people, making the most of your time (and every opportunity) because the days are evil—Ephesians 5:15."

If she had any foreboding of darkness ahead, it was premature.

The waning days of summer 1993 saw improved relationships within the Scaggs family. In late summer, Sarah told a greatly relieved mother that she was getting married. Penny considered sex outside of marriage as "living in sin." Now she could proudly report that Sarah and Cory Munson, the bartender boyfriend (and working college student), were betrothed. She wrote in her newsletter, "The couple will make their home in Austin while working and continuing their undergraduate studies." Again, she did not mention that they were still employed at the strip club she found so objectionable. The engagement was announced on August 25, Sarah's twenty-first birthday.

After excitedly planning for a May 1994 wedding, the pleased parents invited the engaged couple to go on vacation with them. The four went first to New York City to "visit the sights," and then on to spend some time in Yorktown Heights, north of the city, where Sarah had lived with her parents for the first two years of her life.

That Thanksgiving, Penny and Roger drove to the Dallas area to spend the holiday with her family. Their visit was unexpectedly prolonged by a sudden ice storm that marooned everybody for an extra two days. Dallas's ice storms are unlike any other weather phenomenon, in that they literally paralyze the entire metroplex. Streets, bridges, and overpasses are coated with a thin, treacherous glaze called "black ice," which defies movement by any type of vehicle. Since these storms are rarely accompanied by snow, not even tire chains will help maneuver the slick streets and freeways.

The family watched the Dallas Cowboys try to play a Thanksgiving Day football game, but sleet pelted the field through the open roof of Texas Stadium. The sisters' traditional turkey dinner with all the trimmings was delayed until the thaw that weekend.

The holiday gatherings the following month came off much better. Penny wrote that the Scaggses celebrated Christmas twice. The first was with Roger's brothers and their families in Austin, on December 12. After an exchange of gifts, the Scaggs boys and their wives and children enjoyed a fajita dinner at a posh downtown hotel restaurant, followed by dessert back at Winter Park Road. Penny baked three varieties of pecan pie.

Roger and Penny loaded up her van with gifts for a second Christmas with her relatives in the Dallas area. Sarah and Cory joined them for the festivities, sharing their time with his family at nearby Grapevine. Penny described these holiday visits as the "most enjoyable time(s) together."

For Christmas, Penny gave Roger an expensive flight simulator, which could be operated on his desktop computer in his home office. Earlier in the year, Roger had informed her of his intention to learn to fly. He wanted to take private pilot training and buy his own small plane. She was adamantly against the idea, and told a friend that she thought he would be just as happy playing with the flight simulator in the safety of his own home. She would soon discover she was wrong. Roger was dead set on flying the real thing.

"Roger thinks he has wings," she joked in her newsletter. "But he doesn't."

She did acknowledge that he was going to take lessons, and added: "They will mount with wings like the eagles.—Isaiah 40:12." Roger had been called an eagle before, as one of Ross Perot's young "high fliers" almost twenty years earlier, and the metaphorical image of the eagle would soon reappear, to haunt the Scaggs family in an unexpected way.

The newsletter concluded, as usual, with a religious thought:

> With grateful hearts we look back over 1993 and thank God for all our friends, the opportunities to travel, for our health and being able to serve a risen Lord. We look forward to 1994, to teaching opportunities, the May wedding and the possibility of seeing as many of you as God will allow.

The following year, Penny's newsletter was somewhat cryptic and far less informative. The brief note, along with the usual seasonal greetings and biblical quotation, said in its entirety:

> 1994 was such a busy year! Roger did achieve his lifelong goal and now has a private pilot's license. Penny taught 150 women this year how to be more like the Godly women of Proverbs 31. Sarah is working for a computer repair company and going to school part time.

Friends, who were used to receiving the long, detailed accounts of their activities, sensed something might be wrong at the Scaggs home.

*I*f Penny had considered 1993 a banner year for her family, 1994 could only be described as a bummer.

Roger completed pilot training and was licensed to fly a single-engine, light aircraft. His newly earned wings seemed like a license of freedom for a pent-up bird; and several neighbors who had been friends in the past noticed a change in his demeanor.

Apparently, for Roger, who had been a desk jockey in the Air Force and most likely verbally abused by hotshot pilots, getting the pilot's license was important.

Despite her misgivings, Penny threw a party at their home in honor of her husband's accomplishment. Neighbors and a few friends from the office were invited. Penny placed chairs for the partygoers in a circle around the den, similar to the furniture arrangement for one of her seminars. Roger presided over his own party.

One neighbor, retired colonel George Wehling, former commander of the Bergstrom Air Force Base located on the outskirts of Austin, found the event somewhat peculiar.

"Roger said, 'Now, everybody tell a little experience pertaining to me getting my pilot's license,' " Colonel Wehling later told a reporter at the *Austin Chronicle*. When Wehling and another neighbor left, after spending just a brief time with the celebrants, the men were shaking their heads in disbelief.

"Can you believe that guy?" Wehling asked. Both men were stunned by Roger's unabashedly egotistical performance at the party.

Penny ultimately accepted Roger's decision to fly and even took some short flights with him at the controls. His next plan was to buy his own plane. He justified the purchase by saying he could fly himself to some of the closer cities where he had to travel for business.

With that, Penny put her foot down. She demanded that her husband make a list of all the family's assets, including insurance, stocks, and bank accounts. She told him that if he planned to kill himself with this flying foolishness, then she wanted to know just what she would have to live on for the rest of her life.

If Penny was upset by what she considered Roger's midlife crisis—he turned fifty-five that summer—she was devastated by the next family upheaval she faced.

Sarah and Cory Munson were married, as scheduled, in a formal church ceremony at Park Cities Baptist Church in Dallas, on May 19, 1994. An expensive reception for friends and families at the Embassy Suites at Love Field followed the ceremonies. Sarah's half sister, Kerra, flew in from Kansas to be her flower girl, and five friends served as attendants.

To Penny, marriage was the most important milestone in a woman's life. Sarah's wedding was even more significant because of the different lifestyles mother and daughter had chosen in the past. Now Sarah was safely married in a traditional religious ceremony in a Baptist church. Unfortunately, the joy that day brought was to be surprisingly short-lived.

While the wedding in May was one of the happiest events of Penny's life, the couple's separation the following month was the saddest and angriest. After a particularly heated argument between the newlyweds, Sarah called her father, who, with a neighbor, came to remove her belongings from the couple's apartment. When Sarah left Austin for Florida,

Penny told a friend that her daughter would "never, never, never" be allowed back in her home.

"When I got divorced, my dad was there for me a lot more than my mom was," Sarah recalled in an interview with Austin reporter Kayte VanScoy. "My mom was really angry at me for spending all of the money [on the recent wedding]. And my dad was pretty supportive of me. He would never yell at me; he would always just get that disappointed look in his eye.

"After I got divorced, my mom was so angry that she could barely stand to talk to me," she said. "My dad would call and take me to lunch and help me whenever I needed help."

A close friend of Penny's, who had tried to discuss divorce with her on several occasions, felt that Penny's highly emotional reaction to her daughter's divorce was rooted in much more serious concerns than the amount of money spent on a fancy wedding.

"Penny was absolutely adamant that marriage was a holy covenant between Jesus and the couple. It could never be cancelled by a piece of legal paper or a judge," the longtime friend noted. "She literally believed that Eve was made by God from the rib of Adam, and that marriage was the rejoining of the two in one body. It was a permanent physical state, not just an earthly contract."

This friend had tried several times to bring up the possibility that Roger may be "angling for a divorce" after he began trying to coax Penny into putting their spacious house on Winter Park Road on the market.

"After Sarah left home, Roger complained that the Eanes school taxes were too high, and that they should sell their place and move to a smaller house in one of the new developments on the northwest side of town. They actually did list the house with a realtor two or three times," the friend recalled. When it didn't sell by the end of the real estate contract, Penny told everyone, "See, it's God's will that I have this house."

As for her daughter's divorce, it hit Penny harder than it would have in many families because it challenged the very foundation of the godly home she had carefully nurtured over the years. Not only was she the teacher, but also a living example of what the godly wife should be in the Christian family.

Arthur and Diana Coleman had numerous conversations with Penny about the subject. They knew how devastating this divorce in her immediate family was for her. Marriage was the pillar of everything she stood for and professed. For her own marriage, divorce was unthinkable.

"Penny lived what she taught," said Diana, when asked if Penny would ever have agreed to a divorce from Roger. "Divorce went against everything she believed in. Her ministry would have been over."

Another neighbor said, in addition to her religious convictions, there were also more down-to-earth reasons why the idea of divorce alarmed Penny. She had seldom worked outside the home and had no job or professional training to support her comfortable lifestyle.

"Roger also had to be aware that a divorce would cost him dearly," said the friend. Under Texas community property laws, he would have been required to give up at least half his financial wealth, including real property and company holdings.

Just as important, Roger's public and professional image were linked to his status as the head of a Christian home. A messy divorce could have cost him his position as a church elder and the personal credentials as a community and family man that were so vital to his career and every other facet of his success.

Chapter 7

*She maketh herself coverings of tapestry; her clothing is
silk and purple. Her husband is known in the gates,
when he sitteth among the elders of the land.*

—PROVERBS 31:22-23

By early 1995, Roger Scaggs's lifestyle had undergone a
marked change. The once reserved and somewhat reticent executive and church elder had gradually become, over the past
couple of years, more flamboyant in dress and gregarious in
conduct. He still worked hard at building the business of his
division, perhaps harder than ever, with a travel schedule that
had him crisscrossing the nation every month. And he still
attended to his church duties on a weekly basis. But he had
added a broad assortment of grown-up toys and games to his
busy schedule. When weather permitted, he regularly sailed
on the Highland Lakes with peers and employees from his
office, and he hunted quail, dove, and turkey in season. More-
over, much to Penny's horror, the fifty-five-year-old church
elder developed an interest in motorcycles; and not just any
motorcycles—full-sized road hogs.

Roger later conceded that his new interests outside the
routines of work, church, and home could have been partially motivated by "midlife crisis." But he also had a more
practical explanation.

"I finally found myself in a place in life where I had the money and time to do some of the things I had always wanted to do," he recalled. He had earlier taken sailing lessons and became an enthusiastic recreational sailor. Now he had extended that interest to flying.

"I found the freedom to sail, powered by the wind, surrounded by attractive people enjoying themselves, to be quite exhilarating. I then learned to fly and bought a small plane. Both these activities appealed to my daughter, and as she participated with me, we became closer," he said.

"Unfortunately, my wife was afraid of both sailing and flying. She preferred arts, crafts, and church work. Our hobbies pulled us in different directions. We were both happy in our hobbies, but she resented my time with other people sailing and flying."

Even then, Roger said Penny participated, to some extent, from time to time.

Penny had fretted to friends that Roger might be ill, because he had lost a lot of weight. But he easily passed a stringent pilot's physical examination that was required before his licenses were issued by the Federal Aviation Administration.

Roger did seem to be suddenly taking numerous chances with life and limb. He expressed an interest in fast cars, and even racing. Earlier he had traded in his Lincoln for a powerful Lexus SC-series sports car. At the same time, to placate the more practical-minded Penny, he bought her a Ford Aerospace minivan. The van was perfect for hauling the household supplies and groceries, loading up her arts and crafts, and taxiing her disciples to and from church events. Over the years, their automobiles had usually been Lincoln Continentals, one for each of them. Out of frugality, not necessity, the couple had purchased clean, used cars. But this time Roger bought the van and the Lexus brand shiny new, right off the showroom floor.

As much as Roger loved that fast sports car, business demands ultimately forced him to give it up for a vehicle more suitable for escorting visiting clients around Austin. He traded it in for a white Ford Taurus sedan.

He added the crown jewel to his collection of playthings when he purchased his own private airplane in 1993. Penny had stopped protesting, and finally, if reluctantly, accepted that she was not going to keep him out of the air. She even accompanied him on trips to South Carolina, Memphis, and Arkansas to shop for a small aircraft they thought they could afford. He settled on an old but well-maintained, single-engine, low-wing monoplane called the Ercoupe. The small plane got its name, coupe, partially because it could seat only the pilot and one passenger. The two occupants sat in a bubble-domed cockpit with splendid visibility. Roger found the unusual aircraft for sale by an individual owner in Phoenix, Arizona, through a classified ad.

While Penny still expressed fears for Roger's flying safety, and once broke down in tears of anguish while telling a friend of her concern that her husband was going to die in a plane crash, she did occasionally go up in the Ercoupe, with him at the controls. "She didn't enjoy flying as much as I did," said Roger, "but she 'flew the coupe' with me many times." Early in 1995 she accompanied him to a muster of private pilots at an air show in Kalispell, Montana, though they flew on a commercial airline to that event.

But Penny never came around to fully supporting his new flying hobby. The fact was, his numerous other pastimes were also becoming a source of irritation in their heretofore blissful home. One of her intimate friends said Penny became upset about almost everything Roger did "outside the straight line of his work or the church," and described her "suffering long sulks" over his small-game hunting, sailing, motorcycling, and flying. All these activities not only presented some degree of danger, but also took Roger away from home during the small amount of leisure time he had. Since Penny did not enjoy these pastimes, she was increasingly excluded from some of the socializing they involved. At one point Penny complained that Roger had stopped asking her to join his friends from the office on late afternoon sailboat outings. She now said she would like to be asked more often.

As much as Penny feared his flying, Roger loved his new plane. He based it at a small airpark at Lockhart, a forty-five-minute drive from home. Sometimes Roger drove down to Lockhart just to putter around the little aluminum-skinned aircraft. He was frequently seen at the hanger polishing the twenty-one-foot-long fuselage or the thirty-foot wings. Though the plane was old—the last of the Ercoupe models came off the assembly line in 1970—it was in good working order.

Roger was gradually restoring its appearance back to mint condition. The manager of the airpark, Barney Lowe, recalled seeing him cleaning the plane on many occasions when he did not even take it up for a flight. Lowe said Roger always wore skintight rubber gloves to keep the oils and solvents off his hands. The gloves became somewhat of a joke around the airfield, with rawboned old pilots kidding that Roger looked like a surgeon working on his little plane.

Some of the other pilots at the Lockhart airfield did not think the novice flier was a particularly skilled pilot, but neither was he considered reckless. Certainly, they could not fault him on the careful maintenance of his aircraft. He was almost obsessive about caring for the plane and performed maintenance on it after every flight.

The Ercoupe was considered one of the safest private planes ever built for the amateur pilot. It was once described by the Civil Aeronautics Administration as "characteristically incapable of spinning." The plane was ideal for recreational, weekend fliers, with a top airspeed of about 125 miles an hour and an 11,000-foot ceiling. One of its best features was that the cockpit could be fully opened, making it ideal for aerial photography. Roger, like Penny, was already a fairly adept recreational photographer when he took up aerial photography. Now he would buzz low over Central

Texas shooting pictures from the pilot seat of his own plane.

Roger's toy collection did not go unnoticed by Penny's sisters. Sharon Fox felt that Penny had to forgo simple household conveniences to accommodate her husband's costly hobbies.

"While Roger had lovely, expensive toys, Penny used a washer and dryer that were so old they vibrated away from the wall in the laundry room," Sharon said. "He did not give her a full share." After the sister bitterly complained to Roger about his stinginess, he purchased a new washer and dryer for Penny.

During this period, Roger found yet another way to spice up his life and live dangerously.

Texas Chili Parlor is a dilapidated, hole-in-the-wall café with an Austin attitude and a reputation for serving the best bowl of chili in Texas. The little restaurant at 1409 Lavaca Street is almost in the shadows of the great dome of the Texas Capitol Building. Given its culinary fame, when state senators and representatives convene every two years, the place is packed every day for months by a crowd of self-appointed Tex-Mex connoisseurs. It is also a favorite eatery for students and professors from the nearby university, as well as judges, lawyers, city officials, and clerks from the courts and government buildings.

The menu features, at very reasonable prices, such Tex-Mex favorites as the house special, XXX (for triple-hot) chili; ranchero beef with cheese enchiladas; and beef or chicken fajita dinner for two, with Mexican rice and refried beans.

Like any famous eatery that draws a distinguished clientele, Texas Chili Parlor has acquired its own odd collection of folklore. For example, although Lee Harvey Oswald never ate at the place, his daughter, incognito until the end of her employment, paid her way through the University of Texas waiting tables there. *Austin American-Statesman* columnist Michael Corcoran, who knows a little bit about everybody who's anybody in Austin, has for years chronicled the appearance of the rich and famous who brave the establishment's outwardly seedy facade for the zesty cuisine. Roger Scaggs would eventually join the list of former habitués. But it was not until years later that he became well-known enough to make Corcoran's newspaper column, "Austin Inside and Out."

Even though the café was miles away from his office, and too long a drive in noon traffic to be a lunch choice for APS employees, Roger became a regular weekday patron. He was primarily noticed by the waiters and waitresses because of the young, statuesque redhead on his arm when he began frequenting the café in the spring of 1995. The couple always went for the privacy of a back booth.

"Right off, we figured it for a mistress and rich sugar daddy deal," said a bartender named Ron. "She was just too young and good-looking to be anything else with that guy. He was almost spooky. We called him the X-man because of his wrinkled forehead and how he acted."

It was the way Roger treated the girl that cemented the couple in the employees' memories. Only years later did the café staff discover Roger's identity, and they never did know the name of X-man's girlfriend.

"I couldn't get my dog to obey me as much as this one," said Tammy, who had waitressed at the Chili Parlor for fourteen years. "I've seen a lot of important guys—politicians and entertainers—in here with their honeys, and nothing like that. He ordered everything for her. She wouldn't even order tea without his okay. If he said no, she wouldn't have the bun on her hamburger."

If Roger's image makeover as a sports-car-racing enthusiast, motorcyclist, and pilot had surprised his employees and business associates, rumors of an affair with a young woman close to his daughter's age shocked them into silence—a silence they maintained with his friends, neighbors, fellow

church members, and, most of all, his wife Penny. The affair
apparently began in March 1995, and it was not long before
the usual water-cooler gossip was whispered around the offices. The rumor was that Roger had become involved with
someone in the company. Some employees noticed unusually lavish flowers being delivered, arrangements that
seemed to go beyond the routine reward for a job well done.

The subject of the rumors was a twenty-eight-year-old assistant in the accounting section of APS Group, the corporate headquarters operation. The young woman who was
soon identified as Roger's secret lover was Vanessa Ferguson. Although she was almost thirty years Roger's junior, he
was not technically her immediate supervisor.

Vanessa would later say that Roger did not approach her
about having an affair. "He made it a clear prerequisite that
he wanted his life to remain unchanged," she said. "He just
wanted to add sex. I was living with someone at the time, as
well. He loved his wife and daughter and didn't want that
disturbed."

But keeping the affair from his daughter was not in the
cards. Sarah soon figured out that her father was involved
with another woman. She ran into Roger and Vanessa at
Austin restaurants on more than one occasion. Having become serious about pursuing her college education, Sarah
was working toward a degree in criminal psychology, which
she eventually achieved. She had left the waitressing job and
was employed as a dispatcher at a large computer repair
company in north Austin. She had moved to a condominium
complex to be closer to work and the Austin Community
College north campus.

Her new duplex apartment was located in a far-north Austin area where dozens of upscale, multifamily rental properties had been built for employees of nearby computer
hardware manufacturing plants. Austin's computer industry
was rapidly expanding to new areas north of the city. The
vast apartment and condominium complexes offered luxury
housing at affordable rates for the mobile young people

flocking to the industry. Since few of these career climbers stayed in one place long enough to know their neighbors, the sprawling complexes also offered a high degree of anonymity.

Once Roger was confronted and had confirmed Sarah's suspicions about the affair, the father apparently took advantage of his daughter's living arrangements to accommodate his own need for his secret rendezvous. Sarah later insisted she never abetted her father's affair. But after all his support for her during her difficult teen and young-adult years, she may have felt she was in no position to turn down a request for a favor in return. Asking his daughter for the occasional use of her apartment was just one of the more blatant chances Roger was willing to take to further his clandestine dalliance. He was eventually caught in this one by employees from his own office.

*I*n midsummer 1995, Roger continued his uncharacteristic behavior when he announced he was planning to grow a beard. At that time, in the conservative corporate environment of Texas, the look was clean-shaven; the dress code called for suit and tie year-round. It was before the era of Dockers and sport shirts, and even before the introduction of casual Fridays. Roger decided to defy the rules and grow full facial hair.

Soon, a salt-and-pepper beard took growth, much to the chagrin of Penny, if not his fellow execs at APS. Roger brushed off his wife's complaints with the excuse that he was growing the beard to enter the company's annual Halloween costume contest. He said he was going to the party as a Hell's Angels biker.

Neighbor and friend Diana Coleman said the beard upset Penny because she thought it represented more than just a temporary gag for a company party. When she spoke of the beard, "she had tears in her eyes," Coleman recalled. "He had been growing it for several months. One day I saw him across the street. I had not seen him or talked to him since the beard had become so obvious. I called to him and said, 'Hey, Roger what's that on your face?' He came running across the street, and he rubbed his beard against my face and said, 'Don't you just love it?' I said, 'No, I don't. You look like a grub. Go home and shave that off.' He ran back across the street laughing, and shouted over his shoulder, 'You sound just like Penny.' Penny was very upset about the beard."

Apparently, Roger had told his wife that the beard impressed the women at the office.

"The women at the office loved it and thought it made him look very handsome," Coleman said she had learned from a weeping Penny.

Roger went to the company Halloween party as a biker, sporting beard and bandanna, sleeveless T-shirt, dirty torn jeans, and motorcycle boots. He had also purchased a leather motorcycle jacket with a red, white, and blue emblem of an eagle in full wingspread on the back. Roger did, in fact, win a prize for his costume. Penny attended the party with him, though not in costume, and she put up a good front. Despite her strong objections to the beard and motorcycle-gang symbolism, she appeared in photos of the event, smiling broadly.

A month before the party, Penny had been stricken with a serious illness that forced her to cancel all her seminars and most of her other church activities for the rest of the year. A persistent, nagging cold had worsened, until she was finally forced to take to bed. Diana Coleman discovered her immobile when she went across the street to deliver a quart of chicken soup she had made to help speed her recovery. Diana had to let herself in with the house key; the neighbors exchanged keys and checked on each other's homes during absences.

Roger was out of town. Several of Penny's friends were so concerned about her condition that they set up a rotating vigil at her bedside. She had refused to go to the hospital.

Roger returned to Austin at the end of the week, but went directly to his office without coming home to check on his wife.

Penny had told him by phone that she was very sick. His not coming by the house when he returned made her feel "very rejected," a friend recalled. Diana Coleman came back to sit with Penny later that day.

"She was crying," Diana said. "She told me Roger didn't love her, didn't care about her anymore. I told her that was nonsense. A little later, I was in the kitchen getting her something when Roger came in."

Penny's breathing became so labored that she was finally forced to see a doctor. Robert Groves, an internist in partnership with Penny's regular physician, found that she was seriously ill with fluid in both lungs. She still refused to be hospitalized, so he put her on an extra heavy regime of antibiotics. When he saw her again a week later, her condition had worsened. On October 9 she was forced to go to the emergency room at Seton Medical Center, where a pulmonary specialist was added to the team of professionals consulting on her case. Blood tests showed she had a serious systemic infection, in addition to double pneumonia.

Roger continued his business travels while she was ill, but even with no one there to care for her, Penny insisted on being at home. Finally, her condition deteriorated so much that she had to call for help for the first time in her life.

"Penny called me, and she was crying," recalled Sharon Fox, her oldest sister, but still her junior by almost five years. "I was quite surprised by the emotion and distress in her voice. She was very upset, like I had never heard her before. She said she needed help and that Roger was not going to be there to help her."

Sharon flew to Austin on a Saturday and Roger picked her up at the airport. "He had a beard, and we talked about it," she recalled. "He asked me if I wanted to touch it, and I said no. He dropped me off and said he was going on to the office."

Sharon found Penny propped up in bed, looking very pale and having considerable trouble breathing. By then a visiting nurse was coming to the house daily, to administer her medications.

"She was always thin; she always watched her figure and ate very sparingly," Sharon said. "But we were concerned that she had lost too much weight."

Roger left on a business trip the next day, Sunday. This made Penny more upset.

On Monday she was gasping for air, and her sister called 911. The emergency team on the responding ambulance found that she was dangerously short on oxygen. Sharon paged Roger to tell him that Penny had been rushed to the hospital, then stayed with her until she was discharged on Friday. Roger came back from his trip on Wednesday and visited his wife in the hospital for two hours before leaving for work.

Earlier in the week, a woman who worked for Roger had risked her future with the company by almost demanding that he return to his wife's bedside.

Patty Adams, interim marketing and sales director of APS Systems, had accompanied her boss on the trip to Atlanta for major contract negotiations. On the way there, Roger mentioned that Penny was ill, but assured his coworker it was not serious. By this time, of course, Penny had already been hospitalized and was in intensive care.

Later, on the first day of the contract talks, Adams checked in with the home office. A secretary told her that Roger's wife was in "critical condition at Seton and might not even survive" her illness. Alarmed, the thirty-two-year-old subordinate boldly confronted her boss, who virtually held her job destiny in his hands. When Roger told her he had not decided whether to cut his participation in the negotiations short and fly to his wife's bedside, the young woman angrily scolded him.

"I really can't believe you aren't going home," she recalled saying during the tense exchange. "If my husband was in the emergency room, I'd never leave him."

Adams said that it took a call from daughter Sarah to get Roger to finally leave the business meeting. As he left for the airport, he snapped at Adams, "She's going to Dallas [to recover] when she gets out of the hospital. I don't have time to take care of her."

"I was shocked," Adams said. she said Roger did not really have to travel as much as before because APS Systems had added four new sales and marketing specialists during the last part of 1995.

"But he was changing," she said. "In the months after he started growing a beard, there was a change." The acting sales and marketing director even asked him to shave at one point because they were to make a major presentation on a potential multimillion-dollar contract with a new client.

"He looked really scraggily, but said he didn't want to shave the beard off," Adams said. APS Systems did not get the new business, but Adams didn't say whether anyone thought it was because of Roger's unprofessional appearance.

When Penny was discharged from the hospital, her sisters agreed she could not care for herself at home. "I told Roger of our concern," said Sharon. "In my presence he told Penny, 'I don't want you coming home until you can take care of me in the normal way.' "

Sharon drove her back to Dallas, where Penny stayed with her sisters for two weeks while she recuperated. At the end of that period, Roger flew to Dallas and drove his wife back to Austin.

While she was convalescing, Penny sent a note to her friend, Elizabeth Trower, thanking her for having the Seton hospital chaplain visit her each day. Trower had notified the chaplain that her friend probably needed some spiritual handholding.

"Thanks so much for having the Seton chaplain come

visit and pray for me," Penny wrote. "She is so sweet and kind—a real servant of the Lord."

About a month later Penny's extended family took a Caribbean cruise to the tropics, paid for by her elderly parents as a holiday gift. The sisters, their husbands, and the children accompanied their parents on the voyage. The cruise ship *Royal Princess* sailed from San Juan, Puerto Rico, the week before Thanksgiving, with stops in Barbados, Martinique, St. Croix, and St. Thomas. The four sisters spent most of the trip together. When in port, they devoted their time to shopping, while Roger and Sarah went on snorkeling expeditions and sightseeing trips. It was a happy gathering of the large family, and Penny seemed rejuvenated by the experience.

The family got together again in Dallas for their traditional Christmas festivities, visiting each of the sisters' homes and exchanging gifts. Roger accompanied Penny, and, according to the sisters, everything seemed to be going well with the couple.

Penny's 1995 newsletter featured a photograph of her and Roger dressed in formal attire, beaming happily for the camera. She mentioned his hunting trips and chattered gaily about how Roger loved flying his plane around Central Texas, taking family, friends, and coworkers up for rides. She gently chided that the only time she saw him was "when the weather doesn't cooperate and keeps him grounded." She wrote, "His work schedule is heavy, with travel from coast to coast."

She talked about the Christian seminars she had taught early in the year, and lamented that her illness had curtailed those activities for the rest of '95. "I have fully recovered and will begin teaching again in late January," she wrote. She said her illness had also prevented her from taking all but a few business trips with Roger.

She wrote at length about the family cruise to the Caribbean, and joked that it was great having Thanksgiving on a cruise ship, because the food was good and "no dishes to wash!"

Two paragraphs reported on Sarah's progress. One was devoted to her daughter's new job as a "logistics and distribution coordinator for a computer company" and her continuing studies in psychology. The second was about Sarah's new duplex apartment in north Austin, which gave Sarah much more space and a little yard for her half-dozen cats and "a darling little bunny." Penny wrote that Sarah was very busy, "so we try to schedule lunches once a week in order to keep up with one another."

At the bottom of the letter, both Penny and Roger's names were signed in Penny's handwriting. Later, some friends would note that, in previous years, Roger had always put his personal signature on the annual message. The card wished all "a most blessed Christmas," and expressed the hope of "seeing many of you in 1996."

Chapter 8

*She maketh fine linen, and selleth it; and delivereth girdles
unto the merchant. Strength and Honor are her clothing;
and she shall rejoice in time to come.*

—PROVERBS 31:24-25

*P*enny Scaggs's cheerful, upbeat personality seemed to return as 1996 began. She had fully recuperated from her
lengthy illness the previous winter and was excited about
resuming her ministry. According to the positive outlook reflected in the year-end newsletter, her family was flourish-
ing and prospects were bright. But in the real world there is
often a fine line separating an optimist from a Pollyanna. As
was characteristic for Penny, she seemed to be ignoring or
denying some of the more unpleasant realities that were becoming apparent to others in her life.

For example, her positive approach to the New Year was
not dampened by an incident at the Colemans' house that
occurred shortly before Christmas. On December 19, 1995,
she and Roger had been invited for after-dinner refreshments and the traditional exchange of gifts with old friends
Diana and Arthur Coleman. The couples unwrapped pres-
ents and chatted over coffee and cake.

The evening began on a high note. A home video shows a
delighted Penny opening and admiring a decorative teapot.

Roger also closely examined the ornate little pot. "How clever," he said.

But the merriment waned as the evening wore on.

Roger had become noticeably fidgety and began looking at his watch every few minutes. He said he had so much energy he didn't know what to do with himself. He thought he would run over to Barton Creek Mall for some last minute shopping. The parking-lot lights and department-store signs were visible from the Coleman house. Diana looked out the window and reported that the lights were off and the mall appeared to be closed. Roger said he was going anyway, insisting that the stores stayed open late for the Christmas crowds. He said he had something to pick up at Stein Mart. Diana called the store for him and was told they would be open for another twenty minutes. Roger left.

Penny stayed a few minutes longer. She had turned pensive, Diana recalled. And at one point Penny mused, "I wonder where we'll all be this time next year."

Diana and Arthur watched Penny walk across the street to her house, to make sure she got safely inside. Sometime later that night Penny called Diana. She was worried that Roger had not yet come home. The mall was only a few blocks from the neighborhood. The next day Penny told her friend that it was after midnight before Roger returned.

Coleman later confirmed that the stores in the mall had closed well before then. This incident, together with the other uncharacteristic behavior Diana had witnessed in Roger over the past year, was enough to make her suspect that her friend's husband was having an affair. For anyone except a habitué of the bars, the streets were pretty much rolled up at that hour on a weeknight.

*A*ustin was still a small enough place that a married man having an affair could hardly expect to keep it secret for long. Eventually, someone was going to see the lovers at one of their clandestine rendezvous. Predictably, that is what happened with Roger.

Ednoa Harrell, who was managing the APS office properties, accidentally ran across him and Vanessa Ferguson during one noon meeting far from the office. Harrell had dropped her car off at a north Austin auto garage for repairs and later discovered she had left some needed items in the vehicle. A coworker offered to drive her to the garage to retrieve the material. On their way back, they saw Roger pulling out of the Barton Creek Mall. Like almost everyone else in the office, they had by then heard the gossip that Roger was having an affair. They decided to follow him. They drove to the turnaround and tailed him in his white Taurus as he headed north on the MoPac Expressway at a fast clip, unaware that the women were behind him.

"Curiosity got the best of us," said Harrell, who seemed somewhat embarrassed to admit what they had done. "We had heard rumors for a long while that he was having an affair, and decided to see where he was going."

Roger was on his cell phone most of the time. He was not behaving in a furtive manner and appeared to be focused solely on his phone call and his driving. He left the freeway at the Braker Lane exit, drove into a complex of duplexes and condominiums and stopped at one of them. The garage door went up, and he pulled the Taurus inside. Shortly afterward, a dark car pulled into the driveway. A young woman got out and greeted Roger. Ms. Harrell later found out that the woman was his daughter, Sarah. Then a tan Acura drove up and parked on the street.

"I recognized it as Vanessa Ferguson's," Harrell said. Roger and Sarah walked toward Vanessa as she was getting out of the car.

"He hugged her and kissed her," Harrell said. "His daughter drove off, and Roger and Vanessa went into the duplex."

Numerous other incidents at the office involving Roger and the young specialist from the finance department added to the gossip at the company for months.

Talk of the affair became so pervasive around the office that Roger's fellow executives eventually heard about it. A no-nonsense senior secretary at APS finally complained that the fraternization between a high-ranking company officer and a much younger, lower-level employee was having a negative impact on morale. She went to the chief executive with her concerns.

APS Group president Shifrin admitted that he did not act because there was no proof of an affair and he simply did not believe it. He confirmed that the senior secretary had warned him directly about the dalliance. Shifrin recalled having one conversation with Roger about it. He told Roger he had heard a rumor and wanted him to put a stop to it. Roger assured him he would. "I don't think I believed it," said Shifrin, "so I never asked him if it was true."

Roger's fellow employees were not the only ones with suspicions about an affair. Some of Penny's friends, and even some of her former students, were beginning to worry that the perfect marriage she taught by example as well as textbook might not be that perfect after all. Talk circulated about her husband's seeming callousness during her recent illness. His increasingly frequent absences, for both business and leisure, raised some eyebrows, too. Since Penny constantly had friends over for Bible study, to work on arts and crafts, or simply to visit, people noticed that Roger was rarely around the way he had been in the past.

Longtime friend Mary Lowery, a registered nurse at St. David's Medical Center in Austin, openly expressed her concerns about the marriage to Penny. She had taken Penny's seminar in 1985, and continued to keep in touch.

"Everybody loved her, everybody. She was known by all the women in the area for her good reputation," Lowery recalled. "She always tried to make the woman's role in the household an important one, but still something to be enjoyed. She did teach that the husband was the head of the house. She believed that the wife needed to love and respect the husband, but that the husband also had to be loving toward his wife. If the relationship was not loving, the wife had to make it loving."

When Lowery met Penny for lunch in January 1996, the subject of Roger's infidelity came up. Another friend, Pat Muller, was also at the luncheon. They talked about their husbands and children. Penny said she had been sick and that her friends and sisters took care of her.

"I asked where Roger was," Lowery recalled. "Penny looked down and gave a little laugh. She acted embarrassed and said Roger was away more often. She mentioned his boat and plane, and said he had more activities where he was away from her with other things to do. I asked her then if she was sure that there was not someone else involved. She quickly changed the subject. Penny was very private . . . and she never discussed things like that about her personal life. She acted like it upset her. Her whole biblical teaching was taking care of the people you love."

Penny told the women that Roger had stopped asking her to go on trips with him. According to Lowery, Penny said her husband told her, "The work goes much better and faster without you."

*I*n early February 1996, Roger sold a large block of his stock in APS Group, amounting to almost half the shares he had earned in his sixteen years with the company. It was reported that Roger sold over $200,000 worth of stock through a Florida brokerage firm. He still owned 27,000 shares of registered stock and a considerable portfolio of options to buy stock at earlier fixed prices. The company's 1995 annual report indicated that Scaggs had exercisable and unexercisable options valued at about $456,000 and $123,000, respectively. It is not clear if Penny approved the large stock sell-off, or if she was even aware of the transaction.

Obviously, Roger had been able to keep *some* secrets from his wife of thirty-five years. Whether Penny Scaggs knew or suspected that her husband was having an affair and chose to ignore the clues, or actually denied what was becoming more evident every day, is unknown. Many of the employees in Roger's office knew Penny and also knew about the affair. Several considered her a friend, and admitted they had chosen not to tell her because they did not want to bring her pain. If someone from the office did call and tell her about it, she never shared that with her most intimate friends or her sisters.

Nevertheless, something happened in the marriage that caused Penny to seek marital counseling for the first time in her thirty-five-year marriage. She convinced Roger to go with her to a faith-based counseling service. It was outside their own church, and they apparently went without the knowledge of their pastor. Penny and Roger sought help at the Samaritan Center for Counseling and Pastoral Care located at 5425-A Burnet Road in Austin. Their counselor was a licensed Southern Baptist minister named John Cooke. The Samaritan Center specializes in counseling in a spiritual context for individuals, couples, and entire families. It is a nondenominational, professional service that uses spiritual and faith resources to help its patients. Several of the senior counselors are licensed ministers.

"Many of Samaritan's patients are referred to the center through their pastors, priests, or other members of the clergy," according to a statement made by the center. "Counselors frequently will speak to their patients' religious advisers in an effort to help the patient with their difficulties."

Because of the religious nature of the counseling offered by the center, its operators claimed complete confidentiality, including full legal privilege from disclosure of any information on its patients. With respect to the Scaggses, the center exercised that privilege, and nothing was ever revealed about the purpose or content of their sessions. Still, it is clear from the nature of the services offered and the timing of the visits that there was serious trouble in the couple's relationship, which required them to seek outside help. It can also be assumed that they wanted this counseling kept secret from their friends, family, and church. No one in their closest circles knew about it. The Scaggses apparently did not even inform their minister, Reverend Rob Harrell, or anyone else in the clergy at First Evangelical Free Church about the counseling.

Though normally a private person, Penny was unable to hide her emotions as the problems in her marriage seemed to accelerate during the first week of March 1996. Two of her young devotees noticed her apparent agitation on a weekend religious retreat to the Hill Country. The women's retreat, coordinated by Penny's Sunday school class from the First Evangelical Free Church, was held from March 1 to March 3, at Camp Balcones Springs. The camp was just outside Marble Falls, about an hour's drive west of Austin. The sprawling facility, which was one of the most popular summer youth camps in the Austin–San Antonio area, was situated on a beautiful wilderness bay on the shores of Lake Travis. The management rented space for adult retreats during the off-season. The camp featured air-conditioned cabins, sports facilities, an eight-acre private lake, hiking trials, and, most important for Penny, a well-furnished arts and crafts building. Described in promotional material as "a small paradise nestled in the beautiful Texas Hill Country," it offered an ideal location for a weekend of spiritual renewal.

That weekend, however, something seemed to prevent the group leader from taking full advantage of the Eden-like setting.

Risa Pardue, who held up Penny as her mentor, had known the older woman since taking one of her earliest Austin seminars. Through church, they had maintained a close personal friendship over the years. She also knew Roger in his role as an elder of First Evangelical.

Pardue and two other young devotees of Penny's teachings planned to drive out to the retreat with Penny in her minivan. On Friday afternoon, Risa and the other women met at the Scaggs house for the trip. Risa had worked closely

with Penny on the favors committee, which made book-
marks, table decorations, and other small gifts bearing biblical messages to be given away during the retreat. They had
been working on these arts and crafts over the past several
weeks, usually in Penny's home.

The inspirational speaker for the retreat was Ann Ortland, author of the self-help book *Disciplines of a Beautiful
Woman*. Some of Penny's friends were surprised when she
purchased an Ortland videotape on enhancing marital sex at
the book table set up at the back of the conference room.

When the retreat ended on Sunday afternoon, the young
women who were riding back with Penny were in for another surprise. Shortly before the group left, Penny received
a call on her cell phone that seemed to create a feeling of
urgency on her part to return quickly to Austin. Normally,
Penny was a very careful and defensive driver. But on that
particular trip, her driving frightened her passengers.

"Her demeanor that day was calm, and everything seemed
perfectly normal. But on the drive back down from the hills
there were times when I was gripping the dashboard," recalled Risa Pardue. "We were on a very hilly, winding farm
road and Penny was exceeding the speed limit. She was
driving very fast. This was very unusual for Penny. During
that car ride, she seemed to be pensive, deep in thought.
Once she got to the city limits, she got out her cell phone
and called Roger immediately."

Another passenger, Karen Lemens, a young homemaker
whose husband was in graduate school, vividly recalled
Penny's unusual driving behavior on the return from the retreat. Karen was a member of Penny's Sunday school class
and was also attending her latest Creative Counterpart seminar, which had last met on February 29 and was scheduled
to be completed in April.

Like Risa, Karen left her car parked at Penny's house and
rode up with her on Friday, March 1, for the retreat. On the
trip up, Penny's driving was unremarkable—easily within
the speed limit and safe. However, the return trip on

March 3 was anything but safe. It was such a frightening experience that the young woman made a note about it in her diary when she got home.

Penny's driving was "very jerky," said Karen. "She took the corners so sharply on the narrow roads, it made me sick. I don't ride well on trips anyway, but this trip made me ill." When they arrived at Penny's house, Karen collected her things from the van and went directly to her car without going into the house.

Penny's friends and family members who had ridden with her for years could never remember her driving erratically or in an unsafe manner. She drove thousands of miles each year, and was considered an extra-cautious driver. It is not known who called her that Sunday afternoon, but the message she received made her extremely anxious to rush home.

Chapter 9

*She openeth her mouth with wisdom; and in her tongue
is the law of kindness. She looketh well to the ways of her
household, and eateth not of the bread of idleness. Her
children rise up, and call her blessed; her husband also,
and he praiseth her.*

—PROVERBS 31:26-28

*W*ednesday, March 6, dawned clear and balmy over the
Hill Country at 6:51 A.M. It was another of those glorious,
warm winter days, so famous they draw large numbers of
snowbirds from northern cities to second homes or retire-
ment in the Austin area. Of course, those lucky enough to
have second homes can escape back to somewhere else in
July and August, when the triple-digit heat can last for weeks
on end, and the humidity off the Gulf Coast makes even a
short stroll feel like a session in a sauna.

But it was about to turn cold. A northern front was rapidly
sweeping across the Great Plains, propelling arctic air
toward the heart of Texas.

Penny Scaggs seemed to have taken in stride the upset
from the previous weekend, whatever its cause. She was in
the midst of teaching a class of twenty-two women, one of
the largest groups ever to have enrolled in the Creative

Counterpart course, and spent the earlier part of the week preparing materials for the next session. It was scheduled for the following night, Thursday, at her home.

The class was so large that in previous weeks some of the women had sat on the carpeted floor for the lectures. The couches and chairs were arranged in a semicircle, facing the fireplace. At one point, the class broke into small groups of four or five for prayer sessions. One of these groups had to huddle on the floor beside the yellow piano, which also provided a large surface for inspirational tracts and books to be displayed for perusal during the refreshment break.

Lately, Penny's husband had been even busier than usual, if that were possible. For days, Roger and his staff had been preparing a written report and presentation with business charts and graphs for the APS board of directors meeting, also scheduled for Thursday. It would be a busy day for both Penny and Roger, she with her large class to teach, and he with an important business meeting.

This time the news that Roger was going to present to the board about his subsidiary, APS Systems, was not all positive. The primary system that his division had sold so profitably to doctors' groups and hospitals for the past decade had gradually become obsolete. It would require an infusion of at least $5 million to upgrade and redesign the program to make it competitive again. Several board members had already indicated they did not want to put that kind of money into the project. They wanted new, innovative products instead. Roger was somewhat behind schedule in compiling the report, because he had been on a business trip Monday and Tuesday.

On Wednesday he left the house at 7:00 A.M. to drive the short distance to his office. Though normally a ten-minute drive, at that hour of the morning the traffic on Capital of Texas Highway was slowed by commuters, and the jam-ups at exits could add considerable time to the trip.

Penny, as ever, was up and about when Roger left. She always saw him off to work. It was a duty, according to her

teaching, along with the mandate that the wife always cheerily greet her husband's return home, no matter the hour. She
had a special way of making their bed each morning while
she was still in it. That chore would already be done when
she rolled out for the day. She taught her pupils how to do
the trick, along with many other little practical tips she offered up while addressing the greater issues of applying the
rules of the Bible to the marital relationship.

Penny was also interested in learning about a method for
improving her arts and crafts. She had heard about a woman
in a community north of Austin who was using a new technique to make rubber stamps for the reproduction of calligraphy and line art. She asked Risa Pardue, who shared her
interest in calligraphy, if she would like to go with her to see
the new crafts technique.

At about 9:00 A.M. on March 6 they met in the parking lot
of a women's high-fashion specialty store at the Arboretum,
an upscale shopping district in another new Hill Country
suburban area. They drove in Penny's van to the in-home
business, where they reviewed the rubber-stamp techniques
and the kits the woman sold. Afterward, Penny drove Risa
back to the Arboretum to pick up her car.

"We were sitting in her van in the parking lot, talking,"
said Pardue. "It was close to noon. Penny pulled out her cell
phone and left Roger a message: 'I'm waiting for your call.
Call me back.' She wanted to meet her husband for lunch.

"Penny was not a woman to waste a minute. She suggested we visit until Roger returned her call. She had recently learned how to stencil a card and wanted to show me
how to do it. She pulled the material out of her purse and
began demonstrating how to make hearts on the paper, raise
them and shade them. We both liked to send decorative
notes and cards."

When Roger called back, he said he was ready for lunch.
Penny said it would take her "fourteen minutes" to get
home.

Then something happened that Risa found strange. She

had known Penny for years, and although she was closely involved with her at church and through her teaching, she had never seen her become emotional over what seemed to be nothing at all.

"As we said our good-byes, Penny became so misty-eyed and sentimental," Pardue recalled. The friend thought there must be something wrong. "It was such an unusual way to say good-bye, since we were parting company for just a few days and would probably see each other again on Sunday."

The only other times she had seen Penny upset were in response to something serious or tragic, like the illness or death of a friend or relative.

"Once, years ago, she took me to my hairdresser after I had been in bed a long time from surgery and complications," Pardue said. "I told her then how I felt that God had saved my life and returned me to my home and family as a whole person." That conversation made Penny tear up.

But the tears on this day came without warning, without any apparent reason. And Penny could not, or would not, offer an explanation. She just waved her friend away and sped off to meet her husband.

Roger arrived home to have lunch with his wife between 12:15 and 12:30 P.M. They ate soup before he rushed back to work by one o'clock. On the way out he noticed that the trash in the can at the curb where he placed it that morning had not yet been picked up. The Texas flag they were flying that day was flapping in the breeze.

The Scaggses always flew a large flag from a thirty-foot metal pole they had erected in their front yard. The unusual pole made the place look like an official headquarters when compared with the short staffs most neighbors had attached to their homes, to fly flags on special occasions. The Scaggses also had an American flag, which they flew from the pole on alternate days.

With a storm approaching, Roger thought Penny would tend to it. She disliked the expense of replacing flags tattered by the sometimes fierce winds. They could reach near gale force at the top of the hill where their stately home was situated.

Back at the office, several people were helping Roger pull together the figures for his report. As the workday neared an end, Roger called Penny to say he was not going to finish the board presentation on time, that he still had at least two more hours of work on it. Penny suggested he come home, have supper with her, rest for a few minutes, and then return to the office to complete the report.

Around the time that Roger was due home, Penny's friend and former student Shawn Constant telephoned her. The two women shared more than their religious convictions, since Shawn's husband was a computer engineer. They spoke briefly.

"It was a pleasant conversation," the friend recalled. "Penny was working on a lecture she was going to give at another church on the topic of wisdom. I was able to help her, since I had material on that subject. I was excited, because I was able to return something to my mentor after all the things she had done for me."

Shawn said she discerned nothing out of the ordinary during the conversation, and that Penny sounded like she was in a good mood.

"We talked about the weather changing," Constant said. "She told me she had already brought in the flag and needed to bring in some plants." Penny had placed her potted plants on the back deck earlier in the week so they could benefit from the warm sun.

"She was anxious and worried about the lecture and said she felt unsure about herself because of the topic. I had never seen her unsure of herself before," Shawn said.

Roger later said he came home for his supper break between 5:30 and 6:00 P.M. Penny served a vegetable dish of carrots, beans, and barley. After the meal, he helped clear the table and stack the dishes in the sink.

After dinner, Roger changed his clothes from his standard uniform—business suit, white shirt, and tie—to blue jeans, a plaid shirt, denim jacket, and loafers. He also rolled the now empty trash cart into the garage, where it was normally kept. Then he got in his car and drove back to the office.

*T*he first sign of a change in the balmy evening was a rustling in the branches of the eaves-high shrubs along the side of the house. Penny's carefully nurtured potted plants were still out back, on the thirty-foot wood deck. The leaves on the tender plants trembled with the first gusts of the approaching blue norther. The long porch was not visible from the front of the luxurious brick home, and completely hidden from the side street by tall hedges and a redwood fence around the backyard. An attached wooden storage shed further obscured the view of the back of the house from neighboring property.

At around sunset, which occurred at 6:34 P.M. that evening, the leading edge of the approaching cold front roared across Austin at forty miles an hour, setting off car alarms on vehicles rocked by the wind. They wailed like clarions warning of danger invading the town. Austinites, who had been dressed in shirtsleeves for days and frolicked in the city's many parks in shorts and tees, would be ducking indoors from a stinging, icy drizzle by midnight. Freezing temperatures were forecast. In Central Texas the winds come straight out of the flat Texas Panhandle, where it is said "there's nothing between here and the North Pole 'ceptin' a barbed-wire fence in Oklahoma." Penny had not brought her plants in from the elements, almost certainly exposing them to a killer frost that night.

After dinner, she had gone into the den to play her baby grand piano. She was dressed casually in belted black slacks, a light-colored, open-neck blouse, and black, flat-soled shoes. Even in this attire, and home for the evening, she was wearing her favorite diamond jewelry. She needed glasses to read the music when she played. She kept a spare pair on the piano.

That evening she chose a Christian favorite, selecting it from the sheet music of inspirational songs she kept in the bench seat. The hymn was "Lord, Be Glorified," written in 1977 by Bob Kilpatrick as a prayer of consecration to the Lord. She placed the music on the piano rack as she settled on the bench to play. The words reflected what was in her heart, her thoughts, and her actions, every day of her life.

In my life, Lord, be glorified, today. I can think of no other way I'd rather spend my day than with my sisters and brothers all rejoicing in your ways.

*B*etween five in the evening and the time her husband returned home from work shortly after 9:00 P.M., something went terribly wrong in the carefully ordered world of Lou Anne Ehrle Scaggs. Penny's life was suddenly, violently, and prematurely terminated in one of the most brutal homicides that Austin police officers and emergency medical personnel assigned to work the case had ever seen. The savagery of the attack and the gratuitous mutilation of the body added a degree of horror to an act that would already terrify the community because of the unusual circumstances of the victim's social standing and the crime-free neighborhood where it had happened.

Roger Scaggs, according to his statements, was at work completing the business report for the APS board of directors when the assault occurred. He said he returned to the office after dinner and, as usual, drove his Ford Taurus into the underground parking area reserved for officials of the company and rented to tenants of the office building. Then he worked on his presentation for a couple of hours: "Prepared a bunch of slides, did some work on a computer, that kind of thing. Got it all ready . . . laid it out on a table."

APS vice president Jackie Fife confirmed that she had

found the work completed, neatly stacked and ready for distribution to the board members when she arrived at work the next morning.

After the short drive home, Roger pulled his car into the garage, parking next to Penny's van. He had noticed that the yard lights—spotlights installed under the eaves of the house—were lit when he drove up. It was normal for Penny to leave the floodlights on around the outer perimeter of the house when he worked late at night. He also noticed that the Texas flag had been taken down.

He went into the house through the garage entrance, which they kept unlocked. No outsider could get in without first raising the garage door, and that required an access code or programmed opener. Within minutes after his arrival, Roger Scaggs found his wife's dead body lying in a pool of blood beside her treasured baby grand piano.

Directly across the street, Diana Coleman was sitting in her living room, watching something on the A&E channel on TV. Her husband was at a church meeting. She had considered calling Penny earlier in the evening just to talk, but decided against it because she thought Roger was home. She noticed there was one light on inside the house and the porch light was off. She could see the Scaggs house "rather well" from her own front window.

"At 9:13 P.M. our phone rang," Diana said. "It came in on the caller ID. Our eleven-year-old daughter picked up the phone in her bedroom upstairs." Diana checked the number and saw that it was coming from the Scaggs home. She picked up the receiver just in time to hear Roger ask Ariana if her mom was there. "I've got it," she told her daughter.

"Roger said he had just come home from work and had walked into the kitchen and Penny wasn't there. He said that he had called to her and she hadn't answered."

Diana became alarmed. Roger didn't sound like himself. He was hyperventilating, speaking hesitantly.

"Roger, oh my God, what's wrong?" she asked.

At that point she noticed he began to talk "normally." He

said he had gone to the bedroom and Penny wasn't there, that he had "kept checking and found her in a pool of blood."

Roger wanted Diana to come over. She asked him if he had called 911 and he said no.

"Well, you call 911 right now and I'll be right over," she said.

Roger Scaggs called Austin police 911 emergency at 9:15 P.M. In a quivering voice he said, "Hi. I just got home from work and my wife's lying on the floor with blood everywhere and it looks like she's dead."

"Is she breathing?" asked the operator.

"No, not that I can tell," he said. "I had to get out of there. There's blood everywhere."

"Are you positive she's not breathing?"

"No," he said.

"I need you to look at her chest," said the operator. "Okay? You have to do it for me, okay?"

"Oh no," Roger said, "and her face is all bloated. She's not breathing at all."

The operator told him the police and EMS were on the way and that he should get out of the house. Before leaving, he took Penny's address book with phone numbers from the kitchen, so he could make other calls. He phoned a physician friend, who soon arrived at the scene.

When she hung up with Roger, the first thing Diana Coleman did was try to reach her husband. But the church phone was in the kitchen, and no one heard it ring. She then called another neighbor, Colonel George Wehling.

She told him, "Penny is in a lot of trouble. She needs our help."

The retired air-base commander immediately met Diana in her front yard.

"I got a call from Diana Coleman at 9:23 or 9:25. She requested I meet her out front," Wehling said. Two hours earlier, at about 7:30 P.M., Wehling had escorted his daughter to her car in front of their home and had looked directly at the Scaggs house. He noticed nothing unusual there or down the entire length of Winter Park Road. "I did *not* notice the lights on at the Scaggs house.

"[Diana] said she had received a call from Mr. Scaggs and wanted me to go with her. We went across the street together—to the front door. I knocked and rang the doorbell and beat on the door, on and on for three or four minutes. The light on the front porch was not on." Through the beveled glass in the front door, they could see into the foyer and down the hallway that led to the den. They saw "no movement in the house." Wehling was worried about Roger. He was afraid that whatever had happened to Penny might now have happened to her husband. He indicated to Diana that he was going around back to check it out.

"I told her to scream if she saw any movement."

Just as he turned the corner of the house at the driveway, he was met by a police officer, followed by a fireman whose truck had just arrived, with lights flashing and siren wailing.

"I told the policeman and fireman to be very careful, that we didn't know where Roger was," said the retired colonel. "Then I turned around and saw Mr. Scaggs standing there. The policeman went up to him. My wife brought me a jacket because it was cold."

Diana had remained on the front porch of the house.

"I caught a glimpse over my left shoulder of someone walking up to me," she said. "I was startled. He was walking very softly and calmly. I said, 'Oh, Roger, the door is locked.' He started unlocking it and a fireman was now at the door."

A police officer and three firemen entered the foyer, asking Roger where to go. Diana followed them in. A fireman told Roger and Diana to stop and return to the front porch, as the emergency responders rushed down the hall toward the den.

Diana asked Roger what happened. He told her that after he and Penny had eaten dinner together he went back to the office to work

"The whole thing seemed unnatural," she said. "Roger never told me she was dead. There was no anger, no grief, not even surprise. He never asked anyone about her condition."

A neighbor brought a chair for Roger to sit in while they waited. Someone else brought him a blanket and wrapped it over his shoulders. Drawn by the flashing lights and sirens, more neighbors began to gather on the lawn. Within minutes several more police cars arrived. EMS and fire equipment were already on the scene, and the street was blocked off by vehicles with flashing red, white, blue, and yellow lights.

The police officer secured the entrance, as fire rescue teams and EMS personnel poured into the house. Another officer was kneeling down, questioning Roger, who was seated in the chair. Roger stood up and leaned on George Wehling. "I think she's dead," he told Wehling.

Next door neighbors Peter and Elizabeth Brady, who were now joined by the physician friend, Steve Muller, and his wife Pat, suggested they all go to the Bradys' house to get out of the damp, cold night air. While the police officer agreed they should get out of the cold, he cautioned everyone against leaving the area.

"They took me . . . they let me go to the neighbors' house next door," Roger said. "So I got in out of the cold." A uniformed police officer, Thomas L. Sweeney, accompanied Roger and the neighbors into the Bradys' living room. Roger still had the blanket around his shoulders. He sat on a couch and was joined there by two neighborhood women. "They were just kind of comforting me," he said.

Officer Sweeney, a six-year veteran of the Austin police force, was the first officer on the scene and had accompanied the fire department rescue team into the Scaggs home. They had quickly confirmed that nothing could be done for Penny Scaggs.

"The firemen determined that her throat had been slashed," Officer Sweeney said. After that, he cleared everyone from the house except the emergency services personnel. Then he took charge of the victim's husband and asked him what had happened.

"A neighbor invited everyone out of the cold, so I accompanied the victim's husband next door," the officer said, pointing out that he left police officer Michael Burgh in charge at the crime scene. As first responder, Sweeney had to make the crime-scene report. He set up his computer on the table in the Bradys' dining room, which opened onto their living room. From that vantage point, he was close enough to Roger Scaggs, seated on the couch, to observe his actions and ask him questions.

"He was very precise with the details leading up to that time," Sweeney said. "Scaggs was seated eight feet away, with several others around him—friends, neighbors, and, I believe, a clergyman had arrived."

Elizabeth Brady made sandwiches and served them all around. Roger took a sandwich and began eating it between questions from the police officer.

"He was very calm, controlled; his answers were very deliberate," said Sweeney. "When he did show distress he would cry at times. He turned the crying on and off. He was talking with the two women on the couch. But when he looked over and saw that I was watching him he would stop talking, look down at the sandwich plate in his lap, and then raise his head crying. The way he turned it on and off, it was like he realized he was supposed to be upset."

The neighbors, friends, and preacher, along with the uniformed policeman, were soon joined by two detectives from the Austin Police Department. One of the plainclothesmen was J. W. Thompson, who was assigned as lead investigator on the Penny Scaggs murder case. The detectives asked Roger if he was up to coming with them to police headquarters to make a full statement. Roger agreed, but indicated he had to notify Penny's sisters. Detective Thompson said he could call the family from headquarters.

Diana Coleman had accompanied Roger and the others to the Brady home. "His demeanor, his voice, was the type that alarms you, almost like a whimper," she recalled. "He went from fear to calm." Roger repeated to everyone in the room what had happened. She remembered him saying that so many things needed to be done. "His office and Penny's family had to be notified. He said it would be best to tell Penny's sister Marilyn and for her to tell the rest of the family. Roger asked for a pad and pen. He wanted to make notes of things that needed to be done. Roger was very business-like."

Diana went home, devastated with grief at the loss of her best friend. When her husband Arthur returned from his church meeting, she sobbingly related everything that had happened that evening.

Chapter 10

Many daughters have done virtuously, but thou excellest them all. Favor is deceitful, and beauty is vain: but a woman that feareth the Lord, she shall be praised. Give her of the fruit of her hands; and let her own words praise her in the gates.

—PROVERBS 31:29-31

*T*he startling sound of a telephone ringing in the middle of the night instinctively engenders a sense of dread. The unexpected call so often brings news that can change a life forever.

That call came for Penny's sister, Marilyn Muecke, around midnight on March 6. It was Dr. Steve Muller, a friend of Roger and Penny, who had been summoned to the murder scene by Roger. He and his wife Pat arrived almost immediately and went to the Brady home, where neighbors had gathered to comfort Roger. There, Roger asked his old friend to contact Marilyn after learning that he would be taken to the police station to make a full statement.

Marilyn, a tall, willowy blonde who, at forty-five, still looked almost identical to her twin, Carolyn, was considered the most "take-charge" of the sisters. The news racked her with grief. After being comforted by her husband Gus, she decided the best way to tell her other two sisters was on a conference call. With her husband on the line, she set up a link with Sharon and her husband Jim, and Carolyn and her husband Bill. She shared with them everything Dr. Muller had told her about Penny's death. Sharon later recalled that the first information available was that "someone had broken into the house and killed her."

The sisters discussed how they should break the terrible news to their elderly parents. Their mother, Mittie, was eighty-five years old. Their eighty-two-year-old father, S. L. Ehrle, was in fragile health. He had a medical procedure scheduled for early Thursday morning. The sisters arranged to gather in person immediately. Jim drove the three women to their parents' home in McKinney, while the other two husbands stayed with their young children.

"When we got to our parents' house, we called from the driveway to let them know we were there and needed to talk to them," Sharon said. "I sat on my dad's bed and Marilyn and Carolyn sat on Mother's bed." As the sisters gently told their parents that Penny was gone, their mother broke in. She asked if it was a car accident. When one of the sisters explained that Penny had been murdered in her home, the first words out of their father's mouth were, "It was Roger."

S. L. Ehrle voiced the stinging accusation that Roger Scaggs was somehow involved in Penny's death while police were still trying to sort out what had happened at the scene, and while all signs seemed to point to home invasion—robbery and murder by a stranger. Was this immediate response to the devastating news by the elderly father just a knee-jerk reaction caused by extreme grief and the need to blame somebody for an unbearably senseless act? Was it simply that a husband is usually the first suspect in a wife's murder? Or was that first reaction to the news of Penny's death based on something more sinister, a gut feeling resulting from years of observation that Roger Scaggs was capable of such an act of violence?

* * *

Steve and Pat Muller had followed Roger to the police station when he was taken in for questioning, and they waited
there for hours while he was interviewed. It was nearly 3:00
A.M. when the questioning ended, but Roger still had one
more painful thing to do that night. He needed to tell his
daughter. Sarah was twenty-four years old at the time, and a
student at Austin Community College. Roger got into the
Mullers' car and they drove him to Sarah's apartment.

When they arrived, Sarah answered the door. They all
went to the living room together.

"Roger was very distraught, tormented," recalled Dr.
Muller. He said they stayed there for about thirty minutes,
during which time Roger was "sharing his grief . . . expressing his grief with his daughter."

Later that morning the practical realities of funeral arrangements and carrying on some modicum of normalcy for
the surviving family members had to be addressed, despite
the shock and grief of the murder.

Reverend Rob Harrell was contacted early on Thursday.
The Scaggs home on Winter Park Road was sealed off with
yellow crime-scene tape, and police detectives and forensics
teams were swarming over the property. The Mullers had
invited Roger to stay with them for a few days, and it was to
their home that Reverend Harrell went to assist with whatever arrangements were needed. The minister had not only
lost a beloved member of his flock whose work with young
women he admired, but had the pastoral duty to tend to the
spiritual and earthly needs of the husband, an elder in his
church, and a distraught daughter.

"I went to comfort Roger and Sarah," Harrell recalled.
"We all sat around the breakfast table in the home. Roger
seemed hesitant to talk about what he had witnessed the
night before. He said Penny had been beaten up, and asked
who could have done such a thing. He said a transient might
have done it. In all my experience ministering to the newly

bereaved, I have never seen anyone who did not want to talk about it. All people who love someone seem to want to talk, and talk and talk. All he said was, 'This is hard. This is hard.' He seemed anxious to plan the funeral. I said, 'Are you sure you want to do this right now?' He wanted to go ahead and make plans."

The following day, Friday, March 8, the pastor met Roger and Sarah at the funeral home, where Penny's body had been released by investigators after the autopsy was completed.

In a discussion about how Penny should be dressed for an open-casket service, the funeral director indicated it should probably be a high-necked dress, because of the wounds. Reverend Harrell, observing Roger's response, said, "Roger seemed to know that, but Sarah did not understand." It was almost time for the evening news, so they all went upstairs to watch the coverage, to see if there had been any progress in the investigation.

When the report about the murder came on, "Sarah began to sob; she was very emotionally upset," Harrell said. "Roger showed no emotion."

Roger made plans for Penny's funeral while staying with the Mullers. Steve Muller was one of his best friends. They often went flying and to auto races together. His wife Pat had assisted Penny with her Creative Counterpart classes and had actually hosted the first two seminars in her own home. She said the murder of her friend was the most horrific experience of her life. She called it "a night filled with darkness and evil."

One afternoon a day or two after the murder, Mrs. Muller was alone in the house with Roger when he struck up a curious conversation. They were talking about Penny's funeral over lunch.

"He asked me my opinion on what he saw as a problem over the burial plot," she recalled. "He wanted to buy one plot [for Penny], and Penny's family wanted him to buy two." The family assumed he would want to be buried beside his wife. He told Pat Muller that he did not want to go to the burial in Dallas. He felt Penny's parents and family would not want him there, either. But he planned to go anyway, because his daughter Sarah would be upset with him if he did not.

The twin sisters, with their husbands and friends, decided to drive to Austin to assist with the arrangements and attend the funeral. Sharon and her husband were going to bring the elderly parents to Austin by commercial air for just the day of the service, because of their fragile health. The memorial service at the sanctuary of First Evangelical Free Church was set for Sunday.

On Saturday, the sisters met Roger, and they all went to the funeral home for a private gathering of the family. Marilyn rode in the car with Roger.

"We were reminiscing about the pleasant times the family had enjoyed in the past," Marilyn recalled.

The next thing he said stunned her: "I need you and the family to know that I am probably going to remarry; move out of Austin—get away from the tragedy and remarry."

"I didn't doubt that you would remarry," Marilyn replied. "We've already talked about how much Penny did for you, that you would need someone to take care of you, eventually."

Though the subject did not surprise her, she was taken aback by his timing. Less than three days had passed since Penny's death. Why was he talking about this now?

At the funeral home, Roger did not go into the viewing room. The sisters gathered around the casket, sobbing. "Apparently they had to do a lot of reconstructive surgery," Marilyn said. It was a painful reminder of how vicious the attack had been.

Marilyn went to the church to view Penny again before the funeral. "I needed to know her soul was not there," she said.

"Roger indicated that he wanted to have Penny buried next to her father and mother," Sharon said.

The parents had purchased a plot for themselves at Restland Memorial Cemetery in Dallas. Sharon had arranged for that reserved plot to be exchanged for a different location that would make it possible for Roger to buy two other plots next to them. But that was not what Roger wanted. He apparently had no intention of being buried next to his wife of thirty-five years.

The Saturday evening before the memorial service in Austin, the Colemans were invited to join Roger, Sarah, and the sisters for dinner. Diana, her husband, and a daughter went over to the Scaggs house, which by then had been released by the police department. The church had provided a large dinner for the family.

When they arrived, Roger immediately took Diana over to the piano and showed her what he complained was the damage to the yellow finish caused by the forensic team from the police department.

"The black luminescent powder had not been wiped off and he could not get it off," Diana said. "He was upset . . . that the police had ruined the piano."

While standing by the baby grand, Roger told Diana that he "had a lot of important decisions to make."

"I told him, 'You know what they say, you should not make any important decisions for a year [after a tragedy],' " she recalled. "He laughed and said, 'Oh, no, I'm not going to wait any year. By then, I could be married two or three times over.' "

The family asked the Colemans to return with them to the funeral home, but Diana declined. "I just was not up to seeing my friend in that state."

The memorial service for Penny Scaggs was held in the main sanctuary of First Evangelical Free Church at 2:30 P.M. on Sunday, March 10. Over four hundred people attended, including a large number of Penny's former students. Seven men from Penny and Roger's Sunday school class, called the "Cornerstone," served as pallbearers. Reverend Gene Getz read the scriptural eulogy. It was Proverbs 31:10-31, the good wife passages from the Old Testament that Penny had taught for the past dozen years.

Sarah sobbed openly throughout the ceremony, according to one observer; and was pale and badly shaken as she stood in the reception line, along with other members of the immediate family, to receive condolences. The reception was held in the church's new auxiliary building behind the main sanctuary. One close friend who recognized most of the family members, former students, business associates, and neighbors, also noticed a sizable contingent of strangers mingling at the reception. They were officers in business suits from the Austin Police Department's homicide division.

After the funeral in Austin, relatives conferred briefly about the graveside services to be held in Dallas the next day. Sarah asked her aunts what they planned to wear. They all agreed that the women could wear slacks for the occasion. After returning home, Roger showed the sisters a motorcycle jacket he had recently purchased in Las Vegas. He modeled it for them and said he was going to wear it at the grave site. At the time, the sisters thought he was just trying to bring some light relief to the days of grieving they had all undergone since the murder.

The private graveside service was held at Restland Memorial Cemetery in Dallas at 1:00 P.M. the following day, Monday. About thirty-five members of the immediate family and closest friends were in attendance.

To everyone's surprise, Roger did show up wearing his leather jacket with a red, white, and blue eagle in full wingspan emblazoned across the back. The gaudy motorcycle jacket was very disturbing to some members of Penny's family.

"I was surprised that he was wearing what I would describe as a flashy jacket," said Marilyn. "It was inappropriate for a funeral."

But Sarah, who had accompanied her father to the graveside services, believed it was just a misunderstanding.

"The family agreed that the burial in Dallas would be casual dress," she said. Since the weather was chilly, her father had decided to wear the only good casual coat he had—the leather motorcycle jacket. She denied that his wearing it was in any way disrespectful of Penny's memory.

Sarah insisted that her father was emotionally devastated at the burial. "He stayed strong until they started lowering her into the ground. Then he broke down so badly that I had to support him as we walked away from the ceremony. He was so grief-stricken he wasn't even able to walk."

Following the brief services, Roger said he had something important to tell the family.

"We gathered under the tent and he told us that he was planning to hire an attorney," Marilyn recalled. "He believed he was a suspect; and for that reason, for his own protection, he was hiring a lawyer."

She talked to Roger frequently that week. "We were very concerned about him," she said, pointing out that the sisters remained largely supportive of their brother-in-law and had made no judgment that he was their older sister's killer. "We talked several times about attorneys. He felt very threatened about the police interest in him."

*I*f Roger guessed that he might be a suspect in the murder of his wife, the community at large had no such suspicion. They feared a more dangerous killer might be loose in the luxury suburbs of Westlake.

"There was a sense of terror in the neighborhood, revulsion to some kind of evil," said a close friend of Penny's. People retreated inside their homes in fear. All up and down the streets the drapes were drawn. At one house where there had been no curtains before, a sheet hung over the dining room window.

The *Austin American-Statesman* had covered the murder of Penny Scaggs on their inside pages in a three-paragraph crime report the day after the murder. A longer article, also inside, on Friday, March 8, noted, "Police said they had no suspects in custody."

"The rumors were rampant, and fear in the neighborhoods was palpable," said Ed Allen, editor of the *Westlake Picayune*. The seasoned newspaperman was frustrated by the fact that his paper had just gone to press the day after the murder. He would not have another chance to offer facts about the homicide to his readers until the next edition, in mid-week. Allen not only edited the copy turned in by his small staff of young reporters, but also—like most editors of weeklies across the country—designed and laid out the pages, reported many of the major news events of the community, and took news photographs, as well. He had developed good inside sources in the area police departments.

One of his best sources had told him, off the record, that the husband might be a "person of interest" in the case. Allen was almost certain there was no madman running amok in the area, but he could do nothing about it but tell the frequent callers not to be too worried just yet.

There had been only one homicide in the modern history of the Westlake area, and that was four years earlier, in 1992. That equally gruesome crime, in which the victim had been slashed twenty-three times and stabbed sixteen times in the torso and legs, was solved immediately. A forty-one-year-old woman with a history of psychiatric illness had killed her sixty-seven-year-old mother. The suspect was arrested running from the scene when police arrived.

But because the Scaggs crime was still unsolved, and involved the brutal murder of a housewife in her home by herself, this one had a major impact.

By the weekend, almost everyone in the close-knit community was aware that a horrible crime had occurred in their midst, a crime that appeared to be a brutal, home-invasion robbery and murder. That scenario was every resident's nightmare. They had always felt threatened by the prospect of intruders coming over from less-well-off areas of the city to loot and pillage. Gated communities with guards and roving patrols dotted the entire Eanes school district, and security was uppermost in the minds of buyers when they purchased their expensive properties.

"It can't happen here" was the mantra most frequently heard by Allen. "Everyone wanted to know what had occurred and what was being done about it, and there was no place to get any information," he said.

The Eanes school district and the city of Austin had not always enjoyed the best relationship. The property owners of the upscale area made no bones about their distain for the governmental policies of their larger urban neighbor. The wealthier citizens on the west bank of the Colorado consistently fought any suggestion of annexation by the city to share their tax base. Now, many residents of the area were complaining that the Austin Police Department was not doing enough to catch the killer.

The truth was, during the first few days after the murder, Austin homicide detectives simply did not have a suspect, or even a theory about the crime. Thus, there was little the APD could have told the citizens that would have calmed their fears. No one knew who had killed Penny Scaggs. The crime scene, with the victim's body stripped of her valuable jewelry, made it appear that robbery was the motive. The brutality of the murder, with the mutilation of the body after the victim was already dead, was of grave concern to investigators. That did not fit the pattern of a simple robbery. Even if Penny had fought to save her diamonds, a strong, armed robber would normally be expected to use just enough force to subdue his victim. Veteran detectives, some of whom had already said the murder was the most brutal they had encountered in their careers, were sure that the killer or killers probably knew Penny Scaggs. They believed an element of personal rage must have been involved.

The fact that early in the investigation Austin police had no information to offer, nothing that might have comforted neighbors, family, or friends, did not mean the case was being neglected. From the moment the 911 call came in, Austin Homicide had committed the best team of detectives in the department to solving the vicious murder.

Chapter 11

*I*nvestigators assigned to the case of Penny Scaggs, baffled by the gruesome scene they found on Winter Park Road, swarmed over the crime scene like bees to the first blooming of Texas wildflowers. A dozen detectives, uniformed police officers, and forensic technicians spent the remaining hours of March 6 through daybreak on March 7 probing whatever mysteries the house held.

Senior detective Joseph W. Thompson, a twenty-year veteran of the Austin Police Department, headed the team. Officially, he was designated Case Agent Homicide Detective, with the lead role in the investigation from the time the crime-scene tape went up until the case was closed or went to trial.

Thompson had been a homicide detective for five years, joining the murder squad after service as a patrol officer, crime unit specialist, narcotics agent, and member of the elite Criminal Investigation Bureau (CIB). In appearance, he could have passed for a college professor or an actuary, with medium-length graying hair, eyeglasses, and a

neatly trimmed mustache. In personality, though, he was
a cop's cop, with a reputation for dogged tenacity and methodical pursuit of even the tiniest detail of the cases he
worked.

He was backed by a pool of unusually skilled police officers, criminologists, and forensic technologists because of
the unique situation of the city they served. As a center for
the largest educational institution in the state, the University
of Texas, and a dozen other colleges and universities, the
Austin Police Department had an exceptionally large number of college-educated officers. In addition, there was a
free-flowing exchange of human resources between the law
enforcement officers of the city, county, and state. The Travis County Sheriff's Department, which handled crimes
outside the city limits in the contiguous, unincorporated
suburbs, was equally as well staffed with college-trained
deputies. And the headquarters of the Texas Department of
Public Safety, with its vaunted Texas Rangers and modern
crime labs second to none in the country, was located just
north of the university area.

As the police force for the capital city, APD was as well
equipped as, and in some specialties more competent than,
similar departments in the much larger cities of Dallas, Fort
Worth, Houston, and San Antonio. With a consistently good
record for solving felonies of all types, Austin cops were
able to turn a powerful microscope on any major criminal
case they confronted. In the murder of Penny Scaggs, the
commanders sent out orders that all resources were to be
tapped to solve this case as quickly as possible. Lieutenant
David Parkinson, who headed the homicide section at the
time, sent in a half-dozen plainclothes officers early in the
case. In addition, the APD Crime Scene Search team had
immediately been dispatched.

While the forensic teams were probing, dusting, scraping,
bagging, and labeling every speck and sliver in his house,
Roger Scaggs was chauffeured, as a free man, by a uniformed police officer to the Austin Police Department Head-

quarters at 715 East Eighth Street. Roger was cooperating fully. He had given verbal permission to detectives to enter and search his home. He agreed to accompany officers to police headquarters for a statement and expressed his willingness to assist the investigation in any way he could.

Roger did not know that the detective who would conduct the interview was one of APD's best interrogators.

Detective Sergeant David Carter had recently arrived home after working around the clock for two straight days on another murder case when he got the call some time after 10:00 P.M. to return to headquarters. "Hell, I was ready to get some sleep when that damn pager went off," he recalled about the night of March 6, 1996.

When he left the house, he was surprised how much the temperature had dropped in the last couple of hours; but he did not turn back to retrieve a topcoat.

Carter's information about the case was sketchy. The APD communications section told him he needed to interview the husband of a woman who had been found murdered in a tony suburb of southwest Austin. He checked in with the supervisor, Sergeant Hector Reveles, who said the husband was not a suspect but needed to be given a full interrogation because police had learned little from him at the scene.

Carter knew the hilly, upscale neighborhood where the murder had occurred like the back of his hand. He had patrolled it when it was still being developed. He knew the people, too. Unnoticed, he had slowly cruised their streets on many long nights, watching over them, as the first of the newcomers moved into their beautiful new homes. It was the safest neighborhood in the city.

Cold winds gusting to forty-five miles per hour were buffeting his unmarked police sedan before he reached the station. By the time he arrived, he regretted not bringing an overcoat.

He entered the building from the police garage and walked up the back stairs to the second-floor homicide unit.

The place was empty when he arrived. Carter guessed most of the detectives on duty were at the murder scene.

About twenty minutes later a patrol officer came in and told him that Mr. Roger T. Scaggs had arrived and was ready for his interview. Carter looked through the small glass window from the section offices and saw a middle-aged, graying man sitting calmly on one of the chairs along the wall of the hallway. The man was dressed in blue jeans, plaid shirt, dark loafers, and a beige denim windbreaker. Even in casual attire he looked like a meticulous dresser.

Carter studied the man for a few minutes before pushing open the swinging double doors. The detective reached out his hand in a disarming gesture of friendliness as he strode toward Roger Scaggs. He liked to take the measure of a subject's handshake before he began an interview. He found Roger Scaggs's handshake firm but not aggressive. When the man stood, Carter noticed that his clothes were clean and he was not wearing a belt. Carter offered condolences on the loss of his wife and asked him to come into the homicide offices. The man responded with a nod and said something like "Sure" or "Okay" as he followed the detective to an interview room.

"My initial observation was that Mr. Scaggs was polite and cordial, but did not appear to be terribly affected," the detective said. From his interviews with spouses and close relatives of murder victims, Carter remembered—and dreaded—the ones who were hysterical, crying, and too upset to talk coherently. He called that the "emotional outburst" reaction. That was one type of survivor of a homicide in the family. The others he categorized as "denial" and "in shock." The denial type refuses to acknowledge the loved one is dead. The person in shock is too stunned or confused to know what has happened. The detective was not yet sure which type he was about to interview; but at this point, the man was certainly not hysterical.

As they stood exchanging idle conversation, the detective observed that Scaggs, almost as tall as he was, maintained steady eye contact with him.

Carter had served as the department's primary hostage negotiator since 1988. He had been a detective in the auto theft section before joining Homicide, and a patrol officer for eight years before that. He had majored in geosciences at Texas A&M University and left college for a career in law enforcement.

Ramrod straight, Sergeant Carter looked more like an Army Ranger than a cop when he was wearing his tailored, black police uniform with rows of service medals and commendations. He had received over fifty commendations, including the Police Distinguished Service Cross for Valor, the Life Saving Medal, two Meritorious Service Medals, two Meritorious Unit Citations, two Superior Service Citations, and the Honorable Conduct Citation.

Now, as a detective, he wore a sport coat, tie, and dress slacks for this interview. He had been in Homicide for two years and considered himself a personally invisible member of a closely meshed team. Each member of the team had the responsibility to contribute pieces to solving the complex puzzle of a case. There were no stars or heroes in Homicide. The nature of the grisly work made team-sharing essential, not only to resolve a case, but also to prevent any one officer from internalizing the horror of a murder.

"I can't say I enjoy being in Homicide. It can be pretty emotionally tough," Carter said. "I enjoy the teamwork, the challenge; but at times it's a great burden. Investigating criminal deaths can be overwhelming. We take this responsibility very gravely. You have to speak for the deceased's family, the public's safety, and you also have a great responsibility to the suspect. The guilty must be made to understand why he or she must go to prison."

The grim-faced detective said he also felt it was as important to clear an innocent person as to catch a guilty killer.

"One of the most heinous things that can be done to an individual is to take his liberty and, in some cases, his life," Carter said. "Many people today question the police, don't trust that we won't fabricate evidence. I cannot imagine doing that just to close a case. Duty and honor are important in all police work. A homicide officer feels it most strongly of all."

It takes a special set of skills to extract relevant information from a person who has suffered a traumatic event and is under extreme stress. Carter called one of those skills "active listening," which differs from the "casual listening" that people do most of the time.

"People communicate on two levels, the conscious and the subconscious," he explained. "Particularly when they are under stress, they don't always realize what they are saying." To be actively listening means an interviewer must focus on both what the person is saying and not saying; and on all the visual and verbal clues, including body language and mannerisms.

Carter said he personally owed Roger Scaggs the best of his skills, training, and experience that night, regardless of how tired he was from lack of sleep. It was his job, during the coming hours, to help prove an innocent man guiltless or provide a piece of the team's puzzle that would catch a killer.

The detective seated Scaggs in a windowless interrogation room in one of the two chairs placed at a round table. The room had no double-sided mirror like in the movies, so the interviewee did not have the feeling that others were watching from behind the looking glass. There was, however, a hidden video camera mounted in the ceiling, and a very sensitive, voice-activated tape recorder implanted in the wall.

Since the section offices were deserted, Carter had to make a fresh pot of coffee. He thought he would need it before the night was done. While he was waiting for the coffee to brew, and with Roger left to his thoughts in the small interview room, a call came in from the detective in charge, Joseph W. Thompson. Carter took the call in the open reception room, which was surrounded by interrogation rooms and detectives' offices.

"J. W. is very, very methodical and a good mentor for younger detectives," Carter said. "He gave me a rundown on what was known to that point—which was still not much."

While he was talking to the senior detective on the phone, Carter punched the keys of a computer. He pulled up Roger Scaggs's motor vehicle information and checked to see if he had a criminal record. His record was clean, except for a single speeding ticket.

Returning to the interview room with a little more information about the crime, Carter again told Scaggs he was very sorry to have to meet him under these circumstances. He said it would help catch his wife's killer if Roger could give him "as much information as possible. Just start and tell me what happened tonight."

The interview began at 11:20 P.M. Carter brought the interviewee coffee and a small bottle of water.

Scaggs started his story with his return home from work at five-thirty for dinner. He gave his account of every move he had made, up until the discovery of his wife's body when he came home again for the night. He also gave the detective information about his work at APS Systems and told him his office was located less than ten minutes from his home. He went into considerable detail about his daughter Sarah, where she worked and lived, and her current boyfriend.

When he got into the events of the night, one of the first things he told Carter was that he had left home to return to his office at "seven or seven-fifteen—somewhere in there." After giving an account of his time in the interim, he said, "I came home around nine o'clock or so." He described parking his Ford Taurus in the garage next to Penny's van and entering the house through the laundry room.

"I hollered, and I didn't get any response," he said. He had first looked for his wife in the kitchen, where he noticed the dirty dishes were still stacked in the sink, and next checked in the downstairs bedroom.

Then he said he looked into the large living area that served as the family den. "I could see her lying there by the piano. I could see her head. So I kind of panicked, of course, and ran in there, and then came to an immediate stop because it was . . . it's really horrible. She's just lying in blood, and her face was all bloated and bruised and blood running out of her ear."

Scaggs corrected the last part of his statement. ". . . wasn't running; it was there. Her head was in blood." He said his wife was lying "on her side." Carter asked which side. "The left side," Roger said. This meant his wife was facing away from him, toward the piano.

The veteran interrogator did not rush him to give his account. Carter believed that victim survivors were owed every consideration. He gently coaxed him to tell his story at his own pace, in his own words, with a minimum of interruptions or questions.

"I was expecting him to just say 'I found her dead' and leave it pretty much at that. But instead he was giving me a fully detailed account of his every move, everything he saw and felt," the sergeant recalled.

Roger continued talking. "I leaned down a little bit. Of course I just almost threw up," he said. "Of course I didn't know what to do, and so I immediately ran back and picked up the phone and dialed 911." He told the detective the phone was in the kitchen. "I have a portable. It was on the wall. I pulled it off."

He then described his call to 911, where he was soon connected with both the police dispatcher and an EMS operator. He recounted the conversation he had with them.

"The EMS folks made me go back in to see if she was breathing," he said. "Of course that was pretty horrible. Anyway, it was clear she was not alive."

Roger said he was ordered to get out of the house after he determined that his wife was not breathing. He said he had the "portable phone" with him and grabbed Penny's address book. He punched open the garage door and went out the way he had come in. He explained that he always "punched it [the garage door] down" when he walked in the house, "so it's always secure." All this time he was still talking to the emergency personnel, "walking and talking." They were telling him what to do. The 911 operator wanted him to stay on the phone until help arrived.

Roger continued to recount the sequence of events: "I thought a minute. Can I call my pastor and neighbor? They said sure. And so I called my pastor. Or, I called my physician and also good friend of mine from church. That's who is out there—he and his wife." Steve and Pat Muller had come to the station and waited for Roger during his entire interview.

"So you first called your pastor?" Carter asked.

"Uh-huh. Well, actually, I'm sorry. I didn't have the pastor's number handy." Roger explained when he called the Mullers he asked them to come over and to call the pastor for him.

When Carter asked if the Mullers had arrived before the police or EMS, Roger answered, "I made one more call. I called my across-the-street neighbor Diana Coleman. About that time the EMS came up and Diana Coleman from across the street came over."

This chronology was in direct conflict with the account given by Diana Coleman, who later testified under oath that it was she who told Roger to call 911. Both Coleman and Colonel Wehling had been specific about the timing of events that night, and their details were consistent with the time stamp on Roger's emergency call, which came in to 911 at 9:15 P.M.

Roger described unlocking the door to his house, so he could direct EMS to the body, and the scene outside, as neighbors and emergency service crews arrived.

Detective Carter took him back to the events leading up to the discovery of his wife, starting with why he came home for dinner instead of staying at the office to finish his work. Roger told him it was Penny's idea.

"She said, 'Why, don't you come home and have dinner? You can relax a bit and go back and finish.' So I said okay and came home about five, or between five-thirty and six. Probably left at seven or seven-fifteen," Roger stated again.

He described changing clothes from a business suit to casual attire. Back at work, he said he parked in an underground garage reserved for corporate officers and managers. The detective made a special note of that statement. Roger said he was lucky enough to have underground parking in his building so he didn't have to walk outside. Carter thought he seemed a bit anxious to get on to something more important.

The detective had not asked him his opinion about what had happened at the house. Thus, when Roger blurted out his next statement, it caught Carter by surprise.

"Let's see . . ." he began, "I guess my only presumption is . . . it's obvious to me. I guess I need to tell you in case it's not obvious to you, is that it's very obvious to me that this happened not too long after I left. Otherwise, the kitchen wouldn't still be in—the dirty dishes. That's a very obsessive kind of neatnik type of person. Always keeps things squared away and so forth. So I say it would have to have been within an hour after I left."

Carter just responded, "Okay." The detective's expression did not change and he did not look up from his notes. But his pulse quickened, because he realized the subject had just stepped outside the norm of victim reactions. The interview had been under way for more than an hour at this point. Scaggs went on with his hypothetical tale of what happened. The question and answer session that followed became a cat and mouse game. Scaggs opined that the attack must have happened shortly after he left the house to go back to his office.

"Probably thirty to forty minutes. I don't know. Because she might have gone in to play [the piano] and come back. Finished cleaning up. She doesn't let things go around there."

"As close as you can remember," asked Carter, "the time that you left . . . ?"

"I think I was back at the office by seven-thirty. It takes me maybe ten minutes to get up there, something like that. I might have been there at 7:25. It was somewhere between seven and seven-fifteen when I left."

The detective knew now that Scaggs was eager to tell his version of what had happened, so he deliberately went through a long series of routine questions. He then switched suddenly back to how the crime might have occurred, to see if Scaggs would once again volunteer an opinion. Scaggs had told the interviewer that Penny always wore her best jewelry, even around the house. He said that any-one coming to the house could have seen her jewelry through the beveled glass in the front door, even if she hadn't opened it.

"How many doors are there in the house—external doors?" Carter asked.

Scaggs described the main entrances and then focused on the portals to the dark backyard. "In the back of the house there are two doors that go out onto a patio deck," he told the officer.

Carter asked him more than thirty questions about the en-trances to the house, the alarm system, and who else had keys, before he returned to the subject of the back doors.

The front would have been very well lit, "but the back, like I said, is very dark" Roger Scaggs replied.

Now Carter wanted to hear his theory of the murder.

"I don't mean the physical act, but what do you speculate? Did somebody knock on the door? You talked about people—salesmen or people selling."

"She didn't let people in," Roger said. "I've thought about it, of course. The only thing I could come up with is that somebody came around the back. And that back door is dark. It's the most likely one to be unlocked. She goes in and out of it a lot during the day. She goes out on the back porch to make sun tea. She'll take a bottle of sun tea out there, put it on the deck, or she'll go out and sweep some leaves off. She'll go out, water plants.

"I've always kind of harassed her about it. When I come home that's always one of the things that I check. I'll say, 'Dear, you forgot to lock this back door.' Paranoid about keeping the doors locked all the time."

"She sometimes forgets?"

"Yes, that particular one. Like I say, it's quite dark. In the back of our house there is kind of a wooded area off to the side. Somebody could come around there very easily and not be seen—get into our backyard quite easily.

"And once again," Scaggs continued, "this is just all supposition on my part; trying to think about it because she's very careful not to let people in, in the front door, to keep the front door locked. And, you know, she won't even crack the door. When somebody is there she yells through the door—just tells them to go away.

"So, I mean, it's conceivable somebody could have come to the door; she told them to go away; they went back around the back. Or could have been, you know, somebody just wandering down the street."

The detective asked Roger if he wanted more coffee. "Maybe a little sip of water," he said.

Carter said, "Water. Okay. I'll be right back."

But that was not the reason he left the room. Although it was now well past midnight, he knew Detective Thompson would still be at the crime scene supervising and directing the forensic teams. He gave the lead detective highlights of the interview and asked him whether the back door or doors had been unlocked at the time the officers entered the premises. He also asked for an update, specifically if site screeners had found Penny's valuable jewelry. Thompson told Carter that the back door had been found unlocked and nothing but costume jewelry was found at the scene.

Carter returned to the interview room with another cup of coffee for himself and water for Roger.

"We were both very, very tired by that time," the detective said. "But I was focusing on every one of his answers. I didn't jump to any conclusions."

Without further prompting, Roger Scaggs continued to relate his theory of how the homicide had occurred.

"Anyway, the only thing that I can figure is somebody slipped in that back door. Maybe it was unlocked. And I suspect she was playing the piano, because she had two pairs of glasses . . . a separate pair that she keeps around the piano to read the music.

"I do recall when I walked in there, I was so shocked, when I looked around, there was a pair of glasses on the piano bench. There was another pair on the floor, I thought, not far from where she was playing. So I suspect somebody walked up from behind her and grabbed her or, you know, whatever. I don't know.

"That's the only thing I can figure out, because otherwise she wouldn't have been in there unless I think she was probably playing the piano. If she was going to read or something, she generally does that in another room. So that, you know, she was real focused sitting there, her back is kind of to that area—would be to that area when she does that."

Carter's training kicked into high gear, as it had at other times in the interview, particularly when Roger was describing his theory of the murder. A big flag went up when Roger said, "Of course I've thought about it." *When did he think about it?* The detective thought Roger's story too detailed for the short time that had elapsed since the traumatic event.

Sergeant Carter's suspicions were also aroused by the way Roger talked about the back door that opened from the room where Penny was murdered to the unlighted patio. He kept embellishing that part of his story.

"The more he said about the unlocked back door, the more suspicious it made me," Carter observed. "He wanted me to focus on that back door real bad."

Now something else had caught Carter's attention—the kind of nuances of speech that can serve as cues. The detective noticed that Roger had switched from the first person to the third person in telling, hypothetically, how the murder might have happened. He was using the word "I" frequently, because he was describing his best guess, what he thought happened. In just a few sentences he had said, "I recall, I suspect, I was shocked, I don't know." Then, as he kept talking, he suddenly changed to the third person, as if he were there, in the room watching her, watching her from the back as she played the piano. At that moment he also spoke in the present tense and then corrected himself: "Her back is kind of to that area—*would be* to that area when she does that."

"It dawned on me," said Carter. "That's when I decided to take pictures of his hands and feet. It's the responsibility of a policeman to eliminate the innocent. It's also the duty of the policeman to find the guilty out."

About two and a half hours into the interview, Carter asked where the Scaggses kept their valuables. Roger said they had important papers and "maybe some coins" in a safe in the floor.

While he was describing the cases where Penny kept her jewelry, Roger started unwrapping some food one of the neighbors had given him. Pausing in mid-sentence, he asked the detective, "Would you like a little bit of sandwich here?" When Carter indicated no, he said, "But I'm going to eat."

"You go right ahead," Carter said.

In the next forty-five minutes the detective revisited many of the topics they had covered before. Roger was repeating what he did during and after the 911 call, and then started jotting something down.

Carter was curious. "Can I ask what you're writing? Is there something you're remembering?"

"Yes," Roger said. "The investigator said he would give me my house key back."

"Okay," said Carter flatly.

"If they took anything, there would be an inventory," said Roger. "I just—I just got to worrying. They're still there. I don't want them to take anything. Am I going to get all of that back?"

Carter assured him he would.

"I'm a list-maker," Roger explained.

At the end of the interview, Carter typed up a summary of what Roger had told him. After correcting a few minor points, Roger signed the document, which the detective notarized.

When Carter asked Roger if he could photograph his shoes and his hands, he agreed, emphasizing again that he would do whatever he could to help.

The first formal interview with Roger Scaggs lasted until 2:54 A.M., almost three hours and twenty minutes. Now Detective Carter was charged up and had questions about the crime scene whirling around in his head.

"I had a pretty bad headache from all the coffee and lack of sleep. But I went back over Mr. Scaggs's statement after he left police headquarters with friends," Carter said. He was particularly interested in the segment where Roger raced ahead of the carefully planned questions to blurt out a theory of the crime without being asked. Carter was also eager to review his long response to the suggestion that he "speculate" on a crime-scene scenario. The detective had found this series of answers and volunteered narrative too filled with small but important misstatements.

The detailed answers made the husband seem less like an innocent survivor. Overall, the interview had not cleared him of suspicion, but had instead made Carter eager to learn more about his activities. The behavior Roger attributed to himself during the four hours surrounding the homicide was too pat for the detective to accept without further checking.

"He had a window of opportunity," Carter said. "From 5:00 P.M. to 9:00 P.M. No real alibi." Roger had not told the officers that anyone saw him working late at the office after he returned from the supper with Penny.

"I wanted to go home, but I felt I needed to retrace his steps," the detective recalled. "It was colder than blue blazes and I didn't have a coat, but I had to go out there and see it for myself. I decided that on my way home I would go by the Scaggs house and drive from there to his office, just to get the proximity in my head."

Carter knew from the many cases he had worked that a killer usually has something to dump off somewhere— bloody clothes or a weapon.

With the cloudy night reflecting afterglow from the city over the nearest hills, the detective drove past the house on Winter Park Road. He saw the vehicles of APD forensic teams and familiar unmarked detective cars parked all down the block, but did not stop to go inside. His mind was concentrated on the route and travel time from the house to the office, "just like Scaggs would have driven it." He wanted to see what opportunities there might be for discarding things, what hiding places might be available along the way.

"When a person wants to dispose of items that are involved in an offense, he tends to look for a comfort zone, to put them in a place that he or she knows, a place where the items will not be discovered," he explained. "If Mr. Scaggs did have something he did not want discovered, he would not leave it at the house. He had very little time, according to his statement, to dispose of anything. I thought perhaps something might have been discarded at work."

He arrived at the APS office building in less than ten minutes, since there wasn't a single other car on the road at this cold, predawn hour.

He drove around the empty parking lot, seeing nothing of interest. He got out into the cold night and walked up to the entrance to the underground garage. There was a control box at the entrance. He walked around to the front of the building and found a swipe-card lock on the front door. It was the same type of security system they had down at the police station, so Carter knew there would be a record of people who had entered and left on the evening in question.

The detective could not find the big trash Dumpsters that he knew any large office operation needed to handle the daily outflow of waste paper. At the back of the building were three large bay doors. He thought maybe the Dumpsters were in there.

The fatigue, his poor eating habits of the past three days, and the bitter cold finally overwhelmed even this crime-scene-toughened cop. Giving in to the urge for a real meal and a few hours in a warm bed, Carter drove his unmarked police car toward the dawning glow on the horizon in the direction of his home. But he would be back working on his piece of the puzzle soon enough.

Chapter 12

*I*t's called fate, joss, kismet, luck, or chance. In religion it is referred to as God's will. Whatever one chooses to call the mystical force that seems to rule at significant moments in men's lives, it appears to have been in play during the overnight hours between March 6 and March 7.

Somewhere on the windy streets of Austin a noisy and lumbering trash truck with giant arms for hoisting industrial-sized Dumpsters was experiencing mechanical problems. By the time the disposal company's dispatcher could find someone to get a replacement truck out to the driver and a wrecker to retrieve the stalled truck, it was too late to complete all the rounds. The Capital View office park would have to wait one more day for its two big Dumpsters to be emptied.

The trash bins were already overflowing with office wastepaper and such, along with chunks of wallboard and other discarded material from a remodeling project under way in one of the buildings.

Ednoa Harrell, property manager for APS Group, did not

notice that the garbage hadn't been picked up as scheduled when she arrived at work that Thursday morning, but she soon began receiving complaint calls that the trash containers were full.

"The trucks usually picked up the trash between midnight and 8:00 A.M.," the office manager said. "They came every day of the week." The bins were filled up by the janitorial service every night after six when the cleaning crews emptied the waste baskets in the offices. "The trash is first on their list," she said, "before they dust and vacuum, so they will be sure to have that done before the garbage truck comes."

It's a mundane matter of timing. The driver must complete the pickup before 8:00 A.M. Otherwise, the big truck will be unable to maneuver between the employees' cars parked along the narrow driveway that leads to the back of the lot where the Dumpsters are stowed. In the event of a breakdown or delay, trash pickup would have to wait until the next day.

From Roger Scaggs's high office window, the tops of the Dumpsters were visible at the far back of the parking lot behind a low wall. He was also aware of the pickup schedule, having served for a time as the property manager, shortly after APS moved to Austin.

On the morning of Thursday, March 7, the current APS building manager was not the only one pondering the topic of trash handling. Sergeant David Carter woke from a short, fitful nap with trash disposal on his mind. He had been able to grab three hours sleep, his first decent meal in days, a hot shower, and an overcoat before heading back to headquarters. There he met with detectives J. W. Thompson and Hector Reveles. The three veteran homicide officers compared notes from the previous night. Carter explained that he had some concerns with portions of his interview with the victim's husband. He said he wanted to drive the trip as Roger Scaggs had described it in his account, and take a look at his office, in the possibility that something had been stashed or disposed of at that location. After the other detectives concurred with his approach, Carter headed out for the APS offices during morning drive time.

It wasn't all fate at play that morning. A strong application of old-fashioned sleuthing and good investigative procedures allowed the detective to take advantage of the breakdown in the trash disposal schedule.

"I developed a hypothetical situation in my mind," recalled Carter, who now had Roger's route of travel between his home and office down pat, from tracing it the night before. "What if he had done this; what would likely have occurred? If a person had killed his wife at his residence, evidence at the house would be discovered by the crime-scene specialists there."

Sergeant Carter kept in mind every detail of what Roger had said in the repetitive questioning about the timing of his activities. He visually overlaid his steps on a mental map of the ground he would have had to cover. Since nothing incriminating was discovered at the house in the initial search, if anything was discarded, it would have to be between the house and the office, given the time frame involved. There was no pullout or undeveloped property along the route where a sack could be tossed; the road shoulders were wide and well mowed. There was a bridge over the Colorado River, but it was miles down the parkway, with no pull-off lanes at the approaches. The bridge lanes were too narrow and the traffic too heavy at that early evening hour for even the briefest stop. Carter concluded that in the short time available, there simply was no place to hide anything except at the office.

When the detective arrived at APS, he went directly to see the building manager. He got there almost at the same moment as Ednoa Harrell, then introduced himself and said he was a homicide detective. She was not surprised.

"A friend of mine had called on my cell phone and told me about the murder," she said.

The detective asked her questions about access to the

building, how people got into the garage and offices at night. He asked her to run a tape of every entry to the building on the evening of the murder. The data she retrieved showed that Vanessa Ferguson had used her access card early that evening. Roger was one of three executives who had access to a private elevator from the parking garage, so his entry would not have been recorded.

Carter also asked Mrs. Harrell if she had seen anything unusual. She said she went to an early dinner with a friend, who dropped her back at her car around 7:15 P.M. She noticed there were lights on in the area where Vanessa worked and also a light in Roger Scaggs's office. But she did not see either of them that night.

"Do you know what kind of car Ms. Ferguson drives?" asked Carter.

"A tan Acura," said Harrell.

"At seven-fifteen, did you see Ms. Ferguson's car in the parking lot?"

Harrell said yes, she had seen the car in the lot.

The whole time they talked, the detective was scribbling in his notebook.

Then he asked about the trash bins. Where were they located? How often were they picked up? When she told him the disposal company emptied the Dumpsters at the bottom of the lot very early each morning, Carter momentarily thought that one of his investigative trails had probably just run cold. But he wanted to see for himself.

He drove his car down to the bottom of the steep grade below the lot. There were two big trash containers with the logo BFI stenciled on the side. The reason he had not seen them the night before was because they were behind a landscaped terrace or wall at the far end of the property, and from ground level, outside his line of vision. His spirits rose somewhat at the sight of debris topping one of the bins. He got out of his car. When he lifted the heavy steel lid of the first container, he saw that it was full of plastic trash bags. The other one was filled with similar bags, and topped to overflowing with discarded construction material, broken lumber, and wallboard from some construction site.

"At that time I still felt I had to eliminate Scaggs as a suspect," Carter said, noting that everything in the interview that caught his attention could probably be explained away in a subsequent interview. Carter said he had a strong feeling that the containers should be searched, if for no other reason than to show that the husband had been thoroughly investigated and eliminated if someone else were later charged with the crime.

For the search to be sanctioned, he knew it had to be witnessed, photographed, and documented, using accepted forensic practices. Since he could do none of that at the moment, he did not dig into the Dumpsters, even though his curiosity was burning. He went back to the property manager's office, got the name and number he needed, and called the disposal company.

He reached Randy Whitaker, commercial manager at Browning-Ferris Industries. He asked him not to pick up the Dumpsters behind the building complex at 1301 Capital of Texas Highway until the police could look at the contents. Whitaker knew the pickup had been missed the night before because of the delay on the route caused by the breakdown of one of his trucks. He told the officer that the building manager would likely want a special trash run that day, since they had missed the regular one the night before. When Carter advised him that the Dumpsters might contain evidence in a murder case, Whitaker said he would get in touch with a line supervisor and order replacement containers instead.

Meanwhile, Carter called headquarters to make sure that a search of the Dumpsters was technically legal without a search warrant. It was determined that they belonged to BFI; if the disposal company gave permission, nothing else would be required. Even though the Dumpsters were already on property with public access, Carter decided to have them sealed and removed to BFI's facility for the actual search.

The detectives also did not particularly want the employees at APS Systems watching out the windows of their offices as the search was conducted.

Whitaker told a BFI line supervisor what needed to be done and who to contact at the police department if there were any questions.

At 4:30 P.M., when employees had begun vacating the parking lot at Capital View Center, Steve Brinkerhoff, who was in charge of corporate accounts at BFI, personally arrived at the site to collect the two Dumpsters. He brought replacements identical to the ones to be picked up, except the replacements were painted a different color. Because no police officers were with him, there was no reason for APS employees to suspect anything out of the ordinary. It looked like just another late trash pickup.

"I went out with new containers, off-loaded them, and prepared the Dumpsters the police wanted by packing down the overflow materials and tying down the lids," Brinkerhoff said. The supervisor, who had come up through the ranks in the company as a driver, was up to the job of handling the heavy debris. He was very large, with muscular arms, close-cropped hair, and the rugged features of a man who had worked outdoors in the elements most of his life. He rolled one of the Dumpsters onto a truck bed, hauled it back to BFI's yards, and returned for the other. Someone had opened that one and piled in more construction waste material, so he had to repack it before he could seal the lid again.

Once on BFI property at Farm Road 973 in southeast Austin, Brinkerhoff placed the two containers in a secured area behind a chain-link fence in the company's storage and truck parking lot. At 7:30 P.M. on Thursday he called the homicide section at APD and told the receptionist that the Dumpsters were secured and ready to be searched whenever the police wanted them. Since APS was already closed for the day, Brinkerhoff phoned Ednoa Harrell early the next morning and explained that BFI had replaced the company's old containers with new ones. Per instructions, he did not mention that police detectives had ordered the other Dumpsters seized.

If Roger had been standing at the window of his third-floor office late that afternoon, he might have noticed the container exchange. For obvious reasons, he was not at work the day after his wife was found murdered. The executive's absence made the shocking news of Penny's death that much more terrible. The scheduled board-of-directors meeting was postponed for a week, and employees walked through the halls in almost trancelike disbelief. Some cried, because they had known Penny Scaggs personally for years and even been counseled by her, either individually or through the Creative Counterpart seminars. She was better known to the rank-and-file than most corporate wives because of her ministry to young women and the fact that she had traveled with Roger and APS Systems sales reps on business trips in the past. She also made a practice of attending every office party when families were invited.

Stern-faced police officers, some in uniform and others in mufti, had shown up at the APS offices almost with the first employees arriving for work that Thursday, March 7. For the next day or two, the officers moved quietly among the saddened employees, taking some aside for brief questioning. No crime of any sort had ever touched the corporate lives of those working in the glass and tiled offices. The worst on-the-job trauma most had experienced was losing the bid for a hard-sought new client. Several were asked to come down to police headquarters to give more lengthy accounts of information that might help in the investigation. Vanessa Ferguson was one of them. She had an appointment to be interviewed at APD headquarters the following Saturday.

Although there had been rumors about Roger having an office affair, most employees had no reason to think the mild-mannered boss was anything other than a grieving widower, a surviving victim himself. Still, some were curious when the investigators began searching Roger's big corner office. At first, APS management encouraged the employees to come forward with anything they might know that could help. But as the investigation progressed and intruded more and more on employee time and morale, the ardor for carte blanche assistance to the police cooled.

Company cooperation with the news media had already cooled. In fact, the relationship with Austin news reporters was downright icy from the moment the media learned that the husband of the murdered housewife in one of Austin's best areas was a top executive with the publicly traded company. News reporters and cameramen who showed up at APS were barred from entering the corporate offices or interviewing employees. One reporter who got all the way to the executive offices was promptly escorted from the building, with hints that any future trespass would be prosecuted.

Not all employees agreed with the company position on media coverage. Some were far more concerned about the death of Penny Scaggs than about any potentially negative impact on the company's image. A number of APS employees actually knew Penny Scaggs better than they knew her executive husband. Her death was as devastating to many of them as it had been to her seminar students and neighbors.

Patty Adams, who had worked directly for Roger since 1992 and was now interim director for sales and marketing, was one of those employees hardest hit by the news of Penny's death.

"Roger helped me out a lot in the early days [when she was new on the job], and Penny often traveled with us on sales presentations out of the city," said Adams. "Someone called and told me we wouldn't be seeing Roger at the board meeting that morning because Penny had been murdered. Coming in to work, I heard the story on the radio, but I thought they had the address wrong. I saw Penny a lot over the past few years. I loved Penny. I thought she was a wonderful woman. You hear about bad things happening to good people—it's true. I learned valuable things about my own relationship with my husband from Penny."

Curiosity turned to suspicion for some APS employees who were present when detectives zeroed in on the personal computer in Roger's office. Michael J. Shannon, the computer network manager at APS, was summoned into the office by detectives who wanted to access the contents of the hard drive. A mathematician by training, Shannon was responsible for keeping the company's all-important computer systems humming.

Roger accompanied the detectives on Friday. It was his first appearance at the office since Wednesday, the night of the murder.

"They were looking for anything on the computer that might show when Roger was at work," Shannon said. Data retained on the computer hard drive showed Roger had logged off at 8:21 P.M. on March 6. He had printed two files, one at 8:14 P.M. and another at 8:19 P.M. The retrieved data matched, in every detail, Roger's story about his work at the office the night of the murder.

The fact that the Austin Police Department was taking such a close look at the executive sent another round of rumors rippling through the company. Some who had been sympathetic toward the grieving husband felt early pangs of doubt. Over the weeks and months ahead, the unfolding tragedy became a divisive force at APS. A number of employees were upset enough to place anonymous, information-laden telephone calls to Austin reporters, who had been banned from entering the premises or interviewing staff. One reporter assigned to the Scaggs murder said he received more information through anonymous tips from APS employees than from the investigators on the case.

The official shroud of silence that surrounded the investigation from the beginning added to the mystery, fueling rumors and speculation about the murder. While the upscale neighborhood and evangelical community closed ranks in denial that such horror could have happened in their midst, the Austin Police Department was devoting all its resources to solving the heinous crime.

Chapter 13

*A*bout ninety minutes after Penny Scaggs was officially pronounced dead on the scene, the Austin PD's Crime Scene Search team was summoned into the house to begin picking it apart for clues.

Every attempt was made to revive her, but the killer had done the job too well. Once the fire department's rescue team, which had arrived around 9:20 P.M, determined the victim had no pulse, they had quickly begun CPR. While fireman Everett Thomas applied chest compressions, specialist-in-charge Wesley Wright readied the heart defibrillator. It was not until the victim's head was pulled back to start ventilations that they saw the gash across her throat and knew it was hopeless.

Simultaneously, an ambulance with two technicians from Austin Emergency Medical Services arrived at the scene. Cameron Siefert and his partner rushed into the house with their trauma gear. APD told them to be careful because it was a crime scene; the firefighters told them the victim was already dead.

Siefert felt the woman's carotid artery in her neck, examined her wounds, and made an independent determination that there was nothing they could do for her. Penny Scaggs was pronounced dead at 9:40 P.M. The medical examiner's office was notified to send a death investigator to the scene.

Siefert needed to fill out an EMS form for the police, and call the hospital to have a doctor sign off on time of death. He joined the others at the Bradys' home, to escape the cold and finish his paperwork.

The seasoned emergency medical technician had seen grieving relatives dealing with tragedy before—too many times to count. He had been on at least twenty calls where the injured person was either already deceased or died shortly after EMS arrived. Siefert said Roger Scaggs's behavior was "significantly different" from any relative he had ever encountered in that situation. Scaggs seemed unusually calm for the circumstances, he explained, but not as if he were in a trance or in shock. He was sitting on the couch, talking with neighbors.

"He was not traumatized when we asked for information," Siefert recalled. "A lot of family members are emotional when we pronounce their loved ones dead at such a scene. He asked us why everybody was called out. He wanted to know how long this was going to take."

A K-9 unit had arrived at the address. Officer Terry Meadows took his Belgian Malinois on a tour of the outside perimeter of the residence in search of "fear scent," which is often left by a perpetrator fleeing the crime scene in a panic.

"Because the air was cold, the search was easy that night," Meadows said. "The dog found no fear scent on the back deck of the house." Meadows walked the dog along the back fences and down Winter Park Road, but no telltale odors were detected.

"By this time there were too many people and too much news media at the scene to do any more with the police dog," the officer said.

The Crime Scene Search team was authorized to move into the Scaggs home at 11:20 P.M. on Wednesday, March 6. The 911 call had sent emergency vehicles screaming into the normally serene neighborhood with lights flashing and sirens blaring. Squad cars, fire trucks, and ambulances crowded the block around the house, with swiveling lights casting eerie shadows the length of Winter Park Road. Finally, more than two hours after the first claxons had shocked the quiet neighborhood, the emergency vehicles pulled away, leaving darkness and a new fear in the sleepless neighborhood.

The departure of the big, noisy trucks and marked patrol cars did not signal the end of response to the murder scene. Far from it. Once the fire truck and ambulance cleared the scene, Detective J. W. Thompson ordered the property roped off with yellow crime-scene tape. After the barrier tape went up, not even the homeowner could enter the property, a fact soon to become a point of contention between Scaggs and the Austin Police Department.

Detective Thompson waved the team of APD specialists into the house from a van parked in the circular driveway. Most of the search team had stayed huddled in the van to keep out of the cold wind since their arrival hours earlier. They had been summoned to duty from their homes when the first calls for homicide detectives went out from the dispatcher.

The APD's Crime Scene Search team was a relatively new unit, having been funded only three years earlier by the Austin City Council. They went to their first crime scene in January 1994. The core team consisted of a chemist, ID specialist (latent prints), photographer, and ballistics expert, if relevant to the crime; others would be sent, as needed.

Since the special group concept was still being developed, the APD worked closely with the forensics lab of the Texas Department of Public Safety, also in Austin. The APD team, at the time of the Scaggs murder, was primarily responsible for processing crime scenes and gathering evidence to be tested and analyzed elsewhere.

Penny's house was now under the control of someone else for the first time since she had lovingly taken charge of it twelve years earlier, with grand ambitions to make it the perfect Christian home. The cruel irony of what this home—now a crime scene—had become, went unnoticed for the first hours, while emergency vehicles and crews dominated. But with the arrival of dawn and time for reflection, the reality of the night's events would become almost unbearable to many Austinites, particularly those in the evangelical community. Scores, if not hundreds, of young women had come to this room, in this house, to learn from the victim how to make their marriages better by being godly wives, subservient to their husbands. Now the room that had once been sanctified by prayer circles of worshipping women was a scene of unspeakable horror. This place idealized in the memories of many young Austin women as the inspirational example of what they, too, would build someday, was stained with the blood of their mentor. There was nothing left to be done now, but for criminologists to begin sorting out how, and perhaps why, this upscale, suburban home had so suddenly and inexplicably changed from a haven of good to a scene of such evil.

The specialists of the Crime Scene Search team knew they had a real chance to make a difference in this case, because there was no readily identifiable suspect, or even a clear motive for the homicide. The team was ready to devote the rest of the night, and the next one as well, to search for any missing clue that might break the case wide open.

All the members of the team entered the Scaggs house wearing paper booties over their shoes and thin surgical gloves. Coincidentally, they were just getting started as Roger Scaggs was beginning to answer questions at police headquarters downtown. The search team began its work at 11:20 P.M. The Scaggs interview by Detective Carter began at 11:21.

When the team moved into the house, the first order of business was a walk-through of the downstairs area where the murder took place. Detectives had already informed the team that the upstairs bedrooms and recreation room appeared to be undisturbed. The forensic search would be concentrated in the living area where the body was discovered, the kitchen around the sink, and in the master bedroom and bath where Penny's jewelry had been found scattered about. The bathtub contained what appeared to be most of the contents of the jewelry cases. The cases themselves were thrown on the floor, with the drawers removed. This pilferage was the only apparent sign that a burglary or vandalism had been part of the crime. Otherwise, the house looked freshly vacuumed and very clean. Some large areas of the carpet did not even show footprints since the last house cleaning.

The photographer, Cheryl Bowne, was the first to ply her trade. It was her job to assure that every inch of the scene was captured on film in its original state before other members began dusting, scraping, picking, probing, and sampling. She shot the "overalls" of both the outside and inside of the house. She would take additional photographs throughout the coming hours as specific items, locations, and potential clues were tagged and documented by other team members.

Penny's body was photographed in the position where it had been found, between the piano bench and the front of the baby grand piano. Its human value ruthlessly destroyed, Penny's remains became a witness in death against her assailant, the only testimony she was capable of offering about what had happened in her home that evening.

The medical examiner performed a standard postmortem test of internal organ temperature with a liver probe, just before midnight. The liver temperature at 11:54 P.M. was eighty-eight degrees, as Bob Davis, a legal death investigator from the Travis County Office of the Medical Examiner, noted in his report. He also wrote that discoloration had begun and the body was beginning to stiffen. Davis ruled the death a homicide. Only when his work was done could the body be removed from the scene.

After the last photographs documenting the position of the body had been taken, Davis carefully placed paper bags over the hands and taped them securely closed, to preserve any trace evidence that might be present. The body was then transported to the Travis County morgue at 100 Brazos Street.

The crime scene as it appeared when detectives first saw it was now fully documented on film. It was time for the forensic search for evidence to begin.

Uniformed officers remained at the site for security. Michael Burgh and Thomas Sweeney had been the first officers on the scene, hours before. Even though their shifts had ended, they volunteered to stay on the job and assist the crime-scene specialists as gofers, if they were needed. They had a personal investment in finding the killer. This was their regular patrol district, code-named "David Sector." It was their neighborhood "to serve and protect." The worst crime in recent memory had now happened during their watch, and these officers were going to see it through to the end. They were also both fascinated by the forensic phase of the investigation and wanted to observe, firsthand, the team's work. In addition to securing the property, Patrolmen Burgh and Sweeney worked through the night holding tapes, moving equipment, and performing other small but essential chores.

Officer Andy Anderson asked Burgh to assist him in making a detailed diagram, with measurements, of the rooms they were processing. Burgh, who looked like a college jock, with a one-inch whitewall burr haircut and heavy shoulders, patiently held the measuring tape for the tedious job, while the investigator drew the floor plans. They diagrammed the living area where the murder took place before the body was removed, so that exact measurements could be used to fix the location where the body apparently fell during the attack. This drawing would be vital to crime-scene specialists in placing the tangible pieces of evidence they discovered, and explaining where various people were positioned after the emergency response.

When the body was removed, specialists went over the immediate vicinity of the slaying inch by inch with magnifiers, looking for tiny blood droplets. The more obvious blood splatters on the piano and bench had already been identified and tagged for the photographer. There was very little blood at the scene, because Penny Scaggs had apparently died of blunt trauma wounds to the head before the killer ever stabbed her.

Still, the team quickly charted sufficient blood splatter and drop patterns to give the crime-scene reconstructionist ample material to work with. A specialist in that field, Bob Henderson, would later be able to analyze scientifically the spatter and drops, along with photographs and diagrams, to deduce where and how the attack took place. The visual search for blood would be followed later by luminol tests; but this initial work had to be completed before those tests could be conducted in total darkness.

The forensic crew then turned to the old reliable chore of gathering fingerprints. Using the well-known dust and brush technique commonly seen on popular crime shows, the team worked outward from the spot where the body was found, carefully scrutinizing every surface.

Most of their attention focused on the yellow baby grand Kawai piano, for it was there that the victim was apparently struck down. Dozens of fingerprints were lifted from the piano surfaces where people had obviously touched the instrument or leaned against it. However, there were some peculiar prints found on the front left leg of the piano, just inches above the floor. Why had someone touched the piano so low to the floor, within arm's reach of where the body was discovered?

The prints lifted that night would eventually be compared with rolled fingerprints provided by persons with reason to be at the residence. Detective Thompson was already round-ing up prints from the latter group, and eventually would have print sets from Penny, Roger, Sarah and her ex-husband Cory Munson, and some close neighbors and friends who frequented the house. There were too many of Penny's students, who had studied in the room where the murder occurred, to locate and fingerprint each one.

Then the team methodically moved from room to room throughout the rest of the ground level. They gave special attention to the master bathroom, where Penny's costume jewelry had been strewn about. The island in the kitchen was also carefully dusted for prints.

Once the team had swept an area of the house, identification specialist Charles Dean began marking and bagging items that were of interest to the detectives at the scene. The jewelry cases, pieces of costume jewelry, a butcher's block with kitchen knives, and any other objects that might have been handled or moved by an intruder, would be impounded by the police after the crime scene had been completely processed. A piece of gold chain with a diamond heart pendant was found in a small pool of what appeared to be water-diluted blood at the edge of the kitchen sink. The chain was bagged and the bloody droplet was swabbed for further study. The butcher's block, with a Chicago Cutlery logo, was of particular interest, since a knife had been used in the attack. When Officer Sweeney first secured the house, he had noticed three empty slots in the block and two knives lying on the counter. An earring with a broken clasp was found near the body; a matching earring was still in the victim's left earlobe. Two pairs of eyeglasses were removed from that room, too, one from the piano music rack and the other from the floor under a coffee table. One black shoe was bagged after it was found under the piano. Its mate was on the victim's left foot.

Before anything was collected, numbered markers were put down to identify where each item of evidence, small or large, was found. The markers would help others assess the scene, showing the location and relationships of the evidence. The markers, along with coordination and teamwork of those processing the scene, would be important in maintaining an accurate, consistent record of all evidence as it moved through the forensic and legal processes ahead. The photographer documented all evidence that had been flagged with the numbered little "tents." One of the technicians followed with a clipboard, logging it all in.

The last job was the most technical and disruptive. It involved the use of chemicals and equipment that would leave the crime scene badly marked up, and in some cases permanently damaged. But chemical processing was perhaps the most important of the modern techniques for crime solving. Forensic chemist Mary Villarreal was responsible for conducting this test. The process included finding and taking samples from tiny spots of liquid or specks of debris that might yield DNA evidence, including body fluid, hair, skin flakes, and clothing.

Villarreal, who had a degree in chemistry and advanced training at the FBI Academy in Quantico, Virginia, approached her job with the determination of a scientist seeking a breakthrough cure. The material evidence she sought was mostly invisible to the human eye, yet just as damning when presented to a jury.

In addition to the living area, the exact point of the murder, and the kitchen—where some evidence was visually apparent—her team focused on the entryway and foyer. Faint indentations that appeared to be footprints were barely visible in the carpet. The team hoped to pull up even these faint prints, using an electrostatic dust lifter. After several attempts to force the dust particles to adhere to black film using an electrical charge, they determined that the carpet, which appeared so pristine, was actually too dusty to be tested.

The high-tech search of the scene also required spraying luminol—a chemical that could cause damage to walls and floors—to find hidden blood that might have been wiped or washed away by a killer or was too small to be detected by the naked eye. The chemicals in the luminol mixture react to the hemoglobin in blood, to produce a luminescence visible only in a darkened area. The iron in the hemoglobin acts as a catalyst to create a blue glow, which lasts for about thirty seconds, during which time it can be photographed.

In addition to the area by the piano where the body was found, the team also wanted to test with luminol the kitchen, laundry room, and back patio. Since this process would cause some staining that could cover up other evidence, it was the last step in the search. By the time the team completed its other work, it was already too near daylight to conduct the luminol tests. Villarreal told Detective Thompson that they would have to return the next evening, which meant the house must remain sealed, in police custody, at least through Thursday night.

The Crime Scene Search team had spent more than five hours gathering evidence when they stopped their work a little before dawn on March 7. Some of the team members were glad they would have more time on the scene to continue their search. They hoped to get a few hours' rest before returning. When they left the house, they sealed the outside doors with bright orange, adhesive-backed forms, indicating the time and the signature of the officer in charge. These orange sheets were pasted at the seams of the doors so they could not be opened without ripping the seals. Any investigator who entered later would be expected to replace the seal, noting name and time of entry and departure.

Later that morning another important piece of the puzzle was about to be addressed in downtown Austin.

*T*he autopsy began promptly at 10:00 A.M., eleven hours after the body of Penny Scaggs was found in her home on Winter Park Road. It was conducted in the antiquated Travis County Morgue by Chief Medical Examiner Roberto J. Bayardo, MD. Austin PD detective John Hunt was in attendance, along with an assistant and a photographer from the examiner's office. The lead detective, J. W. Thompson, joined the group after the autopsy was under way.

Dr. Bayardo, who held a medical degree from the University of Guadalajara, had practiced medicine and surgery as a hospital physician in Mexico for several years before immigrating to the United States. He had been the medical examiner in Austin for eighteen years at the time of Penny's autopsy. He took charge of the Travis County morgue when county commissioners hired him from a similar post with Harris County in Houston. Bayardo, a tall, distinguished-looking man who spoke with a slight Spanish accent, became a naturalized American citizen while taking advanced medical training in the States. He completed a postdoctoral program in pathology at Baylor University College of Medicine, and served as chief resident in pathology at Methodist Hospital of Dallas and Good Samaritan Hospital in Phoenix. He was board certified by the American Board of Pathology as both a forensic pathologist and an anatomical and clinical pathologist.

As Dr. Bayardo prepared to perform the postmortem examination, he wrote in his report notes and for the record that the subject had been found at approximately 9:00 P.M. the previous day and pronounced dead on the scene at 9:40 P.M. The woman on the examination table was wearing a long-sleeve blouse, unbuttoned almost to the waist. There was a white bra under the blouse. The subject wore a pair of black slacks and a black belt, black panty hose and a black shoe on the left foot. A small silver bracelet with a heart-shaped pendant was removed from the right wrist, and a silver ring with a black stone was removed from the right ring finger. A watch with a black band was removed from the left wrist, and a silver ring with a cross and fish design from the left index finger.

The examiner found blood splatter on the back of the left hand; blood was smeared on the right hand. There was a long earring in the left earlobe. From the left side of the neck a seven-inch section of thin gold chain was recovered. The head was covered with sandy blond hair up to four inches in length. The hair was matted to the skull by blood. Mascara had been applied around gray eyes. There was lipstick on the lips. The mouth contained natural teeth in good condition. The fingernails were trimmed short and neat.

Upon initial examination, Dr. Bayardo observed numerous injuries over the surface of the body. The injuries were of two types: blunt force and stab wounds. These wounds revealed evidence of a massive, violent attack.

The external examination recorded by Dr. Bayardo revealed seven scattered wounds on the head; bruises on the right cheek, the lip, and above the right eyelid; and a torn right earlobe, all caused by a blunt instrument. In addition, there were blunt force injuries evident on the shoulders, and on the right forearm, wrist, hand, foot, and thigh.

The body also bore numerous stab wounds. Because of the low level of bleeding around these wounds, they appeared to have been inflicted postmortem. These stab wounds included a three-and-a-half-inch slashing cut on the neck, which had not penetrated the airway in the throat, and a two-inch-wide, five-inch-deep stab on the right side of the neck, which penetrated to the spine. In the upper front of the chest, a six-inch-deep stab wound in the area of the trachea penetrated the chest cavity, and two stab wounds in the area of the sternum penetrated the chest cavity and the lungs. One of the wounds, which was six inches deep, had passed through both lobes of the lung and ended on a rib in the back. There were other lesser stab wounds on the left shoulder and the upper right arm, and two puncture wounds on the back.

Smears revealed no oral, vaginal, or rectal spermatozoa.

After the autopsy incision was made, Dr. Bayardo confirmed that one of the stab wounds had penetrated the rib cage and both walls of the left lung. The esophagus had been perforated twice by the "stabbing instrument," and the airway passage penetrated. These two stab wounds corresponded with those observed on the neck in the external examination.

The internal examination of the stomach revealed that Penny Scaggs had recently eaten approximately one cup of semisolid food. Particles of beans, barley, and carrots were identified.

However, the damage that was deemed most significant, and that most likely caused her death, was found on the victim's head. The examination revealed massive injury to the back and right side of the skull. There was general internal bleeding in the skull cavity, and the skull in this area had been shattered and broken.

Dr. Bayardo's diagnosis was that the victim had suffered massive craniocerebral injury from seven blows with a blunt instrument, a fractured mandible, and eight stab wounds of the neck, chest, and back. In addition, there were numerous injuries to the extremities.

The autopsy enabled the medical examiner to reach a conclusion as to the manner of death. Dr. Bayardo's official report stated:

> It is my opinion, based on investigation of the circumstances and the autopsy findings, that the decedent, Penny Scaggs, came to her death as a result of a massive craniocerebral injury, sustained by being struck on the head with a heavy blunt instrument.

The autopsy was documented in a series of photographs taken in Dr. Bayardo's presence and under his direction.

Food samples taken from the stomach were preserved for further analysis, to determine approximately when the last meal had been consumed by the victim.

Other samples were sent for testing. Dr. Bayardo scraped tiny amounts of unidentified material from under the fingernails, and with scissors clipped off the ends of the nails. His assistant bagged and marked the samples, beginning the chain of custody. Detective Hunt took the fingernail evidence to police headquarters to log it in before it went to the Texas DPS lab for analysis.

Chapter 14

Roger and Sarah Scaggs asked the detective in charge, J. W. Thompson, to let them into the sealed home on Friday morning, March 8, so they could retrieve a dress suitable for Penny's burial. The crime-scene team had finished the luminol work the night before, searching for additional traces of blood.

The team had also used amido black to look for fingerprints not detectable using carbon-powder dusting. Amido black is a dye that stains the protein in blood, creating a blue-black reaction. It sometimes leaves permanent stains on the surface being tested. In the Scaggs case, it apparently did leave marks on the yellow finish of the baby grand piano. However, the chemical is important to forensics because it is extremely effective in revealing faint fingerprint ridges tinged with blood, even those invisible to the naked eye or that seem to have been wiped clean.

Detective Carter decided to show up at the appointed time to observe Roger's reaction when he walked through the scene of the crime, particularly the room where the murder occurred. At that point in the investigation, although Carter still did not consider Roger a suspect, he was concerned about certain answers to his interview questions.

Detectives Thompson and Carter met Roger and Sarah at the front door, and Thompson removed the police seal. He told Roger that Crime Scene Search would probably release the house later that day. As Roger went through the rooms, Carter hung back a bit, not wanting to make him nervous by following too closely or staring after his every move. But he stayed close enough to observe Roger's reactions.

"Mr. Scaggs's demeanor did not change when he walked into the master bedroom and master bath," Carter recalled. "Sarah gasped when she saw the jewelry and cases scattered in the bathroom. Roger put his arm around her for support."

After father and daughter had selected a funeral dress for Penny, Detective Thompson asked Roger if he could come down to the station again that afternoon to answer a few more questions. Thompson also wanted to interview Sarah, and asked if that afternoon would be okay for her, too.

Shortly after 1:00 P.M., Roger and Sarah walked into the police station, and the receptionist paged the detectives. The lobby of police headquarters is a busy place, with victims and suspects involved in petty crimes milling around and waiting on benches to see specific policemen who had asked them to come in for questioning. Father and daughter did not have to wait. They were met and escorted directly to the homicide bureau's offices.

Roger had already spent more than three hours being interviewed by Detective Carter the night of the murder. He was again assured that police interest in him was not only to gain information that might help in the investigation, but also to clear him of suspicion.

Carter repeated to Roger one of his tenets of police work: "If an innocent person is wrongly tried and jailed, the criminal is free to do the crime again." This seemed to satisfy Roger, who did not complain about the second interview. He did complain, however, about not having his house released back to him and not having an inventory of property the police would be removing for further study.

"While it's on my mind, can you either show us an inventory or the items [you removed]? We tried to make a list so we could compare it," he said to Detective Thompson.

"It's just going to take a little while longer," the detective assured the increasingly agitated Roger. This was the third or fourth time he had asked for a list of his impounded property.

Roger pressed further. He said Sarah had started an inventory of things that were missing from the house—a list "like I asked you about," he told the detective.

"The list is going to grow," Thompson said. "It will take a few days. We want to be accurate."

"I need to know for insurance purposes," Roger said. He then changed the subject to a request for an updated status of the investigation. "I was kind of hoping you can give us some kind of debrief of what all you have done . . . what you know, what your assessment is so far. We just kind of feel in the dark. Obviously we know your people have been here for two days."

Thompson told him that the team had gone over the entire house and was almost done with its work. He said everything collected was being analyzed at the "crime lab." He briefly described the various types of searches they had conducted and what evidence might result from each type.

Sarah raised the question of her mother's more valuable jewelry, asking if Thompson knew whether any of it had been found at the scene or on her mother's body. Sarah described the necklace her mother usually wore, and her mother's diamond ring. The detective told her that neither piece had been found. He asked her to go through family photographs and try to find pictures of her mother wearing the jewelry. He said such photos could be distributed to pawnshops to help identify valuables that a perpetrator might try to hock.

"Anyway, the forensic work has been done. It's being

evaluated at this time," Thompson said. "We're talking to neighbors of yours that would have seen something." He said they were checking fingerprints, blood traces for evidence of foreign sources, and hair and fiber samples. Thompson told the Scaggses that when the evidence was evaluated it would be used to develop leads the detectives would follow until they found the killer.

"Bear with us. It's going to get old," Thompson said of the tediousness of a homicide investigation. "You will get disappointed in us, but don't. Hang in there with us."

At this point he told Sarah he was going to interview her in a separate interrogation room, while Carter resumed questioning her father.

Thompson presumably wanted information about Sarah's relationship with her mother in the months prior to the murder. The police had learned from Roger's earlier statement that although mother and daughter had been estranged after Sarah's divorce, the relationship was on the mend in recent months, with the two meeting regularly for lunch.

Detective Carter's second interview of Roger Scaggs was much more restricted in scope than the one he had conducted the night of the murder. Most of his questions, two days later, pertained to family finances. Roger walked the detective through the details of his bank accounts, his company's expense reimbursement policy, and the types of securities the family held. He said their assets were primarily restricted to mutual fund accounts and IRAs. Roger lamented that there was not much insurance on Penny.

"[We] kind of regret that now," he said. "I guess you never know. We always figured it would be more important if I went first she would need insurance to keep her living [support herself]. I could always make a living if she went first."

The reality now was that the funeral was "going to cost over $15,000," and they had only $1,000 of life insurance on Penny. Her grandmother had purchased the policy when she was a child.

Concerning the family's assets, Roger told the detective that he had sold off a large block of his company stock a few months before the murder.

"I sold a bunch of it around the first of the year because the stock price is real high," he said, adding that he still owned 27,000 shares of APS stock and some options that he had not yet exercised. Oddly, the detective did not pursue the large stock sale so close to the time of the murder, nor did he ask where the proceeds had gone. Either the police already knew about the transaction or had decided that money was not a factor in the murder case.

Carter spent the rest of the interview at the station going over Roger's company—where he fit into the organizational structure and the specifics of his job, including his out-of-town travel requirements. More than once Detective Carter apologized for having to take so much of Roger's time.

"As you may or may not understand, when there is a murder we have to disprove certain things as well," the detective said. "So I'm basically asking some things about yourself and your finances, insurance, things like that. We need to do that because it's, in effect, eliminating you [as a suspect]. I hope you don't take offense by it. It's something that the police have to do."

This second interview took about forty-five minutes. At the conclusion, Detective Carter suggested that Roger take a ride with him to retrace his drive from his home to the office the night he discovered his wife's body.

Apparently, Carter knew that he would shortly be getting into personal aspects of Roger's life. At a homicide team meeting earlier that morning, the lead detective shared some interesting information that had come in to investigators through anonymous phone calls to the Crime Stoppers tip line the previous day.

"Two people—one male, one female—called Crime Stoppers with information about an affair," Thompson told his team at the morning brief.

Carter had already driven the route between Roger's home and office in the early morning hours after the murder. But he wanted to have Roger direct the same trip.

"I asked him if he would show me while I drove the exact route he took that previous Wednesday," Carter said. They left the station in the detective's unmarked car for the reenactment.

"As we drove west on Eighth Street, Mr. Scaggs told me there was something he felt I should know," the officer recalled. "He said he was having an affair with an employee at the office. He named Vanessa Ferguson."

They drove to the Scaggs residence. "We started from the front of the house," said Carter. "I looked at my watch and then followed his directions. It took right at ten minutes, garage-to-garage."

Roger seemed more concerned about the items police were removing from his house than about the affair he had just casually mentioned to the detective.

"He again asked me for an inventory of what had been taken from his house," Carter said. But the affair was on the officer's mind as they drove.

"When he mentioned the affair, I did not react. Affairs are common. They play a role, but are never a surprise," according to the veteran detective. He thought this particular confession might be more significant because Roger had been so insistent about the strength of his marriage.

"Everything he said was strategic," Carter noted.

By the time Roger revealed the affair, he had every reason to believe the police had already learned of it, or were about to hear of it from others. At that very hour, back at headquarters, Detective Thompson was interviewing Sarah, who had been aware of her father's affair for more than a year. Roger also knew that Carter had singled out Ms. Ferguson for an interview when he and other detectives questioned employees at the APS offices. Roger did not know that Vanessa was being interviewed because her car had been seen parked at the office building the night of the murder, and not because officers were suspicious about an affair.

"I told Roger I'd need to talk to her [Vanessa] about the affair," Carter said. "He replied that 'she'd be more than willing' to talk to us. It crossed my mind to ask him how he knew that, but I didn't press it at the time."

At the Capital View office building, Roger used his access code and Carter drove into the reserved area of the basement garage. On the way into the building, Roger again mentioned Vanessa. He said she had been there, that she was his alibi. In the earlier interview, he had told the detective that *no one* was at the office that night. "Now he told me Vanessa had been there," said Carter.

In the third-floor offices of APS Group, they ran into Vanessa in a hallway. Roger stopped and told her that she would need to talk to the police, since she was at the office that night. She had already agreed to an interview with Carter for the following day, Saturday.

"His [Roger's] presence on the floor sent electricity through the offices," Carter observed. "I told those we talked to that we were going to help Mr. Scaggs get to the bottom of this."

Roger told them that the police seemed to be very thorough and professional.

"He showed me Vanessa's office," said Carter. "She was an administrative assistant in another branch, I believe to the chief financial officer."

Carter's later interview with Vanessa Ferguson confirmed what Roger had said about her being his alibi. She told police he had been at the office on the evening of March 6. So Roger now had one eyewitness who could verify that he was at his office working that night—the woman with whom he was having the affair.

An affidavit made by Ferguson read, in part:

> On the night of March 6, 1996, when Mrs. Scaggs was murdered, I had dinner by myself at Jason's Deli near

the office ... I arrived at the office at approximately 7 o'clock P.M. ... I can verify that Mr. Scaggs was present at the office that night. He was working on an important presentation for the next day ... He was at the office between approximately 7:30 P.M. and 9:00 P.M.

This account jibed in every detail with Roger's earlier statement to the police. He said he left home for the ten-minute drive back to his office at 7:00 or 7:15 P.M. He also described what he did at the office between his dinner visit home and finally leaving for the night at around 9:00 P.M.

But before Carter ever interviewed Vanessa, a much more dramatic event took place on the afternoon of March 8. Coupled with Roger's admission of the affair, this next incident was about to give the investigation major new momentum.

Roger had wandered off to talk to his fellow executives at APS while Carter chatted with other employees. The detective's pager rang. He returned the page and reached homicide team leader J. W. Thompson at police headquarters.

"J.W. told me to get back to the office," Carter recalled. "He said they had something. They had found stuff in the Dumpster."

Chapter 15

Among a police detective's many unpleasant but common chores is an old-fashioned, shoe-leather job referred to as "Dumpster diving." It involves simply climbing into a trash bin and carefully examining the refuse.

Shortly after 1:00 P.M. on Friday, March 8, at about the same time homicide detective David Carter was driving downtown on Eighth Street listening to Roger Scaggs admit to an affair with a woman in his office, a team of Austin detectives and forensic specialists was arriving at the gates of BFI.

The company's storage and maintenance yards were located on the southeast outskirts of town. The sprawling facility was the base for a fleet of about fifty garbage trucks and hundreds of trash bins, containers, and Dumpsters being cleaned and refurbished. Two of the Dumpsters, six-foot-tall commercial containers with heavy steel lids and sliding doors on two sides, were set apart for the special attention of the arriving investigators.

The five-member team, under the supervision of homicide

detective Al Eells, had been dispatched by detective J. W. Thompson to search for anything that might be connected to the Penny Scaggs murder. Specifically, detectives were looking for discarded bloody clothing and/or weapons. The police had found two pieces of clothing in the laundry the night of the murder, but when tested for blood, they were negative.

The targeted Dumpsters had been removed the previous day by Browning-Ferris Industries, the disposal company, on an urgent request by Detective Carter. BFI supervisor Steve Brinkerhoff had picked them up on Thursday and hauled them the seventeen miles from APS offices to the storage yards at Farm Road 973 and State Highway 71. The Dumpsters, called Tall Eights, had been off-loaded in an area at the front corner of the property just inside the entrance gate.

Police had told BFI manager Randy Whitaker that the large containers might hold evidence in a murder case. The company officials treated the unusual police request seriously. They cleared out an area that could be easily observed by employees, to make sure no unauthorized person could tamper with the containers, accidentally or otherwise. Although police searches of Dumpsters are not uncommon, impounding them is unusual. The company managers wanted no mistakes at their end that could compromise an investigation.

While Brinkerhoff was picking them up, Whitaker marked off the area where the containers could be separated from others in the yard, to make sure they were not accidentally emptied by the cleaning crews. Brinkerhoff had been careful to tie down the lid of each Dumpster with bungee cords before transporting them, so none of the contents would be lost.

"In terms of evidence, we were looking for anything that might be connected to the case, including weapons, clothing, blood . . ." Detective Eells said.

In his fifteen years on the force, the suave, clean-cut detective had never before been called upon to search inside one of the huge trash receptacles. In his tailored business suit, Eells didn't even look like a cop; he looked more like an advertising executive or Wall Street broker. For the assignment on this particular day, however, he donned the disposable coveralls police call a bunny suit, paper booties, and surgical rubber gloves.

Detective Thompson had asked Eells to put together a team for the search. He selected homicide detective Mark Gilchrist to assist him and asked Crime Scene Search to assign an evidence-gathering crew. That crew included chemist Mary Villarreal, who had completed the luminol testing of the Scaggs home the previous night, photographer Cheryl Bowne, and Kathy Wallace, an evidence specialist.

At the search scene, the team put on the protective Tyvek suits and gloves and divided up the work. Eells and Villarreal searched the first Dumpster, and Gilchrist and Wallace were assigned to the second. The photographer would be summoned to take pictures if anything was found.

The first container was two-thirds full, so Eells had to climb over the top to get into it. "My intention was to remove everything," the detective said. Villarreal waited on the pavement for him to toss out garbage bags and other items of interest. The Dumpster was mostly filled with industrial-type, gray-green trash bags that all looked the same. He slowly removed the larger bags, one at a time, and worked down into the trash. The team at the second Dumpster was duplicating the search process.

About halfway down something caught the attention of detective Eells. "It was darker—didn't look anything like the other bags," he said. The bag was partially buried in leaves and landscaping waste and twigs. When he brushed the leaves away, he could see that the bag was larger and heavier that the others.

"This bag was so different that I decided to open it before tossing it out. I had the photographer climb in and take pictures of the item just as it was found."

Eells pulled open the bag and looked inside while it was still nested in the other trash. The first thing he saw was thin latex gloves and a metal pipe. He rolled the sides of the bag and caught sight of the glint of something that looked like a piece of jewelry. The photographer snapped the shots and Detective Eells called for an evidence identification specialist to rush to the scene.

At 2:20 P.M., ID tech James Bush was on call at headquarters when someone in Homicide phoned and asked him to collect evidence from a trash container at BFI property. He loaded up his processing kit and arrived on scene at 2:55. Detective Eells showed the ID specialist where the evidence was located and told him what he wanted recovered. Bush pulled on a bunny suit and green latex gloves before climbing into the Dumpster. He did not look in the bag; he just closed it back up, to make sure all the contents were intact, and retrieved it.

Bush put the garbage bag and its contents into a large brown paper sack, folded the top firmly in place, and put it in the van. Eells's search team knew they had found something, but did not yet know all the contents of the bag, or the importance of their discovery.

Meanwhile, Villarreal was searching through the other bags the detective had tossed out. She found one containing what appeared to be normal office trash. However, she thought this particular trash might be significant, since it was obviously from Roger Scaggs's office. The bag contained the *New York Times* and *USA Today* newspapers and an envelope addressed to Jackie Fife at APS Systems. It also contained a Federal Express receipt for a package delivered to Roger Scaggs, a Priority Mail envelope addressed to Scaggs dated March 5, and a trip report for travel on March 4, which had been filled out by Scaggs.

After James Bush dusted the side doors of the Dumpster for fingerprints and found none, he took both bags and drove back to headquarters, where he took the evidence to the APD photo lab. Assisted by Villarreal, who arrived at the lab a short time later, Bush opened the first bag. Wearing gloves and using forceps for some of the smaller pieces, he carefully removed each item and laid it on the clean paper covering the lab table. It was only then that the magnitude of the find became clear.

The items recovered were a treasure trove of damning evidence linked to the Penny Scaggs murder. Included were pieces of jewelry the victim had reportedly been wearing that night. Some of the jewelry was blood-spattered. There was a V-shaped diamond necklace, a diamond tennis bracelet, and a diamond ring with a large stone. The necklace and ring were identical to two pieces of jewelry Sarah Scaggs had described to police during her interview.

The other items in the trash bag were even more stunning. Being careful not to touch places where latent prints might be, Bush removed a thin carving knife and a heavy metal pipe, over a foot long, with end caps. The pipe was of a galvanized steel alloy used in commercial plumbing, but not commonly found in residential construction. In addition, there were five latex gloves.

Cheryl Bowne, who had earlier documented the crime scene, shot individual pictures of every piece of evidence. Bush and Villarreal bagged each item separately and tagged each with the APD offense number and other identifying data. They logged the whole cache, including the plastic bag in which it was found, into the police evidence room, a locked, secure facility where evidence is held until released for processing.

The crime-scene specialists gave detective-in-charge Thompson a description of the evidence recovered from the Dumpster. He immediately called his fellow team member, David Carter, with the startling news.

Carter's cop-savvy hunch, which had been seeded in his first interview with Roger Scaggs, had borne fruit. Without this officer's experience and training, in a matter of hours the evidence would have disappeared forever. It seemed almost ironic that justice for the fastidious homemaker might ultimately come, literally, from the trash. Like the legacy of her life, these vital clues that would largely solve her murder could not be so easily discarded.

Austin police suddenly had the evidence they had been seeking. It was now a matter of linking the pieces to a killer.

*F*riday, March 8, had already been a significant day for homicide detectives working on the Penny Scaggs murder case, but more information came their way late that afternoon.

Dr. Roberto Bayardo, the Travis County medical examiner, had completed the autopsy the day before. It came as no surprise to detectives that the autopsy verified the cause of death as massive head injuries from a blunt instrument. With the recovery of the trash from the Dumpster, they now knew that instrument was most likely the galvanized steel pipe.

But the next piece of the puzzle provided by the medical examiner did cause some surprise in the homicide section.

After completing the initial autopsy, Dr. Bayardo set out to narrow the time of death. Detectives had temporarily been using the time period provided by the deceased's husband. Based on that account, the victim would have died sometime after 7:15 P.M., when Roger said he left home to return to the office. He said he completed his office work and arrived back at his house shortly after 9:00 P.M., when he found his wife's dead body.

Dr. Bayardo first examined the stomach contents removed during the autopsy. He found approximately one cup of partially digested carrots, beans, and barley—presumably the victim's last meal. After further analysis, the M.E. concluded that the digestive process had probably continued for at least one hour and definitely less than two hours before it was abruptly terminated by death. In other words, Penny had likely died less than two hours after consuming the meal.

The second piece of evidence he used to estimate the time of death was the liver temperature, taken at the scene the night of the murder by the legal death investigator, Bob Davis. The liver temperature at 11:54 P.M. was eighty-eight degrees.

For his calculation, Dr. Bayardo used the standard assumption that body temperature falls at the rate of one and a half degrees per hour for the first twelve hours after death. Assuming that Penny's temperature was normal (98.6 degrees) when she died, her body had cooled about ten and a half degrees by the time the test was done. That would place time of death approximately seven hours before Davis performed the liver test, or close to 5:00 P.M.

However, as in the case of food digestion, liver temperature is by no means a precise way to calculate time of death. The loss of body heat depends on many variables, including body fat, the temperature of the immediate environment, the surface temperature where the body lies, and whether the body and clothing are wet or dry. Measurements can be skewed if a person has a fever at the time of death. Some forensic pathologists believe that the severe stress or trauma of an attack can cause an instantaneous change in temperature before death.

Calculations of time of death based on food digestion or liver temperature must be used with caution, since they can only provide a range of probability, rather than a pinpointed time. What was significant here was that the calculations reinforced each other. When Dr. Bayardo combined the results, he concluded that time of death was likely between 5:00 P.M. and 6:00 P.M.

According to this calculation, Roger's statement to Detective Carter became problematic. He had told police he had come home that night around five-thirty. He said they "had a nice dinner." He had helped stack the dishes in the sink and changed into casual clothing before leaving between 7:00 and 7:15 P.M. to return to the office.

Bayardo's estimated time of death meant that Roger, by

his own account, would have been at the house at the hour Penny was murdered.

Homicide detectives found this information a cause for serious reconsideration of the truthfulness, or at least the accuracy, of Roger's first statement. But even with the obvious discrepancy between the statement and the medical examiner's findings, it was not evidence of guilt that the police could take to the district attorney.

The new information did not place a "smoking gun"—or, specifically, the steel pipe—in the hands of Penny's husband. As evidence, it was still only circumstantial, since the rates for liver-temperature cooling and food digestion were both subject to interpretation. But the discrepancy, along with the incriminating trash bag found behind Roger's office, caused the homicide detectives to elevate him to the unenviable position of prime suspect.

More precise forensic science could be applied to the evidence found in the Dumpster. And that science was readily available in Austin at one of the most modern crime labs in the United States.

*T*he contents of the bag from the Dumpster search, along with samples from the autopsy and evidence gathered at the victim's home, were delivered to the crime laboratory of the Texas Department of Public Safety on March 12.

The DPS crime lab received high marks compared with other criminal testing facilities in the country, and was ranked among the best in trained personnel and modern equipment. Because of its reputation and its desirable Austin location, the lab attracted some of the best professionals in the field, despite the state's relatively low pay scale for criminalists.

The Austin headquarters of the Department of Public Safety Criminal Laboratory, which is nationally known for its forensic science and criminalistic services, is located in a sprawling complex shared with the DPS administrative of-

fices, Texas Rangers, highway patrol headquarters, and the
state criminal records center. The complex, at 5805 North
Lamar Boulevard, covers over two square blocks in north
Austin, and is one of the city's largest employers.

The DPS crime lab, which began as a one-chemist operation in 1937 in a small building on the Camp Mabry army
reserve post, had a statewide professional staff of more than
235 by the late 1990s. The Austin headquarters was staffed
by 110 employees, of which 78 were forensic scientists and
professional analysts.

The Department of Public Safety makes all its services
available to satellite, state-run labs located in a dozen other
Texas cities, prompting the boast that no Texas law officer is
more than 150 miles from modern crime-lab services.

The huge lab in Austin has the largest Serology/DNA and
Latent Prints (fingerprints) sections in the Southwest, as
well as professionally staffed sections for Photography, Firearms, Questioned Documents, Criminalistics, Toxicology,
and Drug Analysis.

In addition, the Texas crime lab is linked to a national
anticrime network through the Automated Fingerprint In-
dexing System (AFIS) and the Combined DNA Index System (CODIS) run by the Federal Bureau of Investigation. It
also participates in the National Integrated Ballistics Imag-
ing Network (NIBIN) run by the U.S. Bureau of Alcohol,
Tobacco, Firearms, and Explosives.

The Austin Police Department, like the departments in
other Texas cities and counties, was a direct beneficiary of
these crime laboratory services. This was especially true for
the APD, because of the proximity of the lab to the central
police station, just blocks away.

The evidence would be distributed to several of the specialty sublabs at the DPS complex. The Austin PD was developing some in-house criminal lab services, but in 1996 it
basically used its Crime Scene Search team to identify and
gather evidence, not to evaluate it. Two of the specialties offered by the state lab were of particular interest to the Aus-

tin homicide detectives. They wanted the state's crime scientists to focus on fingerprint evidence and potential clues from DNA.

The value of Deoxyribonucleic Acid typing as a criminal investigative tool had only recently been recognized. In 1985 a British geneticist first described "DNA fingerprinting" as a potentially revolutionary, crime-fighting weapon. The important new forensic science gained widespread acceptance in the United States a few years before the 1996 Scaggs homicide. The Texas Department of Public Safety's DNA testing program had been launched only two years earlier, but in that short time became one of the top-rated DNA testing services in the country.

In the Scaggs murder case, DNA analysis was to play an important role. However, before the case was ready to go to trial, Austin police and prosecutors would have occasion to use many of the other forensic services offered by the specialists at the state lab.

Chapter 16

Lawmen have been catching criminals for more than one hundred years using nothing more sophisticated than fingerprint identifications. And savvy perpetrators have countered this almost infallible tool for as many years by wearing gloves during the commission of their crimes.

Even with the broad use of DNA testing by modern crimefighters, fingerprinting is still the most important weapon in the law enforcement arsenal. The simplest and most widely used method for collecting prints is by dusting carbon powder on a surface, spotting the ridge pattern of a fingerprint, and lifting the print with an adhesive no more exotic than Scotch tape. Ten times more murderers, rapists, and other serious offenders are identified by fingerprinting than with DNA and all other types of crime-scene detection combined.

Certainly, suspicions about Roger Scaggs had arisen from the discovery of the contents of the trash in a Dumpster behind his office, and by what appeared to be a conflict between his alibi timeline and the time of death suggested by the autopsy. But there was still no hard evidence linking anyone directly to the murder.

The police ID tech had examined the steel pipe and knife recovered from the Dumpster and found no telltale fingerprints on either one. It appeared that both the weapons had been wiped clean. The five latex gloves found in the same sack with the weapons further discouraged the detectives. Apparently, the gloves had been worn by the killer to make sure that no fingerprints or other trace evidence would be left behind.

At that point detectives believed they were going to have to rely on results of serology and DNA testing to link the husband to the murder.

Austin investigators turned over the initial available evidence to the Texas state crime lab on Tuesday, March 12. Along with items collected at the crime scene, the Dumpster, and the autopsy, they submitted two tubes of Penny's blood, for reference samples.

The DPS lab immediately swung into action, assigning the appropriate specialists to the Scaggs case. The lab returned the first scientific results the Austin detectives were hoping for just three days later. Other analyses and evaluation would take longer—some over a year—but the crucial evidence that led to a break in the case was revealed within days.

When the collection arrived at the lab, it was first sent to Serology/DNA, where each piece was microscopically and chemically examined to identify any blood or other human body fluids. When trace material was found, samples were taken with swabs for future analysis. Donna Stanley, a serologist with more than eleven years of training and experience, was assigned to evaluate the Scaggs evidence. She received it from lead detective Thompson, who asked for both blood typing and DNA analysis, despite the expense of such an extensive workup.

For many of the pieces she evaluated, Stanley used a stereo microscope to scan the item. With two light sources and up to forty times magnification, the stereo microscope was designed for viewing three-dimensional objects. Stanley was able to identify specks of blood that had been undetectable to the naked eye. Almost certainly the killer, who thought the weapons and spoils of the crime had been thoroughly washed, could not have imagined the amount of trace left behind.

Under the stereo microscope the cleanly scrubbed murder weapons yielded new evidence that had been missed by detectives in visual observation. On the galvanized steel pipe, believed to be the blunt instrument that caused the fatal blows, Stanley found a trace of blood on one of the end caps. She found two small spots of blood on one side of the carving knife.

The veteran criminalist found blood on one of the forty-three diamonds set in square-cut bezels on the tennis bracelet. Visible blood was swabbed from the diamond ring. She also tested flakes from the bottom of the paper bags that had been placed over Penny's hands at the crime scene. After identifying stains by scanning each piece of evidence, Stanley took samples of suspicious areas with a moistened cotton swab and placed each cotton tip in a test tube.

Next, Stanley, a graduate of the Serological Research Institute of California and the FBI advanced course in blood-related sciences, prepared the five latex gloves for screening. She had been a serologist at the Department of Public Safety since 1987, working in detection and identification of not only blood, but all other types of body fluids, including saliva, semen, urine, and sweat. Still, the latex gloves offered a unique challenge because of the fragile state they were in when they were discovered.

First, she had to determine which side of the gloves had been worn on the outside and which next to the skin, without destroying trace evidence as she handled them. One of the gloves was ripped and did not look as if it had ever been on a hand. The other four were intact and had obviously been worn. From the direction of the rolled edge at the wrist and the fact that some of the fingers were still folded inward, Stanley believed that, when she received them, those four were inside out, as if the wearer had pulled them off at the wrist.

When she examined the gloves, she found a surprise. In one of the stains she saw something that looked like ridges. To ensure that she did not destroy other evidence when she took her samples, Stanley called in DPS latent print examiner Glenn Unnasch, whose office was down the hall. He concluded there were images on some of the gloves that could be prints, and was anxious to see if they were suitable for identification.

Now the gloves were potentially even more valuable, and Stanley handled them with extreme care.

On glove number one, she found a stain on the palm, close to the thumb. This stain was on what would have been the interior of the glove. There was also a spot of blood on one finger on the exterior side. This was the only glove that had traces of blood on *both* the inside and outside surfaces.

She gently turned the other gloves right side out. On glove number two, no blood was found. Glove number three was torn and appeared not to have been worn; no blood was found on it and there was no blood on glove number four. The fifth glove had blood spots on the tips of two fingers—the thumb and the index finger.

Stanley used a black marker to draw brackets around each stain before she swabbed it, so its location would be visible once the trace was removed. After she had swabbed the blood on the gloves, she passed them to Latent Prints, for that section to begin the next phase of analysis.

Meanwhile, Stanley continued to work on the rest of the evidence provided by the police. She detected four spots of diluted blood on one of three paper towels found in the bag in the Dumpster. It appeared the towels had been used to dry some of the items after the perpetrator washed them. She also determined that a swab taken by the crime-scene team from the countertop next to the kitchen sink contained blood diluted by tap water. This swab sample indicated that the killer had probably used that sink to clean the weapons. There was no blood on the leaves found in the plastic bag that had contained the other items, suggesting the leaves were not connected to the murder. Likewise, she found nothing of interest on the garbage bag itself.

Next, Stanley turned her attention to the nail clippings recovered from the victim during the autopsy. She tested eight of the ten clippings at that time. Using the spectro microscope, she found blood on the right thumbnail, the right index finger, the right ring finger, and the right pinky. On the right middle finger she found little blood, but a lot of dirt and debris. From the left hand, she found blood on the nails of the thumb and the middle finger. There was very little or no blood detected on the clipping from the left index finger, left middle finger, and left pinky. She immersed each nail in a separate tube of solution for DNA extraction.

Preliminary tests revealed that the blood on all the evidence tested was consistent with Penny Scaggs's type. More sophisticated DNA tests would take much longer.

Stanley also examined a small body hair that had apparently dropped onto the paper covering the lab table when she was examining the knife. It was determined to be a small, fine body hair of human origin, probably from a limb. Since DNA testing required removal of the bulb (root), she had hair chemist Juan Rojas examine and photograph it while it was still intact.

Missey Micheletti, supervisor at the forensic lab, took photos of the lead pipe and matched the ridges to photographs of the wounds on the victim's cheek. The comparison indicated the pipe was consistent with the size and pattern of the wounds Penny Scaggs had suffered.

While the crime lab scientists were completing analysis of blood, hair, and tissue, examiner Unnasch began testing the evidence for latent prints as the items were released from Serology. He conducted routine fingerprint processing on the weapons and the plastic garbage bag. The pipe and knife bore some smudged ridges but no usable prints. No prints were found on the plastic bag.

The specialist then turned his attention to the delicate and unusual process of recovering readable impressions from the unstable surfaces of the latex gloves. He knew his chances of developing identifiable evidence was a long shot, but he had already been pleasantly surprised that some ridge detail seemed to be present on the inside of the gloves.

If these prints were readable, this would be only the second time in the lab's history that fingerprints had been extracted from gloves. The first case, several years earlier, involved a rubber glove used in a drug-related crime. Retrieval of prints from latex gloves had rarely been successful in crime labs anywhere in the United States.

Upon closer observation, Unnasch was certain that he saw ridge detail on the fingertips of some of the gloves. Examination of the gloves revealed that while they could have been worn at some point during or after the attack and might, indeed, have prevented latent prints from being deposited on the weapons, there were readable prints left behind—inside the gloves themselves.

Glenn Unnasch and Donna Stanley agreed which side of the gloves had been worn next to the skin. It was on the interior surface that he found the prints. Several of the fingertips of the gloves held images embedded in the talcum powder the manufacturer had added to make it easier to pull the gloves on and off. Apparently, the wearer had perspired enough to moisten the powder. Once the gloves were removed, the powder dried, leaving a mixture of talc and sweat.

After studying each glove under a high-intensity light, Unnasch used a process called "super-glue fuming" to get the best results. This process is particularly effective in developing latent prints on nonporous, shiny or slick surfaces. The items to be examined are placed in an airtight chamber and exposed to heated super glue. The chemical in the gaseous form of the glue reacts with the traces of amino acids, fatty acids, and proteins left on the surface of the object by human skin. The chemical clusters and solidifies around the ridges, leaving a sticky image of the fingerprint. The image can either be photographed or dusted and lifted.

Unnasch found some evidence of fingerprints in three of the gloves.

In glove number one he found an image on the ring finger of the right hand. Although ridges were visible, they were not sufficient for identification.

He found a latent print with nine ridge points on glove number two.

Glove three looked different from the others. It was torn at the wrist and had a uniform surface, with no talc or residue. Unnasch agreed with Stanley that the glove had never been worn and was likely discarded after it was torn.

On glove number four the fuming process produced ridge detail of the right ring finger, with fourteen points.

Glove five was a bountiful source of prints. Ridge detail was found on three of the fingertips and the left palm of the glove. The left little finger, the left index finger, and the left ring finger each had fingerprint ridges with twelve points of identification.

The position of the fingerprints in relation to the gloves indicated that all the prints were consistent with a person having worn them.

After cutting off the fingers with readable ridges, Unnasch inserted a cardboard form into each one and carefully stuffed cotton into the tube-shaped pieces, to give them shape. He then photographed them individually, using various light levels and settings to obtain the clearest shots.

Unnasch and his fellow scientists at the DPS lab were elated with the results of these tests.

"In more than one hundred cases in eighty-three Texas counties, I had never testified about finding prints on a latex glove," recalled Unnasch, concerning the rarity of recovering usable prints from that type of material.

This big break for investigators was not only crucial to

this case, but would be of interest to law enforcement agents across the country. The discovery made by a forensics specialist at the Texas crime lab would likely be quite unsettling for the criminal element as well. When word spread, the criminal could no longer rely with confidence on the single best protection against detection.

Every fingerprint is unique to a single individual. No human fingerprint has ever been found to match the fingerprint of another person, in all of the nearly one hundred years that law enforcement has used fingerprint identification—and there have been billions of manual and automated fingerprint tests conducted.

The ridge patterns of fingerprints make them unique to each individual, and these patterns are abundant on the fingertip. The basic ridge points that the experts look for are called ridge endings, bifurcations, and dots or islands. These basic points are distributed amidst the swirls, loops, and straight lines of the ridges.

A normal rolled fingerprint will produce over one hundred ridge points that can be used for comparison. However, law enforcement officials require a minimum of eight points on a fingerprint to get a match that will stand up in a court of law.

The evidence recovered at the state crime lab from the five latex gloves produced one fingerprint with fourteen points of identification, three fingerprints with at least twelve distinctive ridge points, and one print with nine points.

The crime lab had inked fingerprint cards, provided by Austin police, on Penny and Roger; their maid, Eugenia Hernandez; Vanessa; Sarah; and Sarah's ex-husband, Cory Munson. The prints had been voluntarily submitted, ostensibly for the purpose of eliminating nonsuspects from the fingerprints recovered at the crime scene. Munson had not been at the house in quite some time but had once been a regular visitor, and undisturbed fingerprints can remain on a surface for years.

Comparison of the prints taken from the latex gloves was

completed by DPS lab criminalists on the morning of Thursday, March 15. It had been nine days since Penny Scaggs was murdered.

All of the prints from the gloves matched one set of inked fingerprints taken at the police station on March 8. They were the fingerprints of the victim's husband, Roger Thomas Scaggs.

Several of the lab's experts were called in to verify Unnasch's findings. The results of the fingerprint testing were considered conclusive by these experts.

The combined results of the fingerprint and early serology work had near breathtaking implications. The impact on the investigation was captured in one of the photographs taken by Unnasch. In the picture of the left index finger of glove number five, the ridges were clearly visible. Just as visible, directly behind the ridges, showing through the thin latex, were the black bracket marks that Donna Stanley had drawn. They indicated the place where a spot of blood had been swabbed. The DPS criminalists had found the fingerprint of Roger Scaggs on one side of the glove and blood matching Penny's type on the other.

*R*oger was unaware of the almost frantic pace of the investigation being carried out in the week following Penny's funeral and interment. As the husband of the victim, the last person to see her alive, and the first person to see her dead, he had told Penny's family at the burial that he might be a suspect. But most of his family members, neighbors and friends, and fellow evangelicals at his church still considered Roger the second victim of the tragedy.

When he returned from Dallas, he began trying to put his personal life together without the wife who had taken care of him and his home for the past thirty-five years. Admittedly, he was lost without Penny to tend to the day-to-day details. He told neighbor Arthur Coleman, in a brief conversation, that she had done everything on the home front, that he didn't know where to start straightening out his family affairs.

Toward that end, one of the first things Roger did was contact his insurance company, USAA Insurance. Property claims adjustor Tracey Kendrick, who had been with the company for nine years, first talked to Roger by phone on March 8. He told her his wife had been murdered two days before. He explained that he had just gotten back into the home and needed to replace the bloody carpet immediately, because relatives were coming for the funeral on Sunday. He also said the police had done considerable damage inside the home during the investigation.

"I asked him if anything had been stolen," said Ms. Kendrick. "He said no."

Kendrick gave approval for him to replace the section of bloody carpet in the den and made an appointment to inspect the house on March 12. The petite insurance agent, who felt somewhat uneasy about going there alone, asked a colleague to accompany her. She admitted this was not standard procedure.

When they arrived, Roger escorted Kendrick over to the baby grand piano. There was a bluish stain on the yellow finish that was turning green. The stain was probably from the amido black chemical used to enhance faint, blood-contaminated prints. He also showed her pictures of the bloodstained carpet he had already replaced in that location.

Roger told the adjustor that he tried to have the damage caused by the police investigation in other areas cleaned by a professional service, but they told him some of the chemicals could not be removed and would require repair or replacement of those items.

"He took me through the house where other damage was visible in the hallway and the master bedroom," Kendrick said, noting that the damage was mostly black powder residue left from fingerprinting. There was black dust in the tile grouting, around the bathtub on the walls, and around the doorknobs.

Roger led her to the bathroom. She asked him why the police were investigating these rooms when the crime had taken place in the den. He explained that Penny's jewelry had been thrown in the sunken tub and her jewelry cases thrown on the bathroom floor.

"Why?" Kendrick asked. He told her three pieces of jewelry had been stolen. Kendrick was surprised.

"I didn't know a theft had taken place," she said. "I did not know anything had been stolen."

"We think this is why it happened," said Roger.

He described the missing jewelry to the adjustor. Penny's wedding ring was a one and a half karat diamond with baguettes on either side. The baguettes were a gift for their tenth anniversary. The second piece was a V-shaped necklace, "with diamonds at the bottom of the V" that had been purchased at Service Merchandise several years before. He did not provide details on the third piece, the tennis bracelet.

While they were talking, Roger returned a phone call from his daughter, which gave the adjustor time to estimate the damages. When he hung up, she asked him if there had been forced entry to the house. He pointed to the door from the den to the deck. "No, the back door was unlocked."

Kendrick asked if Roger had additional coverage for jewelry, and he said he did not. She said the loss was obviously going to be well over the maximum coverage on the policy. Nevertheless, she asked him if he had appraisals on the jewelry. He said he didn't have anything on the ring, that it had been purchased as Penny's engagement ring about thirty-five years before. He told her the necklace alone had cost $1,300. She said she was sorry—his limit for jewelry loss or theft was $500. He added that a butcher block was missing in the kitchen because police had taken it.

The agent issued him a preliminary check for $1,300 to

cover the jewelry and the berber carpet he had already replaced.

"I told him to let me know if they were able to clean the rest of the rugs, and about the cost of refinishing the piano," she said. "He showed me a picture of the missing ring." It was a photograph of Penny, wearing the ring on her left hand. "Someone came to the door with flowers from the funeral, and I left."

On Wednesday, March 13, one week after Penny Scaggs was murdered, Roger faxed the additional information the insurance company had requested. They issued a check for $1,900, to cover some painting and having the rest of the carpets cleaned. A short time later the USAA legal department determined that the policy did not cover damage caused by a police investigation and refused payment to have Penny's beloved piano refinished.

During the week following the funeral, Roger also sought legal advice on a probate matter from his neighbor, Arthur Coleman, who was a civil law attorney.

"I said I could not help him with that," Coleman recalled. "The meeting only lasted about thirty minutes. He told me about the affair and that he had ended it." Coleman cautioned Roger that anything he told him was not privileged because, although he was an attorney, he was not representing him. Roger said he understood.

Coleman said Roger told him three things: That he did not kill Penny; that he was sorry about the affair, but it was over; and that "some investigators would be in touch with me shortly."

"The talk—his demeanor—it was pretty strange," Coleman said. "There was no emotion. There wasn't any anger about someone doing this. It seemed like he wasn't very sorry Penny was gone. He missed things she did, like finding the checkbook, writing checks."

Although Coleman ran into Roger once or twice after that, this was the last real conversation he had with his longtime neighbor.

When Roger apologized for the affair, I told him, "It is not for me to judge," Coleman recalled. "I said if I were to be judged on the merits of my life, I would burn an eternity in hell. Roger winced."

Chapter 17

*R*oger Scaggs filed a detailed report of his wife's missing jewelry with Austin homicide detectives on Thursday, March 14. He listed Penny's diamond wedding ring, a diamond tennis bracelet, and a V-shaped diamond necklace. Detectives in the homicide section did not tell him that these pieces had already been recovered from the Dumpster behind his office building.

Discovery of the garbage bag with the weapons, latex gloves, and jewelry made Roger the prime suspect in the murder. But detectives still wanted more evidence before taking the case to the district attorney.

So it was with a sense of irony that the homicide detectives quietly took the list of jewelry Roger claimed had been stolen. Lead detective J. W. Thompson asked Roger if he had filed an insurance claim, and requested the name and telephone number of the insurance contact. Immediately after Roger left, Thompson called Tracey Kendrick at USAA Insurance to confirm that the claim had been filed. It was a minor matter, in light of the possibility that a homicide was involved, but filing a false insurance claim was also a felony in Texas.

The next morning the big break in the case came with a telephone call from the DPS crime lab. As soon as Detective Thompson had confirmed that the lab results linked Roger to the bag containing the murder weapons and missing jewelry, he rushed to the Travis County Courthouse to secure an arrest warrant. Judge Wilford Flowers of the 147th District Court was on call to hear new felony cases that month. The judge went by the nickname "Will" in the casual atmosphere that prevailed around the Austin courts as late as the 1990s. That small-town familiarity was rapidly vanishing as the high-tech boom doubled and tripled the population, along with crime and the caseloads.

Thompson swore an affidavit for an arrest warrant before Judge Flowers around noon, and anxiously waited for the paperwork to be typed up. He was fairly sure the suspect knew nothing about the dramatic turn of events. But the last minute wait for the paperwork when a case was this close to being solved caused jitters in the homicide section. If anything bad could happen at the courthouse, like Murphy's Law, it usually did in a murder case. The Austin detectives did not know the suspect well enough to preclude his fleeing if he caught wind of what was happening. He had the money and he had the means—a private plane parked only a short drive from his house.

The detective's affidavit was typed, sworn, and signed. It provided a detailed description of the crime and cause for the arrest. It was a three-page document, which read, in part:

I have good reason to believe and do believe that Roger Thomas Scaggs, white male, born 6/17/39, on or about the 6th Day of March 1996, did commit the offense of intentional murder, a first degree felony; in that in Travis County, Texas, he knowingly and intentionally caused the death of an individual, Louanne [sic] Scaggs, aka, Penny Scaggs.

After describing the circumstances surrounding the crime, including how police had located the plastic bag of evidence from a Dumpster behind the suspect's office, the affidavit continued:

On March 15, 1996, the affiant [Thompson] was notified by the DPS Crime Lab that a fingerprint had been developed inside one of the latex gloves found in the trash sack that was recovered from the dumpster. The fingerprint was compared to the prints voluntarily given by Roger Scaggs and was found to be his right ring finger.

Judge Flowers issued an arrest warrant charging Roger Scaggs with the murder of his wife. As far as the detectives were concerned, the mystery was solved, but they knew their work was far from over.

With warrant in hand, Detective Thompson returned to police headquarters and telephoned Roger Scaggs. He told him that information on fingerprints taken earlier had been received from the state crime lab and asked him to come to the station house. When Roger arrived a short time later, Thompson immediately escorted him to an interview room in the homicide section.

During a brief interview, the lead detective told Roger he was a suspect in the case and was about to be arrested. With Detective Carter looking on, Thompson read Roger his Miranda rights, which he immediately invoked. He refused to say another word. He was then escorted into the main room of the homicide section, where Detective Carter told the suspect to place his hands against the wall. Roger was holding a portfolio with a legal pad, which he gave to Detective Thompson.

"I frisked him for weapons," said Carter. "He told me he had a pocketknife."

As Carter handcuffed him, Roger asked that his portfolio be given to Sarah, who was waiting in the reception area. Detectives had noticed that he almost always carried the leather portfolio, using it to take copious notes at various times during the investigation. The detectives held onto it.

Roger was escorted by detectives to APD Central Booking, located elsewhere in the building. He was again fingerprinted and had a mug shot taken. A case number was affixed to his file. In custody of uniformed police officers, he was transported several blocks to the Travis County jail, where he was logged in on the charge of murder. After receiving bright orange coveralls and clean bedding, Roger Scaggs began his first experience as a prisoner.

While he had been talking about hiring a lawyer to members of Penny's family and some of his friends and neighbors, he apparently had not yet done so. Because the sudden arrest came as a surprise, he had made no arrangements for posting bail.

Judge Flowers set an appearance bond at one million dollars, pending a hearing. Even for an executive of a midsize corporation, raising the kind of cash required to cover such a high bond would take a little time. In Roger's case, hiring an attorney and making bail took several days, and he spent his first weekend in lockup in a population of felons of every ilk. During that time, he was able to retain temporary counsel, hiring Austin attorney E. G. Morris.

On Saturday, March 16, the Austin Police Department announced the arrest in a press release headed: SUSPECT ARRESTED IN WINTER PARK HOMICIDE. The release stated, along with the regular boilerplate: "The suspect is the victim's husband." It said Roger Scaggs had been charged with intentional murder, with bond set at one million dollars. It also stated an autopsy revealed that "Penny Scaggs had been beaten to death."

The *Austin American-Statesman* carried another small story about the case, noting that Roger Scaggs had been charged with murdering his wife of thirty-five years.

The mainstream news media had still not picked up on the impact the case was having in the upscale, hilltop suburbs, and was treating it like just another domestic violence case.

On Monday, Scaggs's lawyer filed application for a writ of habeas corpus, complaining that the million-dollar bond was excessive and that Travis County sheriff Terry Keel was therefore illegally holding his client. Judge Flowers ordered a hearing for Tuesday, March 19.

The writ said that Roger was a well-respected member of the Austin business and church community and did not constitute a flight risk or a danger to the community. It said he did not have the ability to post bond in the amount of one million dollars.

At the bond hearing on Tuesday, Judge Flowers ruled that the bond amount be lowered to $500,000, half of which was to be posted in cash. Still, it took Roger several more days to pull together that much money.

In the meantime, Roger had contacted his pastor about his arrest. Reverend Rob Harrell of First Evangelical Free Church rushed to console his parishioner and church elder at the Travis County jail. The pastor tried to reassure Roger that he was not alone at this terrifying time. The minister had comforted Roger and the family at the funeral by reminding them of God's light, even in the darkest hours. Now he sought to ease Roger's pain by praying with him, and reading from the 139th Psalm:

> *If I take wings of morning, and dwell in the uttermost parts of the sea;*
> *Even there shall thy hand lead me, and thy right hand shall hold me.*
> *If I say, Surely the darkness shall cover me; even the night shall be light above me.*

*Yea, the darkness hideth not from thee; but the night shineth
    as the day:*
The darkness and the light are both alike to thee.

But Roger was inconsolable about his confinement, although Reverend Harrell visited him three times at the jail. The minister had been at Roger's side since shortly after Penny's murder, and spent hours with both Roger and Sarah in the days following that horrific event.

Scaggs made bail on Thursday, March 21, a week after his arrest. Those seven days—and especially the nights—were undoubtedly a terrible experience for a prominent community leader who had never even seen the inside of a jail except on TV. Now, at fifty-seven years old, he had been forced to give up his freedom for the first time and experience the jailhouse noise, odors, food, and cohabitants he could only have imagined in his nightmares.

Back home that evening, he saw neighbor Diana Coleman working in her front yard and shouted across the street, "I'm free! I'm free!" Like all the other neighbors along Winter Park Road, Mrs. Coleman had been stunned beyond description on learning that Roger was formally charged with Penny's murder. It was only the latest in a series of shocks that had rocked the placid neighborhood over the past two weeks—and there were more to come.

The neighborhood, like the evangelical community and the business community in which Roger was well respected and generally liked, was roiled by confusion. Some thought he might have killed his wife; others adamantly refused to believe the soft-spoken elder and corporate executive was even remotely capable of such a horrendous act.

In terms of their own lives, the announcement that the husband had been arrested for the wife's murder was met with mixed emotions by many of Roger's neighbors and associates. The terror felt in Westlake and surrounding wealthy neighborhoods—that a maniac killer was loose among them—gave way to a macabre sense of relief.

Neighbor George Wehling, the retired colonel who had been among the first people at the scene after Roger phoned neighbors the night of the murder, was interviewed by *Austin American-Statesman* reporter Rebecca Thatcher. He spoke for many when he said that while the news about Roger's arrest was tragic, "the murder charges had allayed fears in the neighborhood that Penny Scaggs's killer was on the loose."

Another longtime acquaintance and friend from Roger's church took the opposite view. Dr. Muller, who had rushed to help Roger the night of the murder, and in whose home he stayed while police kept the house sealed off, was bewildered by the arrest. He doubted that Roger could have done such a thing.

Although the horrible crime had been the only topic of conversation in the communities where the Scaggses had been so well known and active, the top local news organizations had so far barely mentioned anything about the case. It was left up to editor Ed Allen of the suburban weekly *Westlake Picayune* to recognize the importance of the crime and its enormous impact on so many in Austin. With the exception of a three-paragraph article buried inside the Austin daily and brief mention on television newscasts the day after the murder, Allen had the scoop almost to himself. His paper, which circulated on Thursdays, was the first news outlet to cover the story fully. The small-town, tabloid-style paper led with Roger Scaggs's arrest and a most unflattering police mug shot taken at the booking. The story was plastered across the front page of the March 20 edition.

"It was our responsibility to let the community know what was happening," Allen said. "This murder had an awesome impact on everybody. Everywhere you went the murder was all the conversation. And for a couple of weeks, people were really frightened that the crime was a home-invasion robbery and murder.

"The phones at my office and home never stopped ringing," he said. "There were days and days when nobody could learn anything. That caused unfounded horror stories and even worse rumors to grow and spread. I wouldn't describe it as public hysteria, but there was a high state of jitters like I've never experienced anywhere in my years as a reporter and editor."

The murder was an anomaly of huge proportions for that community. Austin has historically been rated among America's top ten safest large cities in the official annual Crime and Traffic Report, compiled by a national mayors' organization. It is usually listed in the top five. But beyond the city's general high standing, violent crime in the specific neighborhood where the homicide occurred is statistically nonexistent. In 1996 the Scaggs murder was the only one recorded for the vast Eanes school district, and there were only three rapes and seventeen aggravated assaults reported in the entire area that year.

So the Scaggs murder was bound to have a disproportional impact on the community, even by Austin standards of relatively low crime. However, it was not the rarity of violent crime in the neighborhood that finally got the attention of the local mainstream media. What ultimately piqued their interest was the discovery by reporters that Penny had devoted her life to teaching young women how to be Christian wives, subservient to their husbands, and the allegation that her own husband was the killer. If true, the tragic irony was simply too great to ignore, even by local journalists who normally didn't give much ink to murder cases until they went to trial.

On Thursday morning, March 28, more than three weeks after the murder, the *Austin American-Statesman* bannered the story. In black, bold-faced type, the headline read:

**Police say Roger Scaggs beat and stabbed
his wife, Penny, to death.
Friends say they were a model couple.
One question lingers.**

That question, printed in two-inch-high red letters, was **Why?**

The experienced investigative reporters, more used to delving into the capital city's plethora of political high crimes and misdemeanors, were Scott W. Wright and Rebecca Thatcher. The lengthy article began with this dramatic description:

> He was a highly successful businessman, a leader in a local evangelical church. On weekends, he hunted dove with buddies, flew to Marble Falls for a cup of coffee in his private plane and went boating on Lake Travis.
>
> She was a Sunday school teacher, the ideal spouse described in the Biblical passage that was the basis for a course she taught on being a noble, Christian wife. She played the piano for an hour every Thursday at a Northeast Austin retirement home.
>
> But on March 6, shortly after Roger and Penny Scaggs cleared the supper table and stacked the dishes in the sink, their impeccably decorated $340,000 home in Southwest Austin would become spattered with Penny Scaggs' blood.
>
> While she sat at the baby grand piano, authorities say, her husband sneaked up behind her, repeatedly beat her over the head with a metal pipe, and stabbed her seven times in the neck, chest and back with a butcher knife.

The article gave the police version of what had happened. More important, the reporters interviewed two dozen neighbors, friends, and associates of the Scaggses. Every person interviewed told an intimate story about the ideal couple, and then described their own horror, grief, disbelief, and shock over the crime and its alleged resolution.

The respondents were about equally divided among those who believed Roger might have committed the crime and those who vehemently denied he could have killed his wife, particularly in the brutal way she was slain.

Roger's attorney, E. G. Morris, was quoted as saying, "Roger Scaggs will plead not guilty. The police have got the wrong man." Questioned further on who might have done it, Morris declined to answer.

Even the spokesman for Austin Homicide, Lieutenant David Parkinson, acknowledged that Penny's murder and Roger's arrest were difficult to comprehend by friends and the greater community. The police lieutenant told the *Statesman,* "Some of them find it hard to believe this has happened, given their [the Scaggses] history, their neighborhood, and their church work."

If the local daily had been slow to grasp the incongruence of the event and to change its policy for handling murder stories, it soon made up for lost time. Reporters were assigned to beat the bushes throughout the Hill Country community in an effort to answer its own question: "Why?" The Scaggs case would become one of the biggest stories of the decade for the award-winning Cox Newspaper Corporation publication. After the banner story broke, the reporters received scores of anonymous tips, crank calls, and even threats. The crank calls included tips on a variety of topics: how and why Roger had been framed, sinister insurance schemes by shady cartels, drug money laundering, and other bizarre theories of the crime. It was the type of mystery that always seems to bring the weird out of the woodwork. However, most of the calls the reporters and editors received appeared to come from people who had actually known the Scaggses. They often asked not to be quoted because the community was rapidly becoming polarized over the case, with some friends of the couple demanding justice for the victim and others adamantly refusing to accept Roger as the real killer.

Since Roger was free on bond and had resumed his activities in the community, the reporters received many calls of "Roger sightings" as he went about his life. A number were from employees of APS Systems and its parent company. These calls mostly involved information about the affair between Roger and a young woman from his office.

Even for those friends who did not believe Roger could possibly have committed the murder, the affair itself was difficult to comprehend. A few days after he was released on bail, Dr. Muller and Reverend Harrell met Roger for lunch at a popular neighborhood restaurant, Tres Amigos. "I told him I had heard about the affair and asked him what it was all about," recalled Harrell. "What he said struck me so profoundly that I wrote it down. He called it 'animal lust.' I left the lunch with the assumption that he was going to give it up."

The shocking story did not stop at the Austin city limits. Long articles about the murder and arrest appeared in all the Texas dailies, and in the Tulsa papers as well. Penny Scaggs, in particular, had a following and reputation throughout Texas and beyond, among the hundreds of women she had taught. She had never published or attained national prominence like her mentor Linda Dillow, but her ministry had touched lives everywhere in the region. She was well known, and apparently well loved, among evangelical Christian women for her teachings in a network that extended far beyond Austin.

After the bold headline in the Austin daily paper, the First Evangelical Free Church took an unprecedented step to reach its own congregation. The church leaders issued a printed press statement about the murder of one of its most beloved parishioners by her husband, a church elder. The statement, headed, "Re: Roger Scaggs," read:

> We at the First Evangelical Free Church are concerned by the events concerning Roger and Penny Scaggs. This is a very painful time for our congregation. Our focus, in this time, is to minister to our people and help them through this very difficult period. The church asks the media to please contact our spokesman, David Chu [a

pastor at the church], with any questions. He can be reached at [phone number].

The public shock and curiosity was nothing compared with the ongoing grief and dismay that beset the evangelical community in Texas, and especially the Austin congregation. After Roger's release from jail and the widespread publicity, there had to be a reckoning in the religious community, and it could not wait for the legal process to run its course. Roger himself asked for a meeting with the board of elders, which they scheduled for the evening of March 28—the same day the bannered story appeared in the *Statesman*. Eight of the ten elders were there, along with Reverend Harrell.

The last time the elders had met was the night before Penny was murdered. Roger had attended that meeting, having just returned from a sales trip, to conduct some routine church business. He had also participated in serving communion to the congregation at Sunday services on March 3.

The elders sat in a circle, which included Roger. He was not asked to sit in the center as an object of judgment. In fact, he opened the discussion. Reverend Harrell took notes, so he had a record of the dialogue that night.

"First, I want to look all of you in the face and tell you I didn't do it," Roger said. He spoke to each man individually as he went around the circle and repeated the words, "I did not do it."

Roger continued, "Secondly, I want to apologize for the affair. I want to apologize for the harm I have done the church. That affair is behind me. God forgives me and you should, too." He expressed his belief that the group was divided into three camps—some who supported him, some who were distant, and "a middle group."

Reverend Harrell said that the men did not hear what they had expected. Roger's public confession of sin involving the affair, as well as his flat denial of guilt for his wife's murder, failed the biblical test.

"He never said, 'I have sinned against God.' He wanted us to forgive him because he apologized, not because he repented," the reverend said. When it appeared that no carte blanche forgiveness would be forthcoming from the elders, the conversation took a bitter turn.

"I need support, prayers, friendship. I need help, counseling," Roger told the men. "It's hard to lose a wife and have your whole world turned upside down. None of us is immune. My pride, my ego, got in the way. I had a lack of accountability."

The more he talked, the angrier he became. He said he felt he had "no friend on this church board." Throughout the session, Scaggs had never shed a tear or shown remorse. But when he accused the church leaders of abandoning him, he began to cry.

"No man here has said, 'I love you no matter what,' " said Roger, sobbing.

Then the tears stopped and he returned to his angry tirade.

"I would be outraged at anyone who would be afraid of me," he said. "I would be outraged if anybody in this church thinks I could do this. My closest friends tell me my support system is being corrupted by the police."

Reverend Harrell had spent many hours trying to console Roger and Sarah after the murder and had visited Roger three out of the seven days he was in jail.

"Do you feel *I* have disappointed you?" the minister asked.

"Yeah, I really do. I'm angry at you," Roger said.

The minister was stung by the charge that he had abandoned one of his flock in a time of need.

"I took that anger seriously," Harrell said. "I'm a pastor. I do lots of counseling. My opinion is that Roger was only interested in himself. He said to me, 'I thought you'd come to the jail every day.' After the session with the elders, I met with Roger only three or four times over the next two years."

Other ministers from the church did try to keep in touch
with Roger Scaggs. If the church leaders took formal action
to strip him of his position as elder or withdraw fellowship,
the church has never made it public, in keeping with the traditions of confidentiality in such matters. However, Roger's
involvement in that church dwindled away after the confrontation.

The murder charge had caused some of his former friends
and neighbors to avoid him. Diana Coleman wrote a note to
Roger stating that because of her deep grief over Penny's
death and "what was coming out," it would be best to sever
the friendship. With her letter, she enclosed the key to the
Scaggs house.

The Travis County Grand Jury indicted Roger Scaggs for
the murder of his wife on June 28, 1996. The one-count indictment stated that he had "intentionally caused the death
of Louanne [sic] Ehrle Scaggs" by "striking her in the head
with a pipe, a deadly weapon, manifestly designed, made
and adapted for the purpose of inflicting death and serious
bodily injury, and in the manner of its use and intended use
was capable of causing death and serious bodily injury."

A short time later Roger auctioned off the furniture,
household items, and personal belongings from the marriage. After having the house professionally cleaned and refurbished to remove any traces of the murder and stains
from the investigation, he placed it on the market. Penny's
beloved house sold on November 5, 1996, two days after her
birth date. Had she lived, on November 3 she would have
turned fifty-five years old.

Roger rented a nearby condominium from a longtime
family friend. The friend, a physician the Scaggses had
known since moving to Austin twelve years earlier, had been
an active member of the congregation with them at Riverbend Church. She was among the many people who knew
them well who would not be convinced that Roger was capable of murdering Penny.

Roger also retained the support of fellow executives and

employees in his business world. Most of these associates could not believe him capable of such violence. Even though many of them had affection for Penny, too, long years of working closely with the affable Roger made it impossible for them to imagine his participation in such a brutal crime.

The indictment caused a dilemma at APS Group because of the potential financial impact on the company. Employees and customers alike were troubled by the news. As president of the APS System subsidiary, Roger was also a key member of the corporate team, and had almost single-handedly developed the highly profitable computer services portion of the business. Most of its customers had a personal working relationship with him. There was no doubt that the loss of his unique knowledge of that part of the business could have been damaging for the company and its shareholders.

The business editor of the *Austin American-Statesman*, Jerry Mahoney, did an unusual business-page article on the impact the tragedy was having on the company.

"When a senior official is charged with a felony or a scandal erupts inside a company, executives are faced with a nightmarish situation for which they've had little or no preparation," Mahoney's story read. "And the fallout may include bailout by shareholders."

That did not immediately occur at APS Group, but there were other repercussions.

Mahoney interviewed Bill Shaw, a University of Texas management sciences professor, about the effects on a company of such an unusual event. Professor Shaw said that when such a scandal unexpectedly strikes a firm, "everyone may be tarnished by a broad brush and embarrassed to say where they work."

The article opined: "There's little to salvage from the bad public relations that accompanies many scandals, experts say. But the company, through its CEO, should assure customers and employees the business will stay on course, and note that the accused official is innocent until proven guilty."

Kenneth Shifrin, the chairman and CEO of APS Group, took what action he could to mitigate the bad situation he faced. He immediately addressed the impact the murder was having on both customers and employees. While continuing to express strong doubt that Roger had killed his wife, Shifrin placed him on leave of absence; he was not to return to his position as president of APS Systems.

Company executives contacted each of the clients that had worked so closely with Roger over the years, to assure them that the service would continue unchanged under Vice President Jackie Fife. Fife flew around the country meeting with clients. Most chose to continue doing business with the company.

Shifrin acknowledged to the business editor that employees were seriously demoralized by the murder and the charges against their boss. He said they were suffering from shock and grief, and that the company was doing what it could to help the staff cope. No doubt the thirty-five-member team Roger headed was traumatized in the days immediately following the murder and its lingering aftermath. They were forced to see their boss's police mug shot on the front pages of newspapers and on television broadcasts on a regular basis. The company offered to pay a hundred percent of the cost of professional counseling for individual employees or groups.

Conventional wisdom says that no one is indispensable in a well-run corporation. But Roger Scaggs had built the computer services business at APS from the ground up. While the company did not return him to an executive position, he was retained on a consulting basis for some time before his case came to trial. Despite the gloomy forecasts by stock analysts about the effects of internal scandals, APS Group common stock shares actually enjoyed a steady price increase. As one analyst cynically noted, "It would be a lot worse if he was arrested for embezzling."

But everyone was not as blasé about the murder as some shareholders seemed to be. Roger, free on bail and loudly proclaiming his innocence, chose not to hide from the world, and attracted unwanted attention as he went about his normal daily routine. In fact, without Penny to run the household errands, his appearances around the community may have been even more frequent than in the past. During the remainder of 1996 and beyond, the local weekly editor continued to receive calls from readers saying they had seen Roger Scaggs in grocery stores, restaurants, the cleaners, or just walking through Barton Creek Mall or along the quaint shopping street of West Lake Hills.

One surprise sighting was uniquely personal.

Commercial pilot Phillip Beall was flying a regular American Airlines route from Newark, New Jersey, to Dallas–Fort Worth International Airport in October. Beall was a younger cousin of Penny Ehrle, who had grown up affectionately calling her "Aunt Penny." Not long into the routine flight, an attendant entered the cockpit with a message from a passenger. She handed Beall a business card and told him the man wanted to speak with him.

The business card belonged to Roger Scaggs. He was a passenger on the cross-country flight.

"I was surprised it was Uncle Roger," the pilot said. "I told the attendant I would take it under advisement. I leveled off and had this rush of emotion. I couldn't believe he was riding in first class in the cabin behind me, collecting frequent flier miles while Aunt Penny was buried in the ground. He was traveling all over the country as if nothing had happened. I did not speak to him. I have a responsibility to my passengers, and I was not sure I could have contained myself properly."

Beall, who was also a veteran reserve police officer, said Penny's murder was especially difficult for him because they had been very close during his childhood.

"She was the most incredible person I have ever known in my life," he said. "Many people were deprived of her continuing good work. Every single person who knew her thought she was their best friend. She made everyone feel very important."

Beall said he and his wife were vacationing in the Texas Hill Country when word came to them that Penny was dead. As they drove to Austin, he had a "very bad feeling about the murder." From his training and experience as a reserve police officer, the viciousness of the attack spoke volumes. He had told his wife that the massive overkill made it a crime of passion and hatred. He said only two kinds of people could commit such a violent murder. It had to be "either a serial killer or someone close—someone in the family."

Chapter 18

As time elapsed after the murder of his wife, Roger Scaggs apparently changed his mind about giving up the affair with the young woman from his company, as he had so often tearfully vowed to do in conversations with friends, fellow church elders, and business peers.

Even though Austin was a booming, midsized city, in some ways it clung to the social mores of a small southern town. People took notice when the now well-recognized Roger Scaggs showed up. On occasion he was accompanied by Vanessa Ferguson, and when they were spotted together, it set the town talking again. Some of the encounters the pair had with townspeople generated more than just idle talk, and would later be cited to further call into question Roger's behavior around the time of Penny's death.

Roger joined a north Austin tanning salon in March or April 1996. He and Vanessa used the facilities of the members-only Tanco Tanning Center at least twice a week, sometimes as often as every other day. A conversation with Stephanie Miles, who had recently been promoted to manager of the facility, was so unusual that it drew the attention of other employees. On that occasion, Roger began making what seemed to be sexually suggestive overtures toward the young woman. His comments might have been shrugged off were it not for the fact that everyone in the place knew about the charges recently filed against him, and that he made them in front of his female companion.

Roger was easily thirty-five years older than Stephanie Miles, who, with her ponytail hairstyle and ingenue appearance, seemed even more childlike than the actual difference in their years. No previous conversation had led up to Roger's advances when he approached her with an invitation to join him and Vanessa on an upcoming trip to California.

"I was taking a break, and he asked me if I had any plans for a weekend in October," recalled Ms. Miles. "He said they were planning a trip to a hotel in California and asked if I would like to go with them." She told him she wasn't interested.

The next time Roger and Vanessa showed up at Tanco, he told Ms. Miles that they had been to California and she had missed a lot of partying at the convention.

"He said it was a swinger's convention," she recalled.

On that occasion, Roger asked Miles if she had ever considered becoming an exotic dancer.

"He said it was a moneymaker. Nothing in our conversations had ever led to that [topic]. He said it wasn't a harmful environment . . . that the men protect the women, walk them to their cars at night."

Another conversation that would come back to haunt Roger occurred on October 4, at a beauty salon where he was getting a manicure. Vanessa had come in with him, dropped off her purse, and left to work out at a nearby gym. Manicurist Sue Bowen and other employees did not immediately recognize Roger, even though his picture appeared regularly in the local news media; and Bowen said she had only been given his first name.

Roger's original appointment was for a silk wrap, but the

manicurist talked him into acrylic, because it was more durable. "He didn't have long nails," she said, "just caps over his own."

Bowen said she liked to make her customers feel relaxed when she did their nails. Her friend Sharon was sitting next to her while she worked on Roger, and the three of them were chatting.

"He mentioned he had been married previously," said Ms. Bowen. "He said his wife had been anal. She did everything, even ironed his underwear. I popped Sharon with my file and said, 'That's why she's the *previous* wife.' Roger laughed. We all laughed. We thought he was talking about an ex." Roger also told them that he and Vanessa frequently went to the Cayman Islands.

After the manicure, Sue Bowen suggested they might want to have their toenails done sometime. She showed them the private room where a couple could have a pedicure together, sitting in leather chairs, drinking wine, if they liked. "It can be a party atmosphere or very relaxing, whatever the client wants," she said. When Vanessa said she was hungry, they left without making an appointment.

While the Hill County residents were fretting about the frequent sightings of a free Roger Scaggs putting his life together, behind the scenes the prosecutors in the Travis County D.A.'s office were building their case against him.

One of the early legal decisions in the case was literally a matter of life or death for Roger Scaggs. Years before, District Attorney Ronnie Earle had established a capital murder review committee comprised of prosecutors in his office. The ten-member committee, which the *Austin American-Statesman* dubbed the "Death Committee," was tasked with deciding whether to seek the death penalty for the murder of Penny Scaggs. The group, handpicked by Earle, considered all the circumstances involved in each murder case that was presented by police and sheriffs' departments before ruling if the crime merited the death penalty. Ronnie Earle took the committee's recommendations to heart. Even though he made the final decision, he had never overruled the committee.

Despite the savagery of the postmortem mutilation of the body, the D.A.'s committee determined that Penny Scaggs's murder did not rise to the threshold of special circumstances that justified asking a jury for the death penalty against her husband. Most death penalties in Texas are imposed for killings committed while in the act of another violent felony, such as armed robbery or rape. Texas statutes also consider the killing of law enforcement agents or children to be prime circumstances deserving the death penalty. Premeditation, ambush, and murder for financial gain are also factors considered under Texas law.

While the decision was made not to seek the death penalty in the Scaggs case, there was reason to be concerned that it might be. It probably would have been in a number of other Texas cities.

With less than 10 percent of the nation's population, Texas has carried out more than a third of all executions in the United States since the death penalty was reinstated in 1976. These shocking statistics were attained even though Texas did not reinstate the death penalty until six years after the Supreme Count allowed capital punishment to resume. The year Penny Scaggs was killed, the state executed 23 inmates for murder, and 443—including seven women—awaited execution in Texas prisons.

A factor that may have prevented Scaggs from facing the death penalty was simply location. When it came to imposing the penalty in Texas, Austin was no Houston, which has been dubbed the "Death Penalty Capital of America." Austin, by contrast, was considered an "island" populated by liberal-leaning jury panels that opposed the death penalty on principle. In the five years leading up to the Scaggs case, Travis County juries were asked to consider the death penalty in only six of the twenty-three murder cases tried by Earle's office.

Austin's statistics were certainly not representative of Texas as a whole. Most other major Texas cities had reputations for being considerably more pro-death penalty, with hard-line, hang-'em-high juries. At the time of the Scaggs indictment, only nine inmates were waiting execution from Travis County, while there were 136 on death row from Houston (Harris County) alone. The two cities are only 160 miles apart in distance, but leagues apart on this issue.

District Attorney Earle delegated criminal prosecutions to a team of seasoned assistants in his office, while he handled political corruption and malfeasance cases. In the years since Earle was first elected to the position in 1976, he had developed a team of highly professional lawyers who specialized in trying various types of felonies. His own assignment was chief prosecutor for the Public Integrity Unit, which dealt with political crimes.

With Austin as the state capital, most of the political crimes in Texas involving state officials or legislators were technically within Earle's jurisdiction. He personally investigated and tried these cases when grand juries handed down indictments. Through 2005 he had investigated or prosecuted more than a dozen elected and appointed state officials. Earle is a Democrat, and despite cries of partisanship, most of the defendants have been Democrats as well. Still, the high-profile investigations of Republicans like Senator Kay Bailey Hutchison and, more recently, former House whip Tom Delay, attracted the most attention. As the state's political watchdog, *Texas Monthly* magazine pointed out, "Depending on your political persuasion, Earle is either revered as principled or reviled as partisan."

With the decision reached early not to seek the death penalty in the Scaggs case, the stage was set for what was shaping up to be one of the most notable Texas trials in recent years. The focus this time would not be on Dallas–Fort Worth or Houston oil dynasty heirs who murdered their wives to avoid sharing the family wealth. The underlying issue drawing early national attention to the Scaggs trial was more subtle. This case was unusual because it focused the hot glare of the spotlight on a peculiar societal trend occurring in large swaths of the country known as the Bible Belt: the questioning of a woman's role in the home and church.

At a time when the women's rights movement was at its zenith, Penny Scaggs had been widely known as a teacher and proponent of a return to a biblically based patriarchal family, where the wife was subservient to the husband. The controversy over a woman's role in the home and the church had already caused growing rifts in Protestant denominations across the country, particularly in the South. It now became one of the central issues in a murder trial in Texas. All that was needed for a national courtroom drama was to complete the cast of characters.

District Attorney Earle assigned one of the most reliable and experienced prosecutors on his staff as his star player when he named his chief criminal trial lawyer, H. F. "Buddy" Meyer, to first chair. Meyer, who was head of the trial division of the Travis County D.A.'s Office, had handled some of the most egregious felonies in Austin for the previous ten years. His assignment to try the Scaggs case was recognition of its importance.

Sporting a drooping, Cossack-cavalry mustache, the unsmiling Meyer had educed many a last minute plea from nervous defendants afraid to face the stern prosecutor before a jury. In actuality, he was well known around the courthouse for his wry wit and sophisticated sense of humor. But he left any momentary merriment at the courtroom door and had a formidable reputation as a tough law-and-order prosecutor. Meyer wore brightly stitched cowboy boots under his dark-colored business suits. He was a 1980 graduate of the University of Houston College of Law, and had joined the Travis County D.A. staff in 1981, straight out of law school. He had been a prosecutor for all of his professional life.

Filling the second chair for the prosecution was Bryan

Case, who, before graduating from the University of Texas Law School in 1983, had been a medical student at the UT Medical School in Galveston, Texas. In his second year of med school he discovered he was not cut out to be a doctor and switched his focus to law. However, his medical background had proved helpful, as criminal prosecutions became increasingly more dependent on scientific and medical evidence. Case also wore a mustache, albeit more neatly groomed and less fear-inspiring than Meyer's. He usually wore dress shoes, rather than cowboy boots, under his conservative business suits.

Assistant District Attorney Case was also a seasoned criminal prosecutor, having headed the child-abuse division and served as chief prosecutor in seventy felony cases for the Travis County office. He was head of the criminal appeals section at the time of the Scaggs murder case, and had successfully fended off four dozen felony appeals.

Both prosecutors were low-key in their courtroom demeanor. They had earned their reputations by winning conviction after conviction in contested cases before Travis County juries. They left the theatrics and fame to the defense attorneys, but consistently sent the defendants they tried to prison.

After the grand jury returned a true bill of indictment for murder, the case of *State of Texas* v. *Roger T. Scaggs* was assigned to Jon Wisser, the senior criminal judge for Travis County. Judge Wisser had presided over the 299th Criminal District Court since 1982. He had been a county court judge for eleven years before his election to the criminal district court, and was a prosecutor for three years before becoming a judge.

A popular figure in courthouse circles, Wisser had presided over some of the biggest trials in Austin. The fact that he rarely drew a Republican opponent and was repeatedly returned to the bench by voters testified to the public's satisfaction with his judicial service. He was not considered an activist or partisan political figure.

Wisser was a graduate of the University of Texas Law School and the National Judicial College. He was known to be highly solicitous of the comfort and well-being of his jury members, often breaking the tedium of a long trial with humorous comments or jokes. At the same time, he commanded a quiet decorum in his courtroom.

Judge Wisser was an Army combat veteran, having served as an officer in the 1st Infantry Division in Vietnam, and an avid, competitive long-distance runner. With his trimmed but full head of sandy blond hair and tennis-pro looks, the judge, even in his somber black robes, always appeared to be in good spirits. He had a boyish smile and cheerful greeting for everyone he met in the hallways of the courthouse.

While Judge Wisser was not personally flamboyant, he was one of Austin's most colorful legal figures. Despite the gravity of his position as a criminal judge, listening daily to some of the vilest acts that humans can commit, he was well known as "Austin's Wedding Judge." He has performed more than five thousand weddings, including many in unusual settings requested by the couples. He has officiated at weddings in hot air balloons, airplanes, barrooms, courtrooms, jails, boats, and at the bedsides of the critically ill who wanted to wed as a last act of life. His services are requested for weddings all over the state, and he has even been flown to California to perform the nuptials for one couple. One of the strangest weddings he performed was for two diving enthusiasts. The wedding was conducted on a sunken platform, forty feet below the surface of Lake Travis. Judge Wisser and twenty attendants donned wet suits and diving tanks to help unite the couple in a totally underwater ceremony.

But when it came to meting out justice, Wisser had a reputation for knowing the law and applying it even-handedly. He lectured on the law at the University of Texas, and had been instrumental in reforming and modernizing a number of the state's antiquated judicial procedures. He designed and helped implement a felony court-appointment system, a drug diversion court system, and a child abuse impact court program. He helped establish the probation department's alcohol treatment program, and established the Criminal Court Administration Office and the Travis County Criminal Magistrate Court. He was among the leading advocates of a major county bond proposition for the construction of facilities to relieve the dire overcrowding in the local jails. His wife, a practicing attorney, also led numerous Austin volunteer and philanthropic projects.

If Roger Scaggs had drawn one of the most eminent jurists in Texas to preside over the trial, he also put together a top-notch defense team, led by an attorney who was reputed to be the best defense lawyer in Austin.

After Roger was indicted for murder, the seriousness of his plight alarmed some of his longtime friends, particularly those who believed he was innocent. One of these friends was Joe Edwards, who had known both Roger and Penny for nearly thirty years. Edwards, who was semiretired from a successful career as a nursing-home developer, had worked with many of the state's best-known lawyers. When Roger called him for advice, Edwards recommended he retain the top legal firm in Austin. He offered to introduce Roger to Roy Q. Minton, Esq.

Roy Minton was legally proficient, successful in both the courtroom and in business, flamboyant, and one of the best all-around civil and criminal defense lawyers in Texas. He was also popular with juries for his colorful, down-home style in the courtroom. He had a hefty portfolio of cases won for famous—and infamous—clients, dating back years. When he agreed to head the Scaggs defense effort, rumors circulated around the courthouse that this was going to be his final criminal defense trial before retiring to the slower-paced practice of civil law. (Later, however, these rumors proved to be untrue.) Minton also had a mustache, just a thin line straight across his upper lip, and cowboy boots under the cuffs of his business suits.

Minton's first love was criminal defense law, even though

his national reputation was largely gained from successful civil litigation in such megabuck cases as *Houston Power & Light* v. *City of Austin* over the South Texas nuclear power plant. He and a partner began a law practice in Austin in the early 1960s, initially focusing on criminal defense work. The young lawyers soon expanded into civil and family law in order to keep the lights on at the office.

He became one of the state's leading figures in the defense of well-known clients accused of white-collar crimes or political malfeasance. He had represented Texas political leaders including governors, lieutenant governors, House speakers, and even a Texas attorney general. He had won acquittals or dismissals of charges brought by the state against some of its own top politicians, but had also been hired to defend the state of Texas in a number of civil cases.

He defended then-governor Ann Richards against two wrongful-termination lawsuits in 1993, in trials before the federal court in Dallas. In one of those suits, Minton was pitted against plaintiff's attorney Harriett Miers, later nominated by President Bush to serve on the U.S. Supreme Court. (That controversial 2005 nomination was withdrawn under pressure from right-wing GOP and conservative Christian political organizations.) Dallas attorney Miers lost the lawsuit her client had brought against Governor Richards, with Minton leading the defense in a jury trial.

Minton, an avid swimmer, could be found practically every morning for the last two decades doing laps at dawn in the chilly waters of Barton Springs, Austin's famed near-downtown swimming hole. His swimming habits led to a physical confrontation at the pool shortly before he assumed the lead defense role in the Scaggs case.

An environmentally conscious fellow swimmer took umbrage at Minton swimming in the natural springs pool at the same time he was representing a land developer accused by Austin greens of polluting the spring's source. The man apparently loudly harangued Minton every morning as he took his swim, until one day the attorney got fed up and confronted his tormentor. The young man accused Minton of a physical assault by shoving, a misdemeanor charge.

"The most I ever did is, I may have put my finger on his chest when I told him to quit yelling at me," Minton told *Austin Statesman* reporter Scott Wright. "I'm sixty-three years old and not a threat to anybody. But I do not like anyone yelling at me while I am swimming in the pool."

The man, who denied belonging to any of Austin's zealous environmental groups, explained that he was only trying to educate other pool patrons about Minton's work. One of Minton's clients had sued the city over restrictions on development in the environmentally sensitive Barton Creek watershed. Minton managed to negotiate a settlement with the protestor at the pool.

The second regular member of the defense team was veteran courtroom attorney Charles R. Burton, a senior partner with his name on the shingle in front of Minton's offices in the center of the city. The firm was so entrenched in Austin legal circles that its brick office building, which prominently fronted on the same street as the courthouse only a half block away, looked almost like an annex of the sprawling justice complex. In fact, one of Minton's office buildings was closer to the main courthouse than the new courthouse annex, then under construction, was going to be.

With a trim white beard, Burton looked and acted every inch a law school dean. He would not only participate actively in the courtroom defense work, but was on hand to perfect the record in the event appeals became necessary. The defense team thought that unlikely, however, fervently expressing a belief in Roger Scaggs's innocence. Burton, who had joined the Minton firm in 1964, had a special interest in precharge investigations and pretrial legal efforts. A University of Texas Law School graduate, he was admitted to practice before all the federal district courts in Texas, the federal appellate courts, and the U.S. Supreme Court. Like Minton, Burton served as defense counsel in some of the biggest criminal and civil suits in Texas during the two-score years he had been practicing law.

Another key member of the defense was a trial lawyer from the younger generation, with a different courtroom technique than the two veteran lawyers on the team.

Randy T. Leavitt, tall, with chiseled good looks, would be the only clean-shaven face among the lawyers at the counsel tables. With his openly expressed passion for defense work, he was the Austin version of Bobby Donnell of the then popular TV show, *The Practice*. His fiery zeal as a defense lawyer stemmed from his belief that if the scales of justice were going to be tilted, they should tilt in favor of a defendant who was presumed innocent until tried before a judge or jury.

All the lawyers in the firm of Minton, Burton, Foster & Collins, which Leavitt joined in 1982, had to accept a large caseload of civil suits to underwrite their criminal defense work. Of the eleven lawyers in the firm, only four were certified to practice criminal law at all.

Leavitt was one of the four, and his caseload was split 65 percent criminal and 35 percent civil. He was a 1980 graduate of the Texas Tech University law school and a Panhandle native, having come to the Austin area to attend the University of Texas and Southwest Texas State University at San Marcos. He first entered college on a football scholarship at Highland University in Las Vegas, New Mexico, after being captain of the Stamford (Texas) High School varsity squad. During college he edited the law review, was on the national mock trial team, and clerked in the local district attorney's office, all the while maintaining a grade point average between 3.4 and 4. After giving up his football scholarship at the small New Mexico school to concentrate on the study of law, Leavitt worked his way through college as a lifeguard, waiter, janitorial service supervisor, and law clerk. It was while working as a lifeguard at Austin's Barton Springs pool that he met and got to know the swimming enthusiast Minton, whose firm he joined after a two-year stint in solo practice.

A private detective named Dennis Dement and a number of legal aides and forensic experts filled out the defense team. The law firm had a total staff of twenty-five, not large by national standards, but one of the largest practices accepting criminal defense work in Central Texas. At one of the Scaggs pretrial hearings, five attorneys were on hand for the defense, prompting Judge Wisser to comment on the size of the defense effort. But even with the talent and depth of the defense team, Austin trial watchers believed Roger Scaggs faced an uphill battle. The well-publicized evidence against him, particularly the fingerprints found inside the latex gloves with Penny's blood on the outside, and the fact that the murder weapon and stolen jewelry were discovered by police in a Dumpster behind his office building, seemed too formidable to overcome.

Many courthouse wags said the defense had already won the only part of the case it could hope for, which was to get Roger a spate of freedom—more than two and a half years—before the trial. His freedom during the preliminaries leading up to the trial was secured by the cash value of his company 401(k) account; the terms of his bail precluded any additional loans against that account.

There was a lingering question over how Roger was going to pay his legal bills, which most knowledgeable observers estimated would exceed one million dollars. A source in Minton's office, who denied the legal fees were even close to that amount, said the firm took the case on a flat-fee basis in the low six-figure range. However, other legal costs, including private investigators, expert witnesses, and forensic tests, were expected to equal or exceed the attorneys' fees.

The defense team was undeterred by the apparently long odds it faced as a result of some extraordinary police work. From the beginning, the defense maintained that Roger Scaggs was wrongly accused, and that the only way the evidence could have ended up in a Dumpster behind his office was if some unknown person planted it and then tipped the police to its location. That, of course, would imply a con-

spiracy to frame Roger Scaggs for the murder of his wife. It
would also imply that someone had reason to hate Roger
and Penny enough to commit the horrible crime in the first
place.

In legal expertise, experience, and personality, the trial
judge and the teams for both the prosecution and the defense
were the most stellar to be found anywhere in Central Texas,
if not the entire state. The expectations for a major show-
down in the courthouse were the highest of any Austin trial
in the past several decades.

The promise of some colorful legal fireworks soon attracted national media attention. Television networks and
cable's Court TV program directors began making inquiries
about sending crews to the upcoming trial, to broadcast live
from Austin.

Chapter 19

As the one-year anniversary of Penny's death came and went without a trial date, her friends and family members began to grumble to authorities and the press about how slowly the wheels of justice were grinding.

Roger was seen frequently around the community, appearing to carry on a normal life. He was living in a condominium at William Cannon Drive and West Gate Boulevard, approximately three miles from the house on Winter Park. Since several of the same shopping and service centers catered to both locations, it was almost inevitable that he would run into his former neighbors.

A reporter for the *Austin American-Statesman*, Dave Harmon, was on the receiving end of the growing number of calls complaining that there had been no trial date set in the case. The long delay was extremely unusual for the Austin courts. Of the previous fifty murder cases filed in Travis County, only four had taken longer than eighteen months to come to trial or be resolved, and three of those were death-penalty cases.

Harmon wrote a story, heavy with quotes from angry friends and kin, that scolded both the prosecution and defense. American Airlines pilot Phillip Beall, who had been shocked to find Roger riding first class on one of his cross-country flights, was among those who complained about the delays. His mother, who was Penny's first cousin, lamented that "she was tired of waiting."

Lead prosecutor Buddy Meyer told the reporter that he was sympathetic to the family and friends and regretted the long wait.

"I understand the frustration," he said, "but there are things that happen in a case that push the trial date beyond the average delay."

Harmon reported that the defense attributed the delays to the long lead times required to get evidence scientifically analyzed by both the prosecution and defense. Some of the same pieces of evidence had to be examined by both sides, since there were disputes over what the evidence showed.

Randy Leavitt acknowledged that in cases where the accused was free on bail, the clock ticked a little slower than when a defendant was waiting in jail for his day in court.

Judge Wisser's ability to move up the trial date was limited, since both the defense and the prosecution agreed on the motions to delay, leaving him nothing on which to make a ruling or set a firm date on the court docket. In fact, the judge set five docket calls in the Scaggs case during 1996, each postponed by mutual agreement of the prosecution and defense. Still, the public and the media were restive over the delay.

If Harmon's story was scolding, an editorial in the neighborhood's *Westlake Picayune* was downright scathing. For over a year editor Ed Allen had been deluged with calls from his readers and residents wanting to know what was going on in the case. When more months passed without a trial, he finally let go with an editorial blast that would have been more typical of a crusading weekly newspaper in the Old West. Excerpts from the editorial read:

They say that "justice" is for those who can afford to pay for it; however, in the case of the state versus Roger Scaggs, perhaps "injustice" would be a better word—depending on the outcome of the trial . . .

If Scaggs is guilty of the crime, then we should all be deeply concerned that we have had in our midst a murderer who doesn't deserve to be set free on $250,000 bond to enjoy life until his trial comes up. If he is innocent, we should all be deeply concerned about the time our district attorney's office staff is spending on this case.

One cannot help but wonder how many other cases involving offenders who pose serious threats to the general public are plea bargained due to prosecutors having their hands full with the Scaggs case and other trials involving people of wealth who can afford an attorney capable enough to drag out the process.

The delays notwithstanding, in reality there had been quite a bit of activity in the Scaggs case. The proceedings to that date might best be described as legal maneuvering rather than forward momentum, but a lot was happening behind the scenes. These activities, other than agreed-upon motions to delay, involved some hotly disputed evidentiary issues. Each required a court hearing, bringing out the judge, court reporter and court staff, lawyers, and the defendant. And each new filing caused further delays in the trial, while the parties concentrated on writing responses or waited for rulings to adjust their strategies.

*E*ven before the formal hearings were held, the defense mounted an aggressive challenge to the prosecution's case. On February 19, 1997, the defense moved to quash a subpoena and issue a protective order to prevent the state from gaining access to the records of Penny and Roger's sessions at the Samaritan Center for Counseling & Pastoral Care. The prosecution had subpoenaed the records and testimony of two counselors from the center. The defense argued that these consultations were protected by the same confidentiality privilege enjoyed by a minister and congregant. Judge Wisser took the motion under advisement and later ruled that these were pastoral conversations and that the state could not have access to them. He quashed the subpoena.

The first formal appearance of the prosecution and defense teams before Judge Wisser in the 299th Criminal District Court was the preliminary hearing held on March 7, 1997, a full year after the murder of Penny Scaggs.

Roger, looking tanned and fit, appeared at the hearing flanked by his trial attorneys Minton, Burton, and Leavitt, and other specialists from the defense team. The size of the entourage prompted the judge to comment that it looked like the defense was ready to go to trial that very day.

Assistant D.A.'s Meyer and Case were in attendance for the prosecution.

The flurry of defense motions filed with the court that day—eight in all—made it clear that Roger Scaggs's attorneys intended to pull out all the pretrial legal stops in representing him against the murder charge.

The first action was a general motion for discovery, stating that the prosecution was expected to provide the defense with a complete list of rebuttal witnesses. Each side had already provided a basic list of witnesses to the other. The same motion reiterated that the defense expected the state to provide all results from blood and DNA testing.

The second was a motion to sequester the jury during the trial. The defense argued that there had already been a huge amount of publicity surrounding the murder, making it potentially difficult to select an impartial jury.

A third motion dealt with a legal technicality that would require a probation hearing before sentencing, in the event a guilty verdict was returned.

The fourth defense motion requested a separate evidentiary hearing to suppress unspecified evidence the defense claimed had been illegally seized by the Austin Police Department.

The next action was a demand for the return of a portfolio with notes that had been taken from Roger Scaggs by Detective Thompson at the time of his arrest. The defense claimed the notebook contained privileged handwritten notes of previous conversations between Scaggs and attorneys, and that this seizure violated attorney-client privilege. The defense maintained that any evidence gathered by police as a result of reading the notes would be tainted as "fruit of the poisonous tree," and thus inadmissible.

A sixth motion demanded that the state turn over all exculpatory evidence in its possession, or other evidence that might mitigate in favor of Scaggs.

A seventh motion asked for a time extension before the trial in order for the defense to retest all the forensic evidence the state had amassed, and to allow its private investigators to interview witnesses and discover new evidence. The defense argued that additional time for retesting was required because the prosecution still had not turned over the reports from lab work done at the DPS crime laboratory.

The eighth and final motion of the day was a demand for transcripts of the grand jury hearings. The prosecution immediately responded that it could not comply with that request because no such transcripts existed.

The lawyers could not even agree on a date for the next formal hearing, the pretrial evidentiary hearing requested by the defense. In response to every date the judge suggested, one or another of the defense team vetoed it for some personal reason or prescheduled court conflict. One lawyer said his wife was scheduled to deliver a baby around the time the judge had suggested; another date was rejected when a second attorney said it conflicted with a big party, arranged long before, for a child or grandchild.

Finally, Judge Wisser, appearing agitated, admonished, "Surely you can find some time on the calendar when everyone can show up."

The evidentiary hearing, tentatively scheduled for May 9, was moved off for various reasons and finally held on July 18, 1997. This hearing turned out to be a dress rehearsal for the pending murder trial. The defense called key prosecution witnesses for full examination, under oath, on the witness stand.

Five defense lawyers showed up for this hearing, with Minton and Leavitt heading the team. The prosecution again had its two assigned lawyers, Meyer and Case, at court.

The state's main witnesses marched to the stand to tell what part they played in the investigation and to exhibit items of evidence. As each piece of the puzzle was described and displayed—whether from the crime scene, the Dumpsters, Roger Scaggs's office, or the state crime lab—the defense made a motion to suppress it.

The defense maintained that all evidence seized in the house on Winter Park Road was illegal because the permission Scaggs gave for the search was obtained under misleading circumstances at a time when he was unable to fully understand his actions. The lawyers further argued that the evidence found in the Dumpster was improperly obtained because no search warrant had been executed. The motion to suppress claimed that Scaggs had cancelled his permission after the first day, and that any searches after that were illegal. According to the defense, Scaggs was repeatedly denied a list of items seized at his property, as had been promised him.

The defense angrily demanded that the personal notebook, which had been seized by detectives the day of his arrest, be immediately returned to their client, contending it contained privileged notes taken during attorney-client conversations. The defense became visibly upset when Detective Thompson stated from the witness stand that he had not brought the portfolio to court with him. The judge ordered the notebook brought from the police evidence room and turned over to the court. Wisser said he would review its contents before he ruled.

An attempt was made to have Scaggs's statements to police excluded on the grounds that he had not been properly informed that he might be a suspect in the case. The defense argued that the statement was nothing more than an informal discussion Roger had with police, in an effort to be cooperative and help find the real killer.

At the end of the evidentiary hearing, the judge declined to suppress any of the testimony of the state's witnesses or any of the evidence. The exception was Scaggs's personal notebook, which the judge kept under seal in the court's possession.

The daylong hearing might have appeared a colossal waste of time, except that the defense now had a full picture of what the state was expected to offer at the trial, or so the defense team thought at the time.

As he adjourned the proceeding, Judge Wisser quipped at the row of attorneys, "I trust I will see all *eight* of you then." There were actually only seven attorneys present—two state and five defense; and two of the defense lawyers were present only to take notes in preparation for any future appeals.

On August 15 the defense filed another motion to dismiss the indictment against Scaggs, claiming that his constitutional rights had been violated by the seizure of his personal notebook containing notes about his conversations with attorneys before the Minton team was hired. According to the motion, this was a violation of constitutionally protected attorney-client privilege. The motion claimed again that all the evidence obtained in the home was derived by unlawful search and seizure. A new alleged violation of Scaggs's rights was introduced, concerning a wiretap that had been placed on the telephone of Vanessa Ferguson. During those recordings, conversations with her attorney had inadvertently been captured. Even though Vanessa was named as a witness, the defense claimed these wiretaps had violated Scaggs's right to a fair trial.

The motion stated that merely suppressing the ill-gotten evidence would not be enough to guarantee a fair trial; therefore, the only remedy would be a dismissal of the indictment.

A hearing on the motion to dismiss was scheduled for August 22 and delayed until September 19. Defense attorney Burton led off this hearing.

Detective Sergeant Hector Reveles and Detective Ismael Campa testified that, on the night of the murder, they had received first verbal and later signed consent from Scaggs to enter and search the home.

"When he signed the consent, he said, 'I hope you get the guy who did this,' " Detective Campa testified.

The Dumpster, which was the property of the waste removal company, BFI, had been searched at the company storage yards. Commercial manager Randy Whitaker confirmed that police had secured permission and made an appointment to search it.

Concerning the seizure of the notebook, Detective Thompson acknowledged that Roger had requested it be given to his daughter at the time of his arrest, but he said he had no intention of complying with the request. The notebook was kept under seal in the court's property room.

The judge ruled against dismissal of the indictment and against the additional requests for suppression of the contested evidence. He ordered the trial to move forward. However, no open date was available on the court calendar for the remainder of 1997. The trial was held over for the spring 1998 docket.

While the courtroom theatrics were playing out, a significant melodrama was unfolding behind the scenes at the DPS crime lab in Austin. On at least one point the defense's argument for delay had some merit. The prosecution had not yet turned over all the forensic evidence. From their perspective, they had good reason for the delay. There were several pieces of evidence at the DPS lab that could potentially raise a question about the state's allegation that Roger, and Roger alone, had murdered his wife.

The questionable evidence involved the DNA analysis of the fingernail clippings and a spot of watery blood found on the kitchen countertop. At this point, the original test results had not yet been turned over to the defense because the lab's conclusions were being questioned within the lab itself.

Serologist Donna Stanley, who had conducted the initial blood tests on evidence taken from the Scaggs home and the Dumpster, also performed most of the DNA testing. She documented her findings in an October 1996 report, which was reviewed by other chemists before going to the head of the section, Irma Rios, for final sign-off.

Most of the evidence tested had shown DNA from only one donor. The blood on the pipe, knife, latex gloves, jewelry, and some of the fingernails, was all of one type, which was consistent with Penny Scaggs.

However, several of the tests gave a different result. Some of the fingernails, scrapings, and a swab taken from a bloody water drop on the kitchen counter had been labeled "inconclusive" in the report. Results for these items showed a mixture of DNA from Penny Scaggs and another person. "Inconclusive" meant the tester could not give an opinion as to the source of the extraneous DNA. Roger Scaggs was excluded from being a contributor to any of the tested evidence.

Donna Stanley believed the tests showed that the mystery DNA from the nails had not come from blood, but from some weaker bodily fluid, such as saliva. In addition to questions on these samples, testing on a small body hair recovered from the knife was also inconclusive. Although it showed some characteristics of the "mystery" DNA, the material in the hair was inadequate to make an accurate analysis.

Stanley had run the inconclusive samples again and obtained the same results.

The DNA findings were important because they could be the basis for arguing that another, still unknown person, might have been in close contact with the victim.

When supervisor Irma Rios received the report for administrative review, she was concerned about the inconclusive results. She believed there was possible contamination in the chemicals used in the control. To determine the source of that contamination, in May 1997 she sent some of the samples for retesting to LabCorp, a respected medical diagnostics company with a major forensics lab located in Research Triangle Park, North Carolina.

Meghan Clement, a senior LabCorp serologist, performed a series of tests on the evidence, the reference samples, and the reagents. She ultimately would conclude that some of the original tests had been contaminated by the chemical reagent used in the testing process. Nevertheless, over the next year the prosecution continued to eliminate other possible contributors to the DNA; and the Texas state lab sent additional samples to LabCorp (some at the request of the D.A.'s office), in an ongoing effort to assure quality control and understand the results of the initial tests. The mystery DNA was compared with the DNA of the scientists who had handled the samples, as well as relatives and other people who had frequently been in the house. No match was found.

Donna Stanley felt confident that contamination had not occurred as a result of her testing procedures.

*T*he next cause for delay in the legal proceedings was more troubling for the prosecution. A potentially important witness went missing on the eve of the approaching spring 1998 trial date. Vanessa Ferguson, who was considered a material witness, had apparently vanished. A week before the trial was set to begin, investigators attempting to issue subpoenas from the D.A.'s office were unable to find her. Since the witness had not yet been formally subpoenaed, she had not committed an illegal act by leaving town without notice.

This latest delay caused a huge furor in the news media, and after the public heard about it, an even bigger outcry in the community. Judge Wisser was at the end of his rope, too.

The trial had been set to begin on Monday, April 20. On Friday, April 17, Judge Wisser reluctantly cancelled the order on a large panel of prospective jurors and postponed the trial again. It had been more than two years since the murder of Penny Scaggs, and this was the ninth delay he had granted. This time the top attorneys in the case, Buddy Meyer and Roy Minton, personally notified the judge that a delay was necessary. The defense lawyers strongly denied that their client had anything to do with the decision of the witness to leave town or had any knowledge of her whereabouts.

Judge Wisser had learned about the required delay on Thursday, only four days before jury selection was set to begin.

"I'm totally at a loss to explain what's going on with this case," the judge told David Harmon of the *Austin American-Statesman*. The chief criminal courts judge for Travis County complained that the trial had already been the most drawn-out in recent memory, which probably meant in the history of the county. He noted that the old settlers believed in swift justice and intended that the accused be tried promptly.

Both sides claimed Vanessa Ferguson's testimony was essential to their case. The state planned to use the girlfriend's very existence as a motive for the murder. The defense planned to use her as an alibi witness, and to prove the office romance was just a casual affair, not serious enough to have compelled their client to kill his wife.

"She has dropped out of sight, and we're almost sure this is intentional on her part, to avoid testifying," complained ADA Bryan Case. "We're very frustrated; but it's not like we can blame someone, it just happened. It's unfortunate, but we have to live with it."

Meanwhile, the defense told reporters that they would welcome the latest delay to continue their investigation. They claimed significant new evidence had surfaced that a stranger might have committed the murder. The defense had fingerprints recovered at the crime scene that did not match anyone in the Scaggses' close circle of friends and family.

"The defense raised the possibility that these are the real killer's fingerprints," the Austin daily reported.

That justification for delay did not impress the judge, either.

"It should have been done, it seems to me, a year and a half ago," Wisser told the newspaper.

The judge, his patience with the legal maneuvering worn thin, let the two chief counsels know that this delay would be their last, unless lightning struck. He gave them time to wrap up all their investigations and forensic tests, and set the trial for October 1998.

Chapter 20

> Made-for-Court TV Murder Trial: The murder of
> Penny Scaggs had it all—betrayal, violence, sex,
> even religion. Perhaps it was these universal
> themes that kept the city riveted . . . .

That was how the alternative newspaper, the Austin
Chronicle, summed up the Scaggs trial when it ranked it
number four in the city's top news stories of 1998.

In this era of televised trials, a high-profile case, with the
theatrics of colorful attorneys in the courtroom and throngs
of media and crowds outside, is often referred to as a "cir-
cus." But because Penny was such a beloved and unlikely
murder victim, and her accused killer so respected in the
church and business communities, the trial of Roger Scaggs
was more like a tragic drama.

Although the Austin murder trial did not attract the degree of interest generated by the likes of O. J. Simpson, the
Menendez brothers, and Scott Peterson, it did garner national television attention.

Court TV, which had announced a year earlier that it would cover the proceedings "gavel-to-gavel," generated the most pretrial publicity, and forced other electronic media to cover the event.

The weekend before the trial began, it was obvious to any passerby that something big was about to happen at the Travis County Courthouse annex the following week. Television trucks with their boom lifts and dish antennae took up the few parking spaces on adjacent streets two days early, to assure themselves a close-in spot and test their links for live broadcasts from the courtroom, hallways, and grounds. The Court TV crew raised a small tent in the outdoor plaza for conducting interviews with witnesses as they left the building.

Of the dozens of reporters from the newspapers, radio, and television stations covering the trial, two led the pack—one a national cable TV star and the other a local weekly journalist. These two women had the rolling scoops throughout the trial because of their almost uncanny ability to get the principals in the case to talk, even as these witnesses were refusing questions from all other reporters. The journalists were Clara Tuma, who was working for Court TV at the time, and Kayte VanScoy, reporter for the *Austin Chronicle*.

Tuma became the face of the Scaggs trial, along with other Court TV commentators and anchors, because of the hourly, live updates from the small, open-sided pavilion set up in the plaza. The award-winning TV journalist collared Penny's relatives and friends, church members, and key investigators after their testimony to gain behind-the-news perspectives. Some of her standup interviews were emotionally charged and ended in tears. All the interviews were insightful and dramatic.

On Monday morning, October 26, jury selection was under way. Immediately, the lead defense attorney, Roy Minton, complained to Judge Wisser that it was going to be difficult to seat a jury because of all the pretrial publicity, particularly in the *Austin American-Statesman*. The local daily, after being initially slow to pick up on the story, had ultimately provided extensive coverage during the two and a half years since the murder. Because of the long lag time between the murder and the trial, several of the paper's top reporters had worked on the story.

In the early coverage, Scott W. Wright had been assigned almost full-time to unearth facts and write about the secret "other life" of Roger Scaggs. When that veteran reporter left the paper to accept a position on the East Coast, he took his files and confidential sources with him. His cowriter on some of the more explosive early articles was Rebecca Thatcher, who also developed an expert knowledge of the case and an extensive list of confidential sources.

As the trial was repeatedly postponed, Thatcher was promoted within the editorial department and Dave Harmon was assigned the courthouse beat. He covered most of the pretrial hearings over the two years the case was bogged down, and then left that beat for other assignments. When the trial finally began, the *Statesman* assigned veteran reporter Leah Quin to cover the proceedings.

The four network-affiliated TV stations of ABC, CBS, NBC, and Fox had sporadically done news reports and in-depth features on the murder, and were on hand with crews during much of the trial. The coverage had been more extensive for this story than any criminal case in recent Austin history. Minton's complaint that everyone in Austin knew something about the case was probably justified.

Reporter Leah Quin's opening-day reportage of the Scaggs trial set the pace for the massive news coverage that was to follow in local, state, and national media for the duration of the trial. She wrote a front-page, twenty-four-column-inch story, recounting all the violent details of the murder and the years of delay. Any member of the panel arriving for jury duty that morning could have opened their morning paper for a full refresher course on the case. Hopefully, the prospective jurors, who had been impaneled the previous week and told to report for jury selection Monday, had heeded the judge's admonishments not to read, listen to, or watch anything related to the case over the weekend.

Quin's front-page story also set the tone of the trial to come, providing details that went far beyond the nuts and bolts of the murder case. The Scaggs murder trial began five days before Halloween. In her article, Quin described the current appearance of the former Scaggs home, decorated with "gauzy cotton cobwebs stretched across bushes and a cardboard ghost and pumpkin on the front door." The story said, ". . . no one has taken over the Bible-based course on how to be an ideal wife that Penny Scaggs pioneered."

The public's fascination with the case extended beyond the forensic evidence to the upscale community where it occurred and the religious background of the people involved. It was as if a certain lifestyle and value system were also on trial.

As it turned out, Minton was wrong about the difficulty of seating an impartial jury. The jury panel of sixty represented a cross section of the community, with twenty males and forty females summoned for final selection. No one was disqualified by the judge solely for having read or heard reports about the case.

In questioning the panel, the defense attorneys were particularly interested in whether the prospective jurors could be fair if testimony revealed the defendant had been involved in an affair with a younger woman at the time of his wife's murder. The issue of the alleged mistress's disappearance also came up.

Out of earshot of the panelists, the judge admonished the attorneys against drawing any conclusion about the absence of this key witness. "Neither the defense nor the D.A. can imply that the other party had any responsibility for the witness's disappearance," Judge Wisser said.

Vanessa Ferguson, who had disappeared seven months earlier, was still missing. In the intervening months, a nationwide search had proved fruitless. A material witness warrant had been issued by the court for her apprehension, and a bond set at $200,000. The warrant had been circulated nationwide and in several foreign countries, and her ID was circulated through the National Crime Information Center.

Local investigators learned that shortly before she disappeared, Vanessa had left her new job with the Texas Employment Commission and closed her savings and checking accounts. Police monitored her post office for mail and checked to see if there had been any activity on her credit cards. They contacted the State Department to see if she had used a passport to leave the country. There was nothing to indicate where she might be, or even that the woman still existed. She had discontinued service to her cell phone, too.

District Attorney Ronnie Earle said every avenue had been explored in searching for the witness. Vanessa had given a lengthy statement to detectives shortly after the murder. However, it could not be introduced into evidence at trial, since the defense would have no opportunity to impeach her testimony.

Attorney Minton said the defense was disappointed, too, because the alleged girlfriend was the only person who could testify that Roger was with her at the office at the time the prosecution contended the murder had occurred.

Off the record, however, insiders with the defense and prosecution said that both parties likely had reasons for being less than disappointed with the disappearance of the key witness. She could have created problems for the prosecution by debunking the contention that the affair was a motive for the slaying. She had told police and her lawyers that it was just a physical fling and that Roger had made it clear he would never leave his wife for her. She could have meant trouble for the defense if her testimony about the affair was used to inflame the jury against Roger. On cross-examination, the prosecution almost certainly would have embellished the affair. So, while the missing witness had caused a substantial delay in the trial, it seemed that both the prosecution and defense lawyers were crying crocodile tears over her disappearance.

ADA Meyer instructed the panel that the sentence being sought ranged from five years to life in the state penitentiary. He pointedly explained to the panel that the death penalty was not being sought by the state because capital murder required that the killing occur during the commission of another felony offense. Ironically, only a week before, Meyer's boss, D.A. Ronnie Earle, had issued a statement that sounded highly contradictory about why death was sought for some killers and not for others.

Prosecutors in the Travis County District Attorney's Office had announced they were seeking the death penalty against a man charged with stabbing his common-law wife to death in front of her home. Leonard Saldana had been charged with the slaying of twenty-four-year-old Sylvia Hernandez. Saldana, who was a mailroom clerk for a local newspaper, had previously been arrested for violating a protective order and had a prior criminal history. Roger Scaggs had no prior record or history of violence against his wife before being charged with her death. But otherwise there were similarities in the crimes charged.

In citing the reason for seeking the death penalty in the Saldana case, District Attorney Earle said: "Domestic violence does immense harm to all of us, including generations yet unborn, and it all too often results in the death of the victim. Violence and murder in the context of a relationship that began in love is especially threatening to that which is most precious to us."

Considering the impact of the Scaggs murder on so many people, some might argue that statement could apply to his case just as well. However, Scaggs did not face the possibility of execution if convicted of his wife's murder. Saldana's lawyer, Jamie Balagia, decried the death decision as "unfair and immoral." His protest was picked up in a three-paragraph article buried inside the *Austin American-Statesman* on the day the docket call went out in the Scaggs case. (Although the state had asked for the death penalty, two years later a Travis County jury gave Saldana a life sentence.)

During voir dire, Minton, using the folksy Texas drawl and country humor that had made him popular with juries in the past, immediately won over the panel. He had them roaring with laughter when he said to one woman, "Speak up, please. I can't hear as well as that young fella," motioning with his thumb toward the assistant district attorney. He asked the potential jurors not to read anything into it if Roger did not take the stand.

"As a Texas boy, I've always presumed that if my sons didn't say anything, they were guilty as sin," Minton quipped, to loud laughter. "But if the state fails to make its case, why should I put my client on the stand? Isn't he presumed innocent?"

The panelists had assured the lawyers they had no prejudices about the circumstances in the case, knew little or nothing about the murder, and could render a fair verdict based solely on the evidence they heard in court. After each side used its peremptory challenges, a jury was selected in just seven hours, a surprisingly short time. The jury consisted of eight women and four men, including one Hispanic-American and one African-American. They retired to chambers and elected a middle-aged newspaper printer as foreman. The trial was to begin in earnest on Tuesday, October 27, but Judge Wisser brought the newly impaneled group together to remind them again that they were not to read or view anything in the news media about the case.

After jury selection, the rest of the panel was dismissed, freeing up the seats in the small courtroom. These seats quickly filled with spectators, eager to see snippets of what was being billed locally as the hottest trial in Austin in a generation. When the jury was called back by Judge Wisser, he commented on the packed room. Spectators were standing two and three rows deep against the back wall.

A small section of the front two rows of seats had been reserved for family and friends of the defendant and the victim. Prominent from the outset were Penny's three sisters—Sharon and twins Marilyn and Carolyn. They would not leave their seats, even for a moment, for the duration of the trial.

Whether sitting in the courtroom or giving interviews on camera, the sisters looked and acted so much alike that they sometimes seemed to think and move as one person. Their closeness was palpable, as was the terrible void the loss of Penny must have left. All three women had short, fine blond hair and flawless porcelain skin that clearly had always been protected from the sun. The twins, who did not dress alike but had their hair styled exactly the same way, would have been difficult to tell apart, except that Marilyn wore glasses throughout the trial and Carolyn did not.

Everywhere they went, the sisters were accompanied—almost guarded—by two female deputies from the Travis County Sheriff's Victim Services Division. Any newsperson who approached was intercepted by one of the attending deputies and politely asked to respect the personal grief of the women. But their guardians could not protect them from the often brutal testimony and evidence that was about to be presented in the case.

Roger's daughter Sarah began the trial sitting with her aunts in the first row. Gradually, as witnesses came forward to damn her father, she moved away from her aunts to the second row.

Sarah, who had turned twenty-six that summer, was a junior at Southwest Texas State University (now Texas State University, San Marcos). She had taken a short leave of absence from school and work to attend the trial.

Occasionally, during recesses or adjournments, she left the courthouse with her father and his attorneys. Unlike the sisters, the daughter had declined assistance from Victim Services. At breaks, she often sat alone in a shaded corner of the courtyard. She listened intently to others expounding on the case and talking about her father to the electronic media, formed up in rows at the entrances to the courthouse. Newspaper photographers snapped images of a forlorn daughter alone with her grief, and more than once TV cameramen drove her from her quiet spot into the security of the building when they approached.

Penny's daughter, torn by the murder of her mother and the arrest and possible long incarceration of her father, became the press corps' most sympathetic figure. The seemingly strong evidence against Roger Scaggs and the horrible details of the murder and mutilation made it difficult for the media to treat him with compassion. His aloof demeanor and refusal to speak to newspeople, let alone answer their rudely flung questions, also caused veteran reporters to keep the defendant at arm's length after a few days.

Roger Scaggs appeared in the courtroom flanked by his three primary lawyers, Minton, Burton, and Leavitt. He wore a white shirt under a dull, greenish-gray business suit, with an even duller gray tie. Once a fastidious dresser, he looked almost wilted in a suit showing wear and in need of pressing. In the two-plus years of frequent court appearances, he had noticeably aged and looked considerably thinner than the 180 pounds he weighed on the day of his arrest. At unguarded moments his six-foot-one frame seemed stooped under the heavy burden of defending himself against the murder charges. On the opening day of the trial, he looked more like a graying grandfather than a roué or accused wife-killer.

He was still associated with the APS Group, but no longer as an executive officer. He had been retained for a good part of the previous two years as a consultant to continue work on the company's computer services systems. Many of his steadfast friends and fellow corporate executives were in the courtroom on opening day, in a show of support and an expressed belief in his innocence. A delegation from the First Evangelical Free Church, headed by associate pastor David Chu, was also in attendance and would be present throughout the trial. A spokesman said the church group was in court to observe the proceedings and update their congregation, and not to offer either support or condemnation. Pastor Chu and one or two members of the congregation sat silently through the trial, occasionally appearing to bow their heads in prayer.

Outside the packed courtroom, employees from the county government offices and lawyers from buildings nearby stopped in clusters to talk about the case and watch the media interview people coming from the courthouse.

On several occasions the event did become circuslike, complete with a street person who could have served as the big top's clown. A tall, bearded man wearing a miniskirt showed up the first day, decked out in finery that included heavy facial makeup, fancy boa scarf, and a feathered hat. This local character returned each day of the trial wearing a different miniskirted fashion, to walk back and forth in front of the entrance to the courthouse. The only harm done was to the TV crews, who had to align their camera angles carefully for interviews, to make sure the self-appointed clown was not caught on evening newscasts of the otherwise solemn proceedings.

During the trial, mysterious people, both men and women, collared reporters with "inside tips" on what had "really" happened. The anonymous tipsters had all kinds of theories about how the police had framed Scaggs or failed to follow leads pointing to other suspects who, these "unnamed sources" contended, had actually committed the crime.

The narrow hallways in the old courthouse annex were crowded by the Scaggs trial and another murder case being tried before a jury on the same floor. At the beginning and end of each day and at break times, the two small elevators serving the building were quickly filled. Those who could not negotiate the steep, three flights of stairs had long waits. Entering the building also posed a delay. Sheriff's deputies screened all incoming people in the small lobby on the first floor. Handbags, camera bags, briefcases, notebooks, and other carried items had to be either inspected or scanned by an X-ray machine. Individuals were required to pass through the single metal detector mounted in a door frame.

The congestion did not prevent the trial of Roger Scaggs from becoming the biggest attraction in town. Judge Wisser's 299th District Court proceedings drew packed audiences for the first time in its history. Some of the pressure was relieved when the public learned that Court TV was providing live, almost gavel-to-gavel coverage. The Scaggs coverage was periodically interrupted when the network went live to a civil lawsuit against action-hero, movie star Jean-Claude Van Damme, being tried in Los Angeles.

However, Clara Tuma, from Austin, and the Court TV commentators quickly caught viewers up on anything they may have missed in the Scaggs proceedings. Their trial coverage also offered a steady banter by guest experts who provided analysis of the testimony and the legal maneuverings inside and outside the courtroom. During the nearly three weeks of the trial, guests discussed forensics, psychology, and legal strategy with Court TV's impressive attorney anchors Fred Graham, Nancy Grace, Raymond Brown, Carol Randolph, June Grasso, Dan Broden, and Beth Karas.

On the ground, Tuma, who by then had been covering famous trials for Court TV for seven years, had another advantage over many of the other reporters. Although she was a national media personality, her home base was Austin. She was also a graduate of the University of Texas. The trial was a homecoming for her. Three years later, Tuma relinquished the national spotlight to assume a reporting position for KVUE-TV, the ABC affiliate in Austin.

Judge Wisser had permitted Court TV to set up a fixed television camera inside the court for continuous live coverage of the trial, on condition that the national cable outlet agree to stream free, live feeds to other TV news stations. Print media photographers were allowed to take still shots from their seats without flash or other extra lighting, but were not permitted to move about the room. All other cameras were banned from the courtroom.

Everyone complained about the lack of space. The room, one of the smallest in the courthouse annex, was of a size more commonly used by a city traffic court than a criminal district court. But the rest of the facilities were already booked with other trials, and this was the only space available. When a particularly interesting witness was scheduled in the Scaggs trial, the crowds overflowed into the hallway, with people lining the passageways, waiting for seating inside. If a spectator left, there was always another, ready to fill the vacant seat.

The size of the room made the environment seem somehow more intimate. The jury box, with seats for twelve, was less than a dozen feet from the attorneys' tables and the judge's bench. This tight squeeze raised concerns that jurors would overhear sidebar comments between the lawyers and the judge. Judge Wisser had to ask the bailiff to escort the jury to an adjoining room when even the most routine disputes erupted. There would be numerous such interruptions throughout the trial.

Even with the many glitches and delays, the long-awaited trial had finally begun. Despite all the news stories and shocking revelations that appeared in the papers and on local television in the previous two years, there had been no answers to the original question posed by the Austin daily. For all those involved and aware of the Penny Scaggs tragedy, the inexplicable *WHY?* was still deeply disturbing these many months later. The families and friends, the town, and the Texas evangelical community were hoping for answers at last.

Chapter 21

While the media show played outside, the legal drama began in the courtroom. Assistant District Attorney Bryan Case opened by damning Roger Scaggs for the murder of his wife, a mentor to hundreds of young women who sought to learn how to be Christian wives and mothers.

"You are going to realize before this trial is over that Penny Scaggs was a devoted woman—devoted to her faith, devoted to her family, and, yes, devoted to that man sitting there, her husband," Case said. "You will hear that Penny Scaggs was found lying in a pool of blood in her home while the vitality of her life was splashed on the piano she loved to play for others."

During his twenty-minute opening remarks, the prosecutor presented a concise, capsule account of the state's case. He told the jury they would hear evidence that Penny's DNA was found in tiny specks of blood on the murder weapons, on gloves worn by the killer, and in a spot of watery blood on the kitchen countertop. Case revealed that the state lab serologist believed she had also identified, in some of the samples, other DNA from an unknown person. He said the state would introduce evidence that the unknown DNA was not human DNA, but rather something akin to DNA.

The prosecutor told the jury that a plastic bag containing five rubber gloves, along with the murder weapons and missing jewelry, was discovered by police in a trash Dumpster behind Roger Scaggs's office. He said the defendant's fingerprints were found inside the gloves; Penny's blood was on the outside.

"Finally, the evidence will show that this defendant had a secret affair with Vanessa Ferguson, an office worker—a secretive affair that only became open, blatant, and notorious after Penny Scaggs's death." With that, Case took his seat at the prosecution table.

Then it was the defense's turn. Spectators in the courtroom, many of them local defense lawyers who had come solely to hear one of Roy Minton's famously eloquent opening statements, were about to be disappointed. Minton waived an opening statement and asked that the judge allow him to defer his remarks until the defense began its case.

For the rest of that day a steady stream of prosecution witnesses took the stand, including first responders from the Austin Fire Department, Austin Emergency Services, and the Austin Police Department, who had arrived at the murder scene after the 911 call. The witnesses described the discovery of the victim's body, attempts to revive her, and final pronouncement of death.

The police officers who questioned Roger Scaggs at the scene described their impressions of his behavior. APD officer Thomas Sweeney, whose patrol area included the Scaggs home, said Roger appeared to fake tears and distress each time he caught the officer watching him. Sweeney told the jury that Scaggs appeared calm and controlled until "he saw me watching. He would stop talking, look down and come up crying. It was like he realized he was supposed to be upset."

Six witnesses, all uniformed emergency and police personnel, underwent questioning and cross-examination that day.

At the end of the first day of testimony, the jurors, accompanied by a bailiff, filed out of the courtroom before the judge allowed the spectators to leave. Scaggs, in a gray suit, accompanied by his attorneys, followed the jurors out of the building, with reporters and cameramen trailing and shouting questions. Roger remained stoically silent, ignoring the questions thrown at him. Outside in the plaza, the TV cameras whirred and electronic media reporters took up the shouting. Roger Scaggs, his daughter Sarah, and attorneys Minton, Leavitt, and Burton cut through the crowd for the short walk to Minton's offices less than a block from the courthouse.

A few reporters caught up with some of the jurors at a bus stop in front of the main courthouse, where they were waiting in uncomfortable silence for the 'Dillo, a Metro Transit bus, to take them back to the parking lot at the municipal auditorium, a mile from the courthouse complex. It was the only parking lot for out-of-town reporters, too.

The 'Dillo (short for armadillo) was a service that provided free rides around town on a trolleylike vehicle most commonly used in amusement parks. It connected the University of Texas campus on the north with the municipal auditorium, where the parking lot was located. The circulator bus, which ran on rubber tires, was a replica of an old-style streetcar, but had a modern diesel engine. This strange trip would become a daily routine, with silent jurors riding along with reporters and courtroom spectators—each group studiously ignoring the other. The court had ordered the jurors not to talk to anyone, especially reporters; and they did not, even when forced together in this close space.

The second day of testimony opened with fireworks. The jury was kept in the adjoining deliberation room while defense and prosecution lawyers verbally flailed away at each other before Judge Wisser.

The subject of the heated argument was Bryan Case's

opening statement that samples of tissue and blood taken from fingernail clippings, a hair on the murder knife, and a small pool of diluted blood contained a mystery substance that was not human DNA. The defense had planned much of its case around DNA analysis from the Department of Public Safety crime lab that described these specimens as a mixture of DNA, including that of Penny Scaggs and an unknown subject.

The defense team angrily told the judge that the prosecution's opening statement was an "ambush."

Defense attorney Leavitt argued, "In March 1997, this court signed off on an order [of evidentiary discovery] that the state would give us all their scientific data from testing." He said from that date forward the state had assured the defense it was turning over *all* the reports on evidence tested as they became available.

"In those seven, eight, nine reports—every single one refers to this DNA evidence as a mixture of human DNA consisting of the victim's DNA and that of another individual," argued a visibly agitated Leavitt. "The reports further excluded Roger Scaggs as the other individual. The district attorney, in discussions before this court, has continually said investigators were trying to determine who this other DNA belonged to. For the first time in two and a half years the district attorney stood up yesterday and said they now have a chemist who is going to opine that, in fact, the mix is not even human DNA. This is nothing we have ever heard before. Judge, we have relied on their reports and on an order of this court, once we agreed to it, that we would get responsive, timely updates about the scientific information. We cannot defend our client without it.

"I am asking the court to make them give us information about who is going to testify to this, to give us the report so our experts have a chance to examine this new information.

"Without such an order, this is a surprise. It violates our client's due process rights," the attorney said. "If they don't have such a witness, then what the district attorney said before this jury is in error; and, Judge, we will have to ask for a mistrial because he has tainted this jury. You have cautioned this D.A. about not giving us timely information. This is exculpatory information. They are tricking this court. They are trying this case by ambush. We have at stake a man's freedom for the rest of his life. We respectfully ask the court to compel them to give us this information."

The prosecution responded that it had turned over all the data, and that the state's witnesses' interpretation of the reports was not subject to discovery or the court's order.

"Our experts can interpret the data and their experts can interpret the data any way they want. We do not have to share our experts' opinions with the defense in advance," Bryan Case argued.

"We have a right to the substance and the opinion that the state experts are going to testify to," Leavitt replied. "There is no such privilege. The state cannot claim that the opinions of its experts are a secret. If their experts are changing their opinions, we are entitled to know that, too. They are sandbagging us. I cannot get my client a fair trial if I am not privy to the evidence."

On the first day of the trial the lead defense attorney, Minton, had said, out of the jury's earshot, that the defense planned to use DNA evidence to show that somebody else was in the Scaggs house on the night of the murder. One of the main elements of the defense case was that DNA evidence from Penny's fingernail scrapings and clippings would prove that her husband was not the murderer.

"We have built part of our case relying on their evidence that there was someone else's DNA there," Minton added to the argument. He said the police had even eliminated Sarah Scaggs as a contributor of the mystery DNA. A prosecutor had secretly seized a water glass she had used at a grand jury appearance to get a sample of her DNA.

The prosecution's one-sentence comment that the mystery DNA was not DNA at all had struck the defense team like a thunderbolt, and blunted the defensive juggernaut the lawyers had planned, even before it could be launched.

In this vitriolic exchange, which took place outside the purview of the jury, the defense accused the state of unfairly flaunting the rules. The adversarial tone for the rest of the trial had been set. The good-old-boy bon mots of Minton and Leavitt toward their longtime associates from the D.A.'s office ended then and there.

The judge asked the prosecution to write down the type of information they had used to reach their conclusion about the "mystery" substance. After taking it under advisement, Judge Wisser determined it was not discoverable (required to be turned over to the defense), and sealed it in the court records.

The second day of testimony was a methodical presentation of the police and crime lab work that formed the nuts and bolts of the prosecution's case. Jurors heard how good police work had resulted in impounding the Dumpsters, and how detectives and crime-scene investigators had discovered the key evidence in a garbage bag. The prosecution skillfully completed the technical portion of its case, with testimony by criminalists and scientists from the state forensic lab that linked fingerprints and bloodstains in and on the latex gloves to the defendant.

On cross-examination of Sergeant Eells, the detective who had found the evidence in the Dumpster, Minton was able to plant the first seed of another defense strategy: Roger had been framed. He asked Eells if his superiors had informed him in advance that he "would likely" find evidence in the Dumpster, implying that someone other than Scaggs knew the incriminating bag was there. Eells emphatically denied the assertion with an adamant "No."

One of the prosecution's main witnesses from the day before returned on Thursday to have his testimony seriously challenged. He was Glenn Unnasch, fingerprint specialist from the DPS crime lab. Charles Burton grilled the expert on the rarity of finding and extracting readable fingerprints on latex gloves. Unnasch admitted that in his long career he had never testified about identifying print evidence on the inside of a glove. But he could not be forced to concede that he had never seen or heard of such evidence. Burton also raised the question of whether it was possible to tell which side of a glove had been worn next to the skin by looking at the roll at the wrist. Unnasch looked at several different latex gloves provided by the defense lawyer and had to admit that the direction and placement of the roll at the wrist was not consistent between brands.

Buddy Meyer strengthened the witness's testimony on redirect when he asked if other experts had also reviewed the print evidence from the latex gloves, and Unnasch confirmed that they had.

"As a regular procedure in a serious offense, other examiners at the lab review the evidence," Unnasch testified. "In this case two other experts examined these fingerprints." He acknowledged that finding such good prints on thin latex was unusual. He said it was such a noteworthy event that the print specialist from the Austin Police Department had made a special point to examine the evidence in person, rather than wait for the report.

Up till now the jury had been spared the grisly details of the murder. The presentations by police officers and lab specialists were mostly academic and businesslike. That ended with the next witness. Dr. Roberto Bayardo, Travis County medical examiner, brought with him to the witness stand a thick sheaf of horrific crime-scene and autopsy photographs. Under direct examination by the prosecution, he revealed the details of the physical injuries Penny Scaggs had suffered in the attack with the steel pipe and knife. One by one he described, with excruciating detail, the size and shape of each wound and how it had been inflicted.

As photos of the victim's battered and bloodied body were pinned on easel-mounted boards in clear view of both the jury and the audience in that tiny courtroom, the impact of this evidence was noticeable. Even some regular trial watchers averted their eyes from the images.

But the impact was greatest on those who knew the victim best. At first Penny's sisters, seated in the front row, just behind and to the right of the jury box, bravely confronted the horrible pictures. They had come to court obviously resolved to see the trial through, no matter what. But the cruelty of the story these photographs told about what had happened to their beloved older sister was too much. Slowly one sister, then another, bowed her head and would not look up again at the terrible sights.

Sarah Scaggs stared with a set jaw at the photographs representing the ordeal her mother had suffered in her last minutes of life.

When a large blowup of Penny's slashed throat was posted on the easel, Reverend Chu leaned forward and stared at it. He raised his hand to his mouth and curled his fingers into a tight fist, pressing it firmly against his lips.

Roger sat passively watching the jury's reaction and taking notes. He could not see the photographs from where he sat at the end of the defense counsels' table.

Dr. Bayardo described what his autopsy had found and what the wounds meant. He told the jury that Penny had been hit seven times with a heavy blunt instrument. Five of the blows had caused massive cranial damage, fracturing her skull; at least one other had fractured her jawbone. She had been stabbed eight times in the neck, chest, and back. In addition, there were blunt-force injuries to her extremities.

He testified that her death resulted from one of the blows to the skull with the pipe. In his opinion, any one of the blows to her skull could have killed her, although not necessarily immediately. He could not determine, from the autopsy, the sequence of the blows.

He said the killer had most likely come up behind Penny while she was playing the piano and struck the first mighty blow with the galvanized pipe to the back of her head. That blow, which fractured her skull, was so forceful it probably rendered her unconscious. Additional blows with the pipe were inflicted as she slumped from the bench to the floor. He added that the stab and slash wounds she received while she was on the floor were gratuitous, because she was already clinically dead from the beating. He knew this because there was very little bleeding from the knife wounds, indicating a lack of blood pressure when she was stabbed.

Roger tilted his head and peered quizzically at the jurors as the medical examiner explained the uselessness of the knife attack.

Buddy Meyer asked the doctor to answer the obvious: "Is this a homicide?"

"Oh, yes, no question about it," Dr. Bayardo responded.

As gruesome as this testimony was, the most damaging evidence the medical examiner presented was about the estimated time of the murder. He explained how he had calculated this from the liver temperature and barely digested food in Penny's stomach.

"Based on these tests, the victim died between 5:00 and 6:00 P.M. on March 6, 1996," Dr. Bayardo told the jury.

At the end of their direct examination of Dr. Bayardo, the state introduced a large color portrait of a smiling, vivacious-looking Penny Scaggs, taken when she was very much alive.

Roy Minton rose to begin cross-examination. He addressed the witness with a personal observation: "We've met before, Dr. Bayardo. We are both avid swimmers."

Minton's first question to Bayardo was, "What opportunity did Penny have to defend herself?" The doctor replied that she had no chance for self-defense from the onset of the attack.

The defense lawyer then grilled the doctor about the meaning of the superficial wounds to Penny's arms and legs. Minton asked if these wounds were not consistent with those suffered by a person trying to ward off further blows. Bayardo replied that they could be defensive-type wounds, but added, "These wounds could also have been inflicted while she was unconscious."

Then Minton challenged the medical examiner's time-of-death estimates. The measurements of time elapsed from death using liver temperature and digestion rates are "rough estimates, possibly erroneous and dubious at best," he said.

"I don't like to say so," the doctor responded.

Minton took the long, steel pipe from the evidence table and handed it to one of the jurors. The pipe, made more ugly and menacing by its adaptation as a murderous weapon, was passed around from one juror to another. Then the grandfatherly attorney, still questioning the medical examiner, did something that shocked trial watchers in the courtroom and television viewers across the country.

Minton described the rage it would have taken to mutilate the victim's body in the way the medical examiner had described.

He demonstrated the violence by bending over an imagined body lying on the floor in front of the jury box and swinging his arm as if holding a lead pipe, down and down and down again against the body. "How often do you ever see a beating as cruel and incredible as this?" Minton asked the doctor.

"Thanks to God, not many times, not too often," Bayardo said.

"In fifteen-thousand-plus times, not many times?" asked Minton. (The medical examiner had testified earlier that he had been involved in the investigation of that many violent death cases.)

"That is correct, not many times," Bayardo replied.

"It would take an incredible rage by some man to make that kind of wounds?" Minton asked.

"I won't disagree with that," Bayardo responded.

"Now, after Penny is already dead we start with the knife, correct?"

Minton picked up the knife and removed it from a protective cardboard sheath. He demonstrated how the killer made two small pricks with the knife to see if the victim reacted. When Bayardo repeatedly protested that he wasn't doing it right, Minton positioned himself in front of the jury box to try again.

"Well, they found Penny with her legs down here," he said, pointing under a nearby table that was serving as the piano, "and her body back there, on her left side." He turned to the prosecutors and asked if they agreed. "I don't want you to get up later and say Minton screwed that up."

He again bent down in the role of the killer leaning over the victim, with the knife in his hand.

"But somewhere like this, and *she* comes over—he— whoever it is, *the assailant*, and punches her down like this." He pushed the knife twice into the imaginary body. This time Dr. Bayardo said he was holding the knife correctly, with the back of the knife toward the victim's head.

Minton then began brandishing the weapon wildly as he acted out the brutal attack, slashing the victim's throat, plunging the knife into her neck, and stabbing her chest through and through.

The reenactment of violence was indelibly imprinted in the minds of all who saw it. Such courtroom antics are not uncommon. It was surprising here because it was such a stunning role reversal. Normally, it is a prosecuting attorney who shocks the jury with a demonstration of the violence of a crime. But in this case it was the defense depicting how savage the attack and how brutal the killer had been. Minton's strategy was apparently to argue, later, that the mild-mannered Roger could never have committed such a violent assault, and therefore could not have been the killer.

During the demonstrations by his lawyer, Roger appeared to grimace with each hypothetical blow. He looked tightly drawn and on the verge of tears. In the front-row seats of the courtroom, two of Penny's sisters wept silently as the horror of the scene was recreated.

It came as a relief to everyone in the courtroom when the

morning session ended and the jury was led out by the bailiff for lunch.

That afternoon, the prosecution called another medical examiner, Dr. Vincent DiMaio from San Antonio, who disagreed, in part, with some of Bayardo's conclusions, but reinforced others. Dr. DiMaio had formed his opinions based on photographs and a number of reports, including the autopsy and lab results. He had not seen the body himself or spoken to Dr. Bayardo about his findings.

DiMaio said he believed the first blow was delivered from behind, while Penny Scaggs was either standing or sitting at the piano. The killer swung the pipe with full force across her right cheek and fractured her jaw. "It would be very painful, but it would not render a person unconscious," he said.

He explained that the normal reaction would be to cringe or try to get away. But she couldn't get away; she was trapped. A horizontal bruise on her thigh looked like it might have been caused by her leg pressing into the edge of the piano. Dr. DiMaio believed, from the pattern of blood spatter, that she had raised her hand to protect herself. When the next blow came over her right ear, it may have also caused the bruising on her forearm.

The medical examiner admitted that he could not say which injuries came next. Some of the blows were "glancing," probably because she was either squirming or falling as she was hit. In his opinion, only one of the blows was fatal. That blow, which he called the "killer blow," was delivered "with such force that it caved in the base of the skull and drove the bone into the brain."

Bayardo had testified that the first blow likely rendered Penny unconscious and that any of the blows to the skull could have been fatal. He had based his opinion on the fact that he saw fractured skull through each of those wounds. However, DiMaio said the blow to the back of the head was so fierce that the fractures had radiated out over a large area of the skull.

The well-known Bexar County medical examiner, who had testified in a number of notorious criminal cases, supported Bayardo's opinion that time of death was around 6:00 P.M., a time when Roger Scaggs's own statement to police placed him at home. He said the fact that the digestion and liver temperature reinforced each other decreased the possibility of error. Pressed by the defense, he said death could "in theory" have occurred as early as 5:30 or as late as 6:30 P.M. He emphasized, though, that the one cup of undigested food in the stomach indicated to him that Penny had died within an hour of eating.

DiMaio hurt the defense case again when Minton asked him about the mystery DNA from the victim's nails. In what may have been his greatest contribution to the prosecution, the expert said that, in his opinion, it was probably caused by contamination, either at the time of collection or in the lab.

"It's not like TV," said DiMaio, indicating that DNA under fingernails is actually very rare. If it were DNA "you wouldn't get seven or eight positives. The most you would get is one or two."

The rest of the day was taken up with testimony by Austin Police Department crime-scene investigators, who identified evidence from the home and Dumpster they had gathered. They described the methods and procedures they followed to assure the evidence remained untainted from the time of collection through delivery to the lab.

On most mornings, when the hallways on the upper floors of the old courthouse annex were filled with jurors, witnesses, and trial watchers trying to get into the packed courtrooms, an odd ritual took place. The sheriff's deputies were also trying to get manacled lines of defendants from the jailhouse on the top floor of the building to courtrooms for plea hearings. With the brown-uniformed deputies leading and following, chains of orange-clad men—mostly unshaven, with scraggly hair—mingled with the human traffic jams in the hallway. Accused thieves, rapists, robbers, addicts, and wife-beaters, though well guarded, came too close for comfort to the panicky spectators. For several minutes there was a melee of motion, with deputies loudly asking everyone to make room to let their orange, human train pass; people pushing themselves against each other and the walls to make room when there was no place to go; then small *eeks* and squeals as the prisoners shuffled past, close enough to smell them. As quickly as this confused little dance began, it ended, as everyone made it to their destined courtroom.

Travis County needed a new courthouse badly, and one was being built adjoining the building where the Scaggs trial was held. The loud banging and high-pitched bleeps from warning horns of heavy equipment backing up frequently disturbed the testimony inside Judge Wisser's courtroom. At one point the trial was postponed for half a day, due to construction noise.

When testimony resumed the morning of October 30, the prosecution called Tom Pachalos, an APD fingerprint expert. He described the location and quality of fingerprints that were lifted at the Scaggs home the night of the murder. On cross-examination, the defense was able to introduce the first evidence of a possible intruder at the scene, by getting Pachalos to admit that a number of unidentified prints were taken from around the piano where Penny was killed. He was specifically grilled about fingerprints found a few inches above the floor, on the front left leg of the piano, not far from where Penny Scaggs's battered head and shoulders came to rest. The person who left these prints was never identified, even when the fingerprints were sent to the FBI for comparison.

In the midst of the forensic and expert testimony, a motive witness was called by the prosecution to tell the jury that Penny may have suspected Roger was having an affair. Mary Lowery was a registered nurse and longtime friend of Penny.

Lowery said she had mentioned the possibility of another woman at a luncheon meeting when Penny was distressed over Roger's frequent absences and his lack of attention during her extended illness. Minton ridiculed the testimony. He said in the first place it was hearsay, and nothing more than idle gossip between some women having lunch and surmising that one of their husbands might be having an affair. The judge disallowed the comment about an affair but let Ms. Lowery testify that Penny was disappointed in something her husband had "not" done.

The prosecution got permission to call witness Karen Lindell out of order, in consideration of her travel to Austin from Seattle, where she was now a forensic chemist in the Washington State crime lab. In her previous job at the Texas DPS lab, Lindell had been assigned to do some of the serology testing in the Scaggs case in 1997.

She had received, in an envelope, the necklace with a small heart that police had found on the kitchen counter the night of the murder. When she tested the flakes of blood that had dried and fallen to the bottom of the envelope, results showed only one DNA profile, consistent with Penny Scaggs. This would become important because the necklace was lying in the spot of watery blood that, when previously tested, had shown a possible mixture of DNA.

In March 1997, Lindell had also typed Roger's DNA from both blood and saliva. She compared his profile with tests on blood evidence that she was running and with the table of results in Donna Stanley's earlier report. Lindell testified that Roger Scaggs was definitely eliminated as a source of the DNA in any of the blood evidence tested in the case.

The final witness of the week was Mary Villarreal, the chemist with the Austin Police Department who served on a number of special teams, including the Crime Scene Search team. Her testimony covered the scientific methodology used to recover the hardest-to-find fingerprints, blood spots, and footprints.

The first week of the Scaggs murder trial ended late in the

day on Friday. Judge Wisser said he hoped the weekend would be "a well-deserved rest for members of the jury," and again admonished them not to read, view, or listen to anything about the trial during their days off. By then the trial was receiving heavy coverage in every media outlet in Austin.

As the jurors left the courtroom, eager to begin a break from the horrible things they had seen and heard, they encountered the jury from another murder trial. Those jurors had just delivered their verdict in the adjoining courtroom. After only fifteen minutes of deliberation, they had found David Martinez guilty of capital murder for the robbery, rape, and killing of twenty-four-year-old Kiersa Paul. The murder had taken place in July 1997, on the Barton Creek Greenbelt. Martinez had allegedly stabbed the young woman eight times and carved an X on her chest. Two weeks later the Martinez jury would sentence him to death.

Chapter 22

On Sunday morning, November 1, several thousand people were gathered in downtown Austin, shivering in the morning chill in flimsy, silken shorts and tank tops. They were waiting for the starting gun to begin Austin's 5K Race for the Cure. Running in the pack were Travis County judge Jon Wisser and Texas governor George W. Bush, both competing in the male fifty to fifty-four age group. In that category, Judge Wisser came in first, beating Governor Bush, who finished fifth, by three minutes and six seconds.

On Monday morning when he opened the second week of the Scaggs trial, Judge Wisser proudly announced his weekend win to the jury and courtroom. Attorney Minton rose to congratulate him and added that every morning before the trial, he was at Barton Springs pool, swimming laps.

The first and only witness of the day on November 2 was perhaps the most critical witness of the trial—paradoxically, for both the prosecution and the defense. Donna Stanley, a senior serologist at the state crime lab who did most of the blood and DNA testing on evidence in the case, had recently moved from the state job she held for eleven years to the Austin Police Department's crime lab.

She was key to the prosecution because she was the expert who had discovered Penny's blood on the outside of a latex glove in which Roger Scaggs's fingerprint was found. This was the single most important piece of evidence the state could present to tie Roger directly to the murder of his wife. She showed the jury the photograph that the fingerprint specialist had taken of the left index finger of glove number five, with the fingerprint on one side and her marks from where she had swabbed the blood on the other.

However, before the day was over, the highly trained serologist would testify that she had also found a mixture of DNA belonging to Penny Scaggs and an unidentified person on three items of evidence taken from the crime scene and the Dumpster.

At first she bolstered the state's case and was treated like a valued expert witness for the prosecution. Then she was morphed, under cross-examination, into a witness for the defense.

Stanley testified for most of the morning about how DNA tests are conducted, what safeguards are used to prevent contamination during testing, and the specific results of tests on the weapons that killed Penny, the blood on her purloined jewelry, and other vital blood samples.

The state's witness, who at the time of the trial had been hired by the Austin Police Department to assist in setting up an in-house forensic lab unit to support the crime-scene investigators, was placed in the unusual position of defending her lab work—not from defense lawyers, but from the prosecution side. This was the second time the jury witnessed a reversal of roles in the Scaggs trial, close on the heels of Minton acting out the murder. Now the defense was taking the unusual position of supporting the credentials and efficiency of a state expert, rather than trying to discredit the DNA evidence.

It was a difficult task, because the complexity of the relatively new forensic science was clearly baffling—not to mention boring—to almost everyone in the courtroom, including the jurors. Even the attorneys seemed a little less sure of their questions when dealing with the vocabulary of biochemistry. The use of multiple charts depicting DNA typing strips of Penny Scaggs and Roger Scaggs did little to make the mind-numbing explanations more comprehensible.

By the time the state passed the witness to defense lawyer Leavitt, the jury had clearly wearied of the technojargon. The defense directed the questioning to several pieces of evidence: a tiny hair the analyst said came from the knife, Penny's fingernail clippings, and a swab taken in a pool of water-diluted blood on the kitchen countertop. The lengthy and highly complex descriptions of DNA testing had put some spectators to sleep, including a snorer. Though some jurors were still taking notes, others were fidgeting.

"Let's cut to the chase," said Leavitt. "You do not believe, Ms. Stanley, that you contaminated any of the test runs in this case, do you?"

"I feel that I did not," she said.

"You spend most of your time in courtrooms defending what you have done and explaining that you did it without contaminating evidence?"

"I testify, a lot, yes," the forensic expert replied. "I do some crime-scene work, too. But the majority of my time is in the lab with evidence from police departments, the DPS, or Rangers."

"You found DNA under the nail clippings of Mrs. Scaggs that did not belong to Penny," Leavitt pressed.

"Yes, sir."

"On the nail from the right pinky, you found mixed DNA?" the defense lawyer asked.

"Yes," she answered again.

Stanley testified that the DNA mix strongly indicated Penny's type was in the samples, and a weaker sample of another type of DNA was present as well.

Leavitt got Stanley to agree that the weak showing of the second, unknown DNA could have been the result of how it was deposited on Penny's fingernails. Leavitt used a hypothetical case to illustrate why one type of DNA might be stronger than another in a mixed sample. He suggested that it could have come from a weak source, such as saliva. This could occur, for example, if the victim's fingers were briefly shoved into the assailant's mouth during a struggle. He asked Stanley if that scenario could produce a weaker trace of DNA than would appear in a blood specimen.

The witness, unenthusiastic about being led into the role of defending the alleged murderer, replied, "I guess so."

On redirect by prosecutor Bryan Case, Stanley told the jury about the different ways a sample could be contaminated. But she held fast to her position that she had not made a mistake in the lab.

"I do not think that happened with the tests in this case," Stanley said. "I don't believe it is possible that it happened at any time I was in the lab."

The mystery DNA had been firmly planted in the jurors' minds. Leavitt had used a state's witness to set the first brick in the wall of the defense.

On Tuesday, November 3, the prosecution set out to prove that Roger Scaggs had a powerful motive to kill his wife. The double life of Roger Scaggs became the subject of the prosecution's next line of witnesses, who were called to establish a motive for the murder.

Diana Coleman, whose family lived across the street from Penny and Roger, had known them for the dozen years they had been in Austin. During that time, she became one of Penny's closest friends, as well a reliable neighbor whenever she needed a favor. They exchanged keys and looked after each other's homes when either was away on a trip. It was from that close association that Diana had observed the slow but distinct changes in the marriage.

She spent most of the day under intense examination by the prosecution to map the relationship for jurors. She painted a verbal picture of the strong and successful Christian marriage, and of Penny sharing the secrets of its success with young women through her classes.

After almost ten years, which Mrs. Coleman described as the happiest of times, things began to change in her best friend's home. Roger was away a lot—mostly on business, everyone, including Penny, believed. But his behavior changed, too, as he spent more of his leisure time flying, sailing, or hunting. She told the jury how the always well-groomed businessman suddenly grew a shaggy beard and played out the biker role in dress and conduct.

Diana recalled how Penny tried harder than ever to be the perfect wife, even as she felt overwhelmed by changes beyond her control. Her reverence for Roger was evident in many ways. Photographs of Roger and of the couple together were tacked up all over the refrigerator and displayed throughout the home. Under one picture of her husband, Penny had lettered the words: "The Greatest Man I Know."

For his birthday in July 1995, the Colemans gave Roger a plaque engraved with the words: "The man who walks with God always gets to his destination." He displayed the gift in his home office. Penny liked the thought so much that she later calligraphied the statement on gifts she made for the other men in her family.

Diana went on to describe how the idyllic marriage began to falter in the last few months of 1995. For Penny, this was a time of illness and the beginning of doubts—about her husband, and herself as well.

Defense counsel Minton had objected each time Mrs. Coleman ventured to tell a story that verged on besmirching his client's character. As the sad tale continued to unfold late into the day, Minton rose to object forcefully again.

"This is all prejudicial to my client," the angry attorney told the judge. "I object to all of this line of questioning. It's hearsay, it's not relevant, it's prejudicial."

Prosecutor Case argued that the testimony was pertinent to the motive, saying that all these incidents were leading to the ultimate death of Penny Scaggs.

"When Penny began to question his conduct, his loyalty, and confronted him, he decided, I'm not going to take this anymore. He has a girlfriend; and when his wife gets sick, he won't even come home. He wants to get out of the marriage any way he can," the prosecutor said, pacing before the bench.

Equally impassioned, Minton rose to argue. "They are trying to show he's a bad guy in general. This is not admissible. So he had a girlfriend. They are trying to show that made him murder his wife."

Judge Wisser overruled the defense objection. "The relationship between the victim and the defendant is relevant," he said.

Diana Coleman's damning testimony continued almost without pause for questions by the prosecutor. She described the Christmas gift exchange and Roger's leaving the party for a shopping trip to a mall that had already closed. She told of Penny confiding that she did not believe Roger loved her anymore, and of comforting the grieving wife as the perfect marriage seemed to be disintegrating.

The defense objections intensified. Each time, the judge overruled them.

"We should soon be out of this minefield," the judge suggested. "How much more time do you need, Mr. Case?"

"I'm going to take this witness up to the murder, Your Honor," he replied.

Finally, late in the day, Case asked Diana Coleman about the night of the murder in her neighborhood. Her description was both tragic and frightening. She testified that she was the first person Roger called to tell he had found Penny in a pool of blood. Mrs. Coleman and a male neighbor arrived at the scene before anyone else. When Diana described Roger's conduct that night, bitterness edged her voice and she stared at the defendant as she spoke. Roger stared back for a few seconds and then turned his gaze to the jurors, as if trying to gauge their reaction to her testimony.

The lawyer asked Diana about the first time she saw Roger that evening.

"While we were knocking on the door, he walked up behind us, very softly and calmly," she said. She went on to testify about Roger's comments just before and after Penny's funeral, which continued to shock her and her husband.

The personal testimony of the people who had come in contact with Roger or Penny during the last year of her life, and the year of his strange behavioral changes, held the jury rapt after the tedium of the DNA presentations. Over the next two days the prosecution called a parade of witnesses from the couple's family, church, workplace, and neighborhood, including stores where they had shopped. Each witness added another dimension to the saga of the deteriorating marriage. The aberrant behavior of the business executive, church elder, and model husband was carefully related by witness after witness, to illustrate the gradual transformation of the man they had known into the stranger who could have committed this murder.

The intimate look into the life inside the home on Winter Park Road provided in the testimony of longtime friend and neighbor Diana Coleman seemed to carry considerable weight with the jurors. Several of them never stopped taking notes during the almost two days she was on the stand. And some were visibly jolted by her answer to the final question the prosecutor posed to her. For a moment in time it brought Penny back to life and established her as a real person, not just a murder victim.

Bryan Case asked, "Does this day have any particular significance to you, Mrs. Coleman?"

The witness's composure broke and her body convulsed.

"Yes, it does," she said, choking out the words between sobs. "Today would be Penny's fifty-seventh birthday."

Diana Coleman's testimony, reinforced and embellished by the stream of other motive and character witnesses, made a strong case that the wheels had been coming off the "perfect Christian marriage" at the time of Penny's death. But was this cumulative testimony enough to establish motive for murder?

The defense team thought not.

Chapter 23

The challenge for the defense was to convince the jury that while Roger had admittedly betrayed his marriage vows to Penny, there was nothing in the testimony of the people who knew them that rose to the level of motive for murder.

Defense attorney Charles Burton took the cross-examination of prosecution witness Diana Coleman, whose soft-spoken and often tearful description of the last days of Penny Scaggs had riveted the jury's attention.

In a staccato barrage of questions, he sought to dismantle each point the neighbor had made from the witness box in the previous two days.

On the topic of Roger's peculiar late night shopping trip, Burton got Coleman to admit that Roger had bought, "at a store in that mall," an angel band ring that Penny proudly showed off at Christmas.

"But not that night," Mrs. Coleman said.

"Didn't you call Detective Thompson about that incident because you wanted to raise suspicion about Roger?" Burton probed.

"I did not ask to go to the police station for questioning. I was called," she said. "I told them about Roger's shopping trip only because Penny was upset that he didn't come home until after midnight. It was obvious the mall was closed."

About the frequent sailing trips Roger took without Penny, the defense lawyer had Coleman admit that it was the wife's choice not to go because of the damage the wind and sun did to her fair skin. Burton listed a dozen trips that Penny had made with Roger piloting his own plane.

"Penny did tell me she had been in the plane," Diana Coleman acknowledged.

The defense lawyer pointed out that Penny took trips without Roger as well, citing the March 2-4, three-day women's retreat as an example.

"She asked me to keep an eye on Roger while she was gone," Mrs. Coleman added.

Penny's longtime neighbor and friend held firmly to her critical testimony under the battering cross-examination. While continuing to speak in a controlled, low voice, she was clearly hostile to the defense effort to excuse Roger's conduct.

Finally, the attorney asserted that "Penny was a strong-willed, controlling person."

Coleman responded, "She cared for the people close to her family, particularly Roger and Sarah."

The prosecution rounded out its case with testimony from members of the APD homicide investigative team that had cracked the case.

Sergeant David Carter, who had transferred to a supervisory position from Homicide a year after the murder, and other detectives from the homicide section, detailed how careful police work led to the trash bin behind Roger's office, and how the key evidence had been discovered in the impounded Dumpster.

The state introduced into evidence, but did not play, a videotape of Carter's initial interview with Roger. Carter read excerpts from the transcript to explain parts of the interview that had first tweaked his interest in the husband as a potential suspect rather than victim. He was on the stand for hours describing his activities before and after the interview on the night of the murder, as well as his perceptions of Roger Scaggs. The previous day the defense had tried to keep out much of Carter's personal impressions, but the judge ruled against them. At the end of the direct examination, some court watchers were surprised when the defense declined to cross-examine the sergeant at that time.

Employees from APS Systems and the parent company were subpoenaed to testify about how they learned of the office affair their boss was having with a young subordinate. Roger's conduct on the business trip when Penny was hospitalized a few months before the murder was detailed by a fellow worker, and his behavior after the funeral at the tanning and beauty salons was described by employees from those facilities.

The young women enrolled in Penny's courses on how to be a godly wife traced the day-by-day, hour-by-hour events leading up to the fatal events of March 6, 1996.

Roger's own minister described how the revelation of a long-term extramarital affair by one of the church's lay leaders had tested the very foundation of the congregation's faith. Coming as it did on top of the murder accusation, the disclosure of the affair became the main point of contention between Roger and his fellow elders. He was never directly confronted by the church about his innocence or guilt in the homicide.

Amid all the evidence and factual testimony, Roger's behavior before and after the murder was an underlying theme of the prosecution. Patty Adams, former sales manager at APS Systems, was asked to describe another example of what the prosecutor contended was Roger's callous behavior. The incident occurred shortly after he had been charged with the murder. Since APS had retained Roger as a consultant, he still worked with the same people at the company, although he no longer had an office there.

Patty Adams explained, "He was still my boss. Jackie [Fife] and I would meet him off-site, usually for lunch." On one such occasion, two or three weeks after the murder, the women were waiting at a Mexican restaurant.

"When Roger came in he made a joke about Penny's murder," Patty recalled. "I said, 'How can you joke about this? There's no humor here.' Then Roger said—and I will remember this as long as I live—'If you don't see the humor of it, it will drive you crazy.' "

Such inappropriate conduct attributed to Roger by numerous witnesses testifying to different aspects of the case added heavily to the impression the jurors were forming about the man they were there to try. His own behavior, described in these vivid verbal snapshots throughout the trial, was slowly eroding his positive image.

But a ruined reputation was not the main concern for the defense. Preventing their client from spending the rest of his life in prison was a far greater challenge. The prosecution had placed dozens of pieces of murder-scene evidence, crime-lab reports, and painful-to-look-at photographs before the jury, to be reviewed over and over again.

On the ninth day of the trial, the prosecution rested, after calling Penny's sister Marilyn Muecke as their last witness. The state's two-man team had expertly presented damaging testimony from more than thirty credible and sympathetic witnesses. Almost three hundred items and photographs had been numbered and placed into evidence. Most critical, the prosecution had shown the jury the heavy pipe and knife, along with the latex gloves that had covered the hands that wielded them—the damning gloves with the victim's blood on the outside and the defendant's fingerprints inside.

The prosecution's case had effectively wiped away Roger Scaggs's facade of respectable business leader, devout Christian and church elder, and bereft, loving husband of a murder victim. Witnesses testified, instead, that the defendant was a man capable of cruel neglect of a seriously ill wife; a man in midlife who indulged in pricey possessions for himself—a fast car, airplane, motorcycle, and sailboat— while keeping his wife on a frugal budget. But perhaps most dastardly of all by Texas family-value standards, Roger was depicted as a man who had brazenly pursued an illicit affair with a woman young enough to be his daughter, a man who betrayed the sacred obligations of a Christian marriage and scorned a devoted wife of thirty-five years for self-gratification.

At the close of the state's case, the defense team stared up the sheer rock walls of the mountain of evidence the prosecution had erected. The team would have to climb hard to keep their client out of prison. The court's rulings on their objections to vilifying testimony had not gone their way; but one of the best defense teams ever assembled in Austin had the experience, skill, and resources to scale that mountain. At midpoint in the trial no knowledgeable local court watcher doubted that Roger Scaggs could still walk free.

*T*he prosecution rested its case at 11:40 A.M. on Friday, November 6. But before they did, the jurors were sent out one more time while the lawyers argued out of their earshot.

The defense immediately moved for a mistrial for prosecutorial misconduct. They accused the prosecution of deliberately leading the last witness, Penny's sister Marilyn, to recount Roger's graveside statement to the family that he had to hire an attorney, even before he was considered a suspect in his wife's death.

She had described talking to Roger about lawyers the week after the funeral. In one of those conversations, Roger said someone had told him, "If you're not guilty you hire somebody who knows their way around the hill, and if you're guilty you hire Roy Minton." Although the jury never heard this inflammatory statement, Minton objected to any reference to Roger needing a lawyer.

The judge denied the motion for mistrial, but chided the prosecutors that a previous court order had specifically barred them from presenting such testimony. He agreed to give a jury instruction to ignore all of Marilyn's testimony on the subject of Roger retaining counsel.

Then Randy Leavitt made a routine motion for a directed verdict of not guilty on the grounds that the state had failed to make its case against Roger. The judge denied that motion as well.

Finally, the defense moved again for a mistrial based on ADA Case's opening statement that some DNA found at the scene had proven to be nonhuman. The defense claimed that the statement was deliberately misleading because the state had not shown any evidence that the material found on Penny's fingernails was "not DNA." Leavitt argued that the statement was intended to prevent the defense from making its case that the DNA was from an unidentified person—possibly her real killer. The judge ruled that Case's opening remark did not rise to the level of error that required a mistrial.

After these arguments, the jury was brought back into the courtroom. With only about fifteen minutes left before the noon hour, the defense began its case in chief. And again they did not make an opening argument, which Minton had indicated they might do when he waived his statement at the beginning of the trial.

Instead they began by recalling a leading state's witness to bolster the defense claim that the mystery DNA found at the murder scene was possibly that of the real killer and not Roger. Although Donna Stanley had already been exhaustively cross-examined about the DNA evidence, the defense needed to establish a firm basis for the presence of an intruder in the Scaggs home the night of the murder.

Stanley was asked to restate her testimony on her conclusions that an unknown person's DNA was present in the sample taken from the nail clippings and the small pool of watered-down blood on the kitchen counter. She repeated that additional tests had definitely eliminated Roger's DNA from the samples.

When court resumed after lunch, the defense called Dr. Edward Thomas Blake, a forensic serologist from Oakland, California, who was widely published on the subject of DNA evidence. He had reviewed Donna Stanley's report on the DNA testing she had done at DPS, as well as the results of the LabCorp retesting. He had examined the work done on the Dumpster evidence, and testing on the hair from the knife, the fingernail clippings, and samples from the kitchen counter.

Attorney Leavitt asked Dr. Blake to go into a very detailed description of the DNA analysis process and directly apply his scientific explanation to the evidence in this case. Once again, many jury members became restless during this complicated scientific exchange, but some tried to follow along, taking careful notes.

Describing Stanley's testing as "pretty straightforward," Dr. Blake testified that there were detectable traces of a second DNA mixed with Penny's DNA in some of the samples. He said, in his interpretation, the retesting done at LabCorp "further supports the work done by Ms. Stanley."

Bryan Case took the cross-examination. He immediately established that Dr. Blake was being paid $550 an hour as an expert defense witness. On cross, Dr. Blake contended that the reason for the weak showing of the mystery DNA in the tests was possibly because it came from Penny's fingers being jammed into the assailant's mouth during a struggle.

"I don't think most people go around putting their hands in other people's mouths," Case stated, wryly. "If she had suffered a severe blow to the head with a pipe, how could she get her fingers into the assailant's mouth?"

"I would think that if she had been incapacitated by the first blow, the biology would have had to get under her nails before the attack," said Blake. He suggested several ways that could have happened, including during making love or a violent struggle, adding that the nail samples certainly seemed to be from saliva.

The expert witness reiterated that he had examined Donna Stanley's work notes and there was no indication that anything had been done that could have caused the specimens to be contaminated.

"You are aware, aren't you," said the prosecutor, "that the reason LabCorp entered into this situation is because a supervisor at DPS looked at the results and thought they might be contaminated from the positive control?"

"Yes, there is a note here that suggests that," Dr. Blake replied. "I just saw it for the first time a couple of days ago."

When this document came up, Leavitt again asked for the case against Roger to be dismissed or a new trial granted on the grounds of prosecutorial misconduct. Testimony had ended for the week, and the jury was excused until Monday morning, with apologies from Judge Wisser for the trial lasting longer than he had predicted.

An angry argument between the adversaries ensued. Leavitt produced the note Blake had referred to during questioning. It was a LabCorp submittal sheet that had apparently accompanied the request for retesting samples in May 1997. On the sheet, DPS Serology manager Irma Rios had indicated her growing concern that there was possible contamination in the positive control of the original tests done at the Texas lab.

"I have all the other LabCorp submission sheets except the one that mentions contamination," said Leavitt. "It's an obvious attempt on the state's part not to give it to us because they knew the value it might be to the defense, given the time to work with it. We don't have that time now. It is something I have continuously brought up to the court. We get no relief. We're finding stuff—not from them—they *still* haven't given it to me. The Department of Public Safety made a complete copy of that file and gave it to the D.A.'s office. DPS assumed we had it." Leavitt claimed he first became aware of it when he saw it in Karen Lindell's file when she was on the stand, several days earlier.

Buddy Meyer calmly responded. "To the best of our knowledge we have provided the defense with all this material." Meyer told the judge he and Leavitt had gone to DPS together to talk to the people who did the work and reported the results. "There was never an attempt to hide anything," he said.

In an unusual move, Leavitt then called prosecutor Bryan Case to the stand. Case looked at the submittal form in question and testified that he would have given the defense anything he received that said LabCorp on it.

"Is it in your file right now?" asked Leavitt.

Case, who said he would have to look, pulled from his briefcase a manila envelope from LabCorp and a file folder from DPS. "I made you a copy of the entire file that Lab-Corp sent me," he said, indicating the papers in the envelope. Case sat on the stand, grimacing and sighing as he flipped through the pages of the LabCorp file, the sounds amplified by the microphone in front of him. When he didn't find the form in that stack of papers, Leavitt showed him the file from DPS, where there were two copies of the submittal sheet in question.

"You never gave that to me, did you?"

"I did not," said Case.

"Have you ever mentioned to me—*ever*—that you all thought there was contamination with the DPS work done in this case?" Leavitt asked.

"I don't think so," Case said.

Then Leavitt took the stand himself, to preserve the record, in the event of an appeal.

"In March 1997, the court ordered all the handwritten notes, reports, and worksheets on the DNA evidence turned over to the defense," he testified. "Subsequently, [the state] got these additional lab reports, and prior to this trial had not turned them over to us. At no time, in two and a half years, have they ever suggested there were problems with the testing." To the contrary, Leavitt said, the state had represented the results as a mixture of DNA and said they were testing a series of people to try to find an explanation for it.

Case rose to explain that although he had looked at the DPS file, the first few pages said "DPS" at the top and he never realized there was a LabCorp form in it.

Leavitt said that stretched credulity. He pointed out that during the prosecution's opening statement, when Case referred to a non-DNA substance, "he saw our surprise."

Case countered by stating, "While I did not want to reveal my theory, I made it clear at that time that I thought it was in the papers you had." I said, "It is in the reports. The words are there. Read it. Look in the reports—it's there!"

Leavitt responded that he had looked repeatedly and it was not there.

"We have been harmed, Judge," said Leavitt. He gave a list of remedies the defense was requesting, in descending order: dismissal of charges against Roger Scaggs, short of that a mistrial, and short of that exclusion of all LabCorp testimony and evidence.

The judge examined the LabCorp paper in question. He implied that the defense team thought they were entitled to more discovery than they were because the attorneys were primarily accustomed to litigating civil cases.

Judge Wisser said that under Texas criminal law, the defense was entitled only to state's evidence that might clear a defendant or mitigate guilt. He did not think this qualified as mitigation since the state was trying to impeach its own witness's testimony. He noted that the state had turned over "reams and reams, beyond any case I have ever seen."

Minton protested that the judge was reversing his own court order, which said the state would give the defense everything.

Wisser replied that he had gone along with an agreement between the two sides, which the law itself did not require.

When the state and defense no longer agreed, he had the right to make his ruling more specific, based on the law.

"With the volume of discovery and the number of expert witnesses, how one piece of paper could change the strategy of the defense escapes me," he said.

Leavitt then requested that if the judge was not going to declare a mistrial, the defense should be granted a one-month delay in order to obtain further DNA tests, in light of the "surprise" evidence.

"I'll delay the trial until 8:45 Monday morning," Judge Wisser said, "and take this under advisement over the weekend."

On Monday morning, November 9, Judge Wisser gaveled the court to order for the tenth day of the trial, and promptly overruled all the defense motions from the previous Friday.

"The state does not have to reveal its strategy. There has been no violation," the judge opined. "Therefore, I deny the defense request for mistrial and I deny the motion for continuance. The motion to restrict the contamination evidence is also denied."

Roger Scaggs's attorneys did not pause to lick their wounds, which were considerable. The mystery DNA was a linchpin of their strategy for convincing the jury that a stranger, and not Roger, had committed the murder. Their job now was to dismantle the rest of the prosecution's case, which at this point in the trial looked like it was leading to an almost certain conviction. Key witnesses would have to be discredited in order to mitigate what appeared to be irrefutable physical evidence. And while it was impossible to restore Roger's image as a paragon of civic or domestic virtue, it was important that the jury be made to doubt that the meek, aging man sitting before them in the dock was capable of so brutal a crime.

Before launching its attack on the state's investigators, defense lawyer Charles Burton called a character witness to the stand, to remove some of the vile taste left about Roger by former associates and family members.

Dr. Steve Muller, a longtime friend, was the person Roger had called for support the night of the murder. Muller said that when he and his wife Pat first arrived that night, he saw a grieving Roger standing on the front walkway. "He was crying and distraught." This testimony rebutted the police officers and others who said Roger had appeared to be either feigning grief or showing no emotion over his wife's murder. Muller also described how tormented Roger appeared when he told his daughter of Penny's death.

Roger had stayed with the Mullers for several days after the murder, until police released his house to him. Dr. Muller said during that time Roger's expressions of grief were appropriate for some types of people. "He is a very methodical person. Everyone expresses grief in a different way. Some are more outward, others more withdrawn or in denial."

The state was not going to budge on its contention that Roger's behavior immediately after the murder was inappropriate. Bryan Case vigorously challenged Dr. Muller's observations. He first established that the doctor was a personal friend of Roger's who had attended the same church and shared flying and other activities with him. Nevertheless, Dr. Muller admitted that he did not know about Roger's affair until sometime after the murder.

"Did you know that he used his daughter to facilitate the affair?" Case asked.

"No," Muller said.

Case probed further. "Did you know that he made Sarah let him and his lover use her duplex to conduct the affair?"

Again the answer was no.

"Would that change your mind about him?" Case drilled.

Still, the answer was no.

Next, lead counsel Minton recalled the state's star witness, police sergeant David Carter. The videotape of his long interview with Roger was dissected and closely examined. This was the first and only time the jury would hear Roger giving his own version of what happened the night of the murder. The attorney played more than two hours of the tape, stopping to question Carter and sometimes replaying a section several times to underscore a point.

Minton pointed out that the detective himself had urged Roger to speculate on what had happened, and that Roger had not just spontaneously offered his opinion about how the murder occurred.

"What I found unusual was that a person would give such a specific response," Sergeant Carter said.

The defense lawyer pounded at Carter's contention that the statements Roger made during the taped interview were the source of his suspicion, saying it appeared only that Roger was trying to be cooperative and helpful.

"It was not any single thing he said that concerned me," Carter answered. "It raised a question in my mind. Clearly he was methodical and organized. It was odd to me that he would not be wearing a belt. There was no rush to judgment based on this interview alone. I didn't know at the time that the unusual scenario about how the murder was carried out was close to how it actually happened."

Minton then began a line of intense questioning about what had led Carter to conclude that the Dumpsters behind Roger Scaggs's offices should be impounded. The veteran investigator did not budge from his earlier testimony that it was completely his own decision; there had been no tip or suggestion from anyone else that the Dumpsters be searched. The former homicide detective was polite in his responses, but doggedly stayed with his original testimony.

Fingerprint evidence, not DNA, had been the prosecution's primary link between Roger and the murder, and the defense next brought an expert witness to attempt a rebuttal. Claude Stephens, a former FBI fingerprint instructor and top investigator in the special crimes unit of the Amarillo Sheriff's Department, was called to discuss the unusual fingerprints found in the latex gloves. He had worked in fingerprints for more than twenty years and testified in 320 criminal trials. Stephens was the director of security for a hospital association at the time of the trial. Before addressing the gloves, attorney Burton led him through fingerprint evidence on each piece analyzed by the Texas state crime lab.

Stephens agreed that the fingerprints in the gloves belonged to Roger, but disputed that they were used during the crime.

"Would a latex glove worn by a person wielding a pipe or knife leave readable fingerprints?" Burton asked.

"It is less likely that this type of glove could yield prints because these heavy activities—gripping and twisting—would greatly distort or wipe out any detail," said Stephens. "I have never been able to get a suitable fingerprint from a latex glove."

The expert testified that his review of the police record on the case revealed that a fingerprint found in the kitchen was suitable for comparison but had not been identified. He also noted that prints suitable for comparison, but of unknown subjects, had been lifted from the crime scene low on the left leg of the piano and on the piano bench and lid.

"I was surprised that other areas of the house were not processed for fingerprints," he testified. "There were no latent prints taken at points of entry or exits—not at the front, back, or garage of the house."

On cross-examination by ADA Meyer, the out-of-town expert could not be shaken in his opinion that it was highly unlikely that readable prints could be taken from latex gloves that had been used in an extreme activity like pounding with a pipe or repeated stabbing with a knife. He did, however, admit that prints on the piano could have been put there sometime before the night of the murder.

Deborah Draper, a former vice president for production at APS Systems, testified that she had helped Roger prepare for the board meeting the day of the murder. She bolstered the idea that although Roger's reaction to the tragedy may have seemed unusual or unnatural to some, it was characteristic of his personality in general.

"Roger was always methodical, cool, and calm, almost scientific in his approach to problem-solving," she said.

Barney Lowe, operations manager at the Lockhart Airport, told the jury that Roger always wore latex gloves when he cleaned his plane and that everyone at the airport took note of it. He said nobody else used gloves like those while working on their aircraft. Lowe, who had also given Roger flight instruction, said the executive sometimes drove down to Lockhart just to work around his plane. He always brought latex gloves for the job.

Detective Thompson was called as a defense witness in another unusual reversal of roles for a murder case. Leavitt had him go over the progress of the entire investigation in detail, before it became obvious why the defense had called the lead detective in the case against their client.

"You concluded the crime was committed by someone with rage, hate, and extreme anger?" Leavitt asked.

"Yes. Because of the postmortem stabbing," the twenty-four-year veteran police officer answered.

The defense lawyer led the officer to agree that none of the evidence gathered at the house linked Roger Scaggs to the killing of his wife. He then turned to the evidence from the Dumpster.

"You received tips from Crime Stoppers and other anonymous calls and letters, did you not?" the attorney asked.

The detective described the tips received from all sources.

"You also received another call about the Dumpsters, didn't you?" Leavitt snapped.

"Never," the detective shot back.

"This is the only time you ever sent a crime-scene team to search a Dumpster, isn't it?"

"Yes," Thompson said.

"You never had the prints from the piano leg compared against anyone in this case, did you?" Leavitt continued.

The defense lawyer then ran through a litany of other finger-prints that had been lifted but never matched to anyone.

"You videotaped the funeral, too?" Leavitt appeared to be opening a new line of questioning, to make the detective admit that the police were looking for another suspect who might have attended the funeral.

The last questions caused the prosecution attorneys to rise in protest, and the jury was excused while the lawyers approached the bench. During the ensuing argument, the prosecutor asked Thompson about law enforcement efforts to locate the alleged girlfriend, who had disappeared the year before and was still missing. Thompson recounted de-tails of the yearlong search to find her.

Prosecutors told the judge they wanted to question the de-tective about the search for the girlfriend in front of the jury to illustrate how thorough the investigation had been. The defense objected on the grounds that it would make it ap-pear that Roger or the defense had something to do with her leaving town.

"The state is not going to contend that the defense is se-creting this witness," the judge said, allowing the question to be raised on cross.

Meyer had Thompson describe the futile, exhaustive search for Vanessa Ferguson, using all law enforcement re-sources. The prosecutor then asked if the homicide detec-tives had any outside information that caused them to impound and search the Dumpster.

"Detective Carter came to me with that idea," Thompson answered. "I thought, 'Why?' at the time, but I value this detective's knowledge and experience. I got permission and secured the Dumpster."

While the defense had questioned the legitimacy of the Dumpster find, they took the opposite approach when it came to evidence found on the victim's body. Bob Davis, the medical examiner's representative at the crime scene, testi-fied that he had properly handled and bagged the victim's hands at the scene to assure they did not come in contact with any contaminants. Homicide detective John Hunt verified that the hands were bagged when the body arrived at the morgue and were not exposed to contamination before the clippings were taken during the autopsy. Once again Roger's lawyers were in the position of defending the police forensic work when it applied to the DNA evidence, which they claimed was exculpatory to their client.

Chapter 24

The defense attorneys badly needed to restore some part of Roger's image, if not as a perfect man, at least as a person incapable of committing such a violent attack on his wife of thirty-five years. In rapid order they called eight witnesses, who either had worked with Roger, were close friends of Roger and Penny, or could directly refute previous state testimony.

Ken Shifrin and Jack Murphy, who had both directly supervised and worked with Roger at APS Group, gave him the highest commendations. Murphy, now retired, was the founder and former chairman of the board of APS. Both men said Roger was incapable of such violence and they would never believe he was the killer.

Longtime friends Theresa Neal, Bill and Nancy Snead, Robert and Phyllis Culp, and Dr. Jacqueline Jeffery testified that they had never seen Roger angry and had certainly never witnessed him committing an act of violence toward Penny or anyone else. They stated that in their long associations with the couple, they had seen only a loving and caring marriage. All these defense witnesses agreed that Roger was not capable of committing an act as violent as this murder.

Steve Holyfield, a victim's services counselor for the Austin Police Department, also testified for the defense. On the night of the murder he had been called to the scene to assist the family of the victim. He said Roger was crying at times and at other times appeared to be calm. He testified it was hard to judge what was going on with relatives of a victim at a murder scene because different people react differently when first confronted with this kind of violence in their lives. On cross-examination Holyfield admitted it was very unusual for him to be called to counsel the suspect in a murder. However, on that night, he noted, Roger was a surviving family member, not a suspect.

A doctor and nurse who treated Penny during the serious illness several months before her murder were called to the stand to refute claims that she had been abandoned by an uncaring husband during that episode. Dr. Robert Groves testified that Penny had refused several times to stay at the hospital for treatment before she finally relented. Registered nurse Vanessa Nunnelly said it was Roger who finally talked Penny into being admitted.

Jackie Fife, who had replaced Roger as APS Systems president, confirmed that he left the office at 5:30 P.M. on March 6, 1996, to have dinner with his wife. Fife and Scaggs were both working on the board presentation. From her office, which was adjacent to Roger's, she heard him talking on the phone. He said, "Okay, I'll just come home for dinner then, but I've got to come back." Then he stuck his head in Jackie's office and told her he had to run home for dinner. She said he was pleasant, smiling.

It was 5:30 P.M. She took note of the time because she had a standing appointment for 6:00 P.M. and wanted to know if she needed to cancel it. But Roger told her to go ahead, that he would finish the report himself. A minute or so later she saw him drive away. She said when she came to work the next morning, she found the board presentation in her locked office. Roger was one of the few people in the company who had that key.

She also testified that the charges against Roger had been devastating for the company.

"The days after he was put in jail were frantic," she said. "A *Wall Street Journal* reporter was sitting in our office; clients who had heard the rumors were calling. There was unbelievable turmoil."

She told the jury that in the years she had worked directly for Roger she found him to be completely honest, upstanding, and of "great" integrity. Even under business pressure she had seen "no anger, no violence—a person with a very even temper, who would walk away from a conflict."

Under cross-examination by attorney Case, Ms. Fife said that Penny also shared the admiration of clients because she frequently called on them with Roger. "They were presented as the model couple," she said.

Two other defense witnesses were called to verify Roger's statements about the time frame and his whereabouts on the night Penny was murdered. They were Michael Shannon, the computer technician for APS Group, who had checked Roger's computer usage at the request of police; and Patty Edling, one of the last people to talk to Penny on the day she died.

Patty Edling had spoken by telephone with Penny that afternoon, and according to her, Penny seemed fine. Although they had known each other only six or seven weeks, Edling did not believe Penny could have continued teaching her classes if anything had been awry in the marriage. During their conversation, Penny told her that Roger was under a lot of pressure preparing for an important board meeting, and asked her to pray for him.

"What did you do after you hung up the phone?" defense lawyer Burton asked.

"I prayed for Roger," she said.

At 5:00 P.M. on November 11, the twelfth day of the trial, the defense rested its case.

* * *

Shawn Constant, who had been an earlier witness for the state, was the prosecution's first rebuttal witness. She had taken two of Penny's Creative Counterpart courses, one in the fall of 1995 and the second in the spring of 1996. Penny had not completed that nine-week course at the time of her death, and was scheduled to teach another session in her home on the evening of March 7, the day after her murder. Mrs. Constant and a member of Penny's Sunday school class, Karen Lemens, who was also enrolled in that last course, were called to testify about the few days leading up to Penny's murder, including the weekend church group retreat to Lake Travis. The women told of Penny's unusual behavior on the rushed trip back to Austin.

Lemens answered questions about the last session of Penny's seminar, the Thursday before she was killed. She said a group of women had been seated on the floor near the piano for part of the meeting, and that she herself had handled one of Penny's jewelry boxes.

Neighbor Diana Coleman was recalled by the prosecution and testified that Penny would never have willingly agreed to give Roger a divorce because it would have been against her basic belief system and destroyed her ministry to young women. To Penny, marriage was a union of two people made by God and could never be broken, she said.

The state then called Meghan Clement, assistant director of Laboratory Corporation of America (LabCorp) of Research Park, North Carolina. She was called to refute the main defense contention that the mystery DNA found at the murder scene and under the victim's fingernails belonged to an intruder. She testified that eight different genetic tests were conducted on DNA evidence submitted by the Texas crime lab for retesting. Samples collected from the fingernails and the kitchen counter showed positive results matching Penny Scaggs's DNA, according to Clement.

"We found absolutely no additional person, only a single profile in the tests," she said.

Other tests she conducted showed "definite product contamination" from the test reagents. According to Clement, any tests originally run with those reagents could not be relied upon, because retesting "clearly indicates contamination of those chemicals."

When questioned about additional tests that did *not* show that type of contamination, she said that in those instances the residual DNA left over from the work done at the Texas lab was either so degraded or in such minute amounts that an accurate reading was no longer possible.

The jury had now been presented with dueling experts. Two highly qualified experts had offered diametrically opposed analyses of the original test data.

On cross, Randy Leavitt asked Clement if she was aware that Dr. Blake, a defense witness who had talked to Donna Stanley and reviewed her work, did not believe her tests were contaminated. She said she was not aware of his testimony.

Leavitt was standing at the witness box, leafing through Clement's file. He was stern when he asked her, "In all of these reports, did you ever tell me, tell Roger Scaggs, that you believed there was contamination? Did you ever write those words?"

"No, sir. We document that there is additional activity, but—"

"Were you trying to hide something in these reports?" he asked.

"No, sir." Clement was composed and undaunted. "The report is to document the results we obtained from the testing we were requested to do, and to draw conclusions," she said. "We were never requested to completely review the case file and give an opinion on that."

"You weren't asked to do that until this morning. Is that correct?" asked Leavitt.

"That's correct," she said.

When he passed the witness, the prosecutor asked, "Ms. Clement, how long does it take to look at photographs like I showed you this morning and render an opinion on what alleles [DNA markers] show up and what the reagent blank shows? How long does that take?"

"Ten or fifteen minutes—at most," she said. "Really, only a couple of minutes to look at it, maybe write something down and make comparisons." She repeated her conclusion about contamination and was dismissed.

The judge said, "Thank you and good luck," as she left the witness stand.

Irma Rios, supervisor of Serology at the state testing lab, was called to bolster Clement's testimony that the mystery DNA resulted from contamination during testing. She explained why she had questioned the results from the beginning, when she did the first administrative review of the October 1996 report. Her opinion was unequivocal, and unchanged, as she described why she sent the samples to Lab-Corp in the first place. "We knew there was contamination," she said. "That was never a question. We were trying to find out where it was coming from."

Given that statement, Ms. Rios was asked how it could be that other chemists in the unit had agreed with Donna Stanley's report. Rios said they agreed with the *results* of the report—which included the fact that some of the calls were "inconclusive." For the same reason, she herself stood by the report to that day.

In surrebuttal, the defense called Donna Stanley, the serologist who had conducted the initial DNA tests while she was still at the state lab. She said that nothing she had heard in testimony from her former supervisor at DPS or from Meghan Clement at LabCorp had changed her opinion. She still believed the mystery DNA belonged to a second, unidentified person. Based on the way she conducted the tests, she said once again that she did not believe it was possible for the reagent to have become contaminated.

The prosecution next called Penny's sister, Carolyn Pittenger, to address the issue of Roger Scaggs's capacity for violence. She related the incident the family had witnessed during the mountain vacation the sisters and their husbands shared with Roger, Penny, and Sarah in 1989. Mrs. Pittenger somberly recounted how frightened the family felt that Roger was going to strike Penny because she had forgotten to pack one of his favorite bath towels.

She was asked to address Roger's clothing preferences. Previously, Sergeant Carter had testified how odd it seemed to him that a man like Roger was not wearing a belt in his jeans, the night of the murder. He thought it was an indication that he had dressed in a hurry. Carolyn confirmed that Roger was a very conscientious dresser and that a belt would be part of his normal attire, even with blue jeans. In fact, she said, members of the family would give him special belt buckles for birthdays and other occasions.

While the sister was testifying, defense lawyer Roy Minton had gone back to confer with Sarah. She appeared very animated and was talking excitedly with her hands as she explained something to her father's attorney.

On cross, Minton approached Carolyn and showed her four photographs of Roger in different situations, wearing blue jeans without a belt.

Then he questioned the sister's memory of the fight about the towel. Sarah, who had been on the cot in her parents' room the whole time, had a very different and less disturbing recollection of the scene. In her version, it sounded more like two people who had gotten on each other's nerves after days of living in close quarters. However, the sister stuck to her version of events, and claimed that Sarah had not been involved.

Pat Muller, wife of Dr. Muller, who had testified that he did not believe Roger was capable of committing the murder, was called by the state to describe Roger's behavior during the four days he stayed with them while police had his house sealed. She told of Roger's conversation about not wanting to attend the graveside services of his wife and his desire to buy just one burial plot. Pat Muller was the last witness in the guilt phase of the trial.

Before the jurors were dismissed for the evening, Judge Wisser told them that the summations of the case would begin at 9:00 A.M. the following morning. He said the trial had reached the stage where they would be sequestered for deliberations, and suggested they bring an overnight bag when they returned the next day.

Separating the jury from the participants in the trial had not always been possible in the small courtroom. At one point, during a break, the news media noticed one of the jurors standing at the defense table, cheerily talking to the defendant. The judge was informed of the breach of protocol and he admonished the juror about future contact with lawyers or the defendant in the case.

*F*inal arguments began on Friday, November 13. After Judge Wisser read the charge, he announced that each side had two hours to sum up its case. First up was the prosecution. Bryan Case opened his remarks with an appeal to jurors to use their life experiences to evaluate the evidence the state had brought against Roger Scaggs.

"There are probably eight or nine of you," he said to the jurors, "that for one reason or another know in your heart, or in your gut feeling and from the evidence you have heard, that the armor of presumed innocence once enshrouding that man has come tumbling down, and he stands naked. And you are going to say he's guilty. Then there are two or three of you who are going to say, 'Whoa, wait a minute.'

"I would simply ask the ones who know this man stands naked to be patient with those who want to retain the idealism we would all like to have. Be patient with those who don't want to believe that when they consult a businessman who is prominent in our community, he may be contemplating killing someone. I understand that some of you do not want to think that when you go to church or see a religious function on television where there are preachers, deacons, or elders, you have to wonder if that man is running around with a twenty-eight-year-old woman and planning to get rid of his wife. We don't want to live in that kind of a world.

"During jury selection a woman raised her hand and said, 'You can never understand the mind of a murderer unless you have done it.' You people have not done it. You have been raised to follow the ideals, pursue the dreams of what is good in life—to help others, to take care of others.

"Haven't you seen more denial and hypocrisy here than you have in all your life?" Case asked. "There was denial on Penny's part and hypocrisy on Roger's part. There was a lot of love in that home. A lot of people in this city got a lot of love from it. But it was not a real world because, as much as Penny believed and as much faith as she had, and as much love and guidance and strength as she gave to other women, she was never able to have it flow over to that man." He pointed to Roger.

The prosecutor said the testimony had shown that in her last days, Penny had lost confidence in her ability to continue her ministry because she sensed that her "very foundation was about to be wiped out from under her. She could sense it from the time of her sickness in the fall, the meeting in January when someone suggested her husband might be having an affair, to the weekend before, when she was so frantic to get back to see him. Penny sensed the foundation was crumbling and she was about to lose the entire meaning of her life, which was her ministries. It was coming. She could feel it. On March 6, 1996, she was uncertain that she could continue her teaching. And on that same day, this man came home and killed her.

"Don't ever think that this defendant was not fully, fully aware of their social position in this community, of the importance of their relationship to his clients. How much of Roger's image of integrity at APS Systems depended on Penny Scaggs? Do you realize how much of his business success actually came from Penny? Everything good in Roger Scaggs's world came from Penny.

"You may think he is a smart man," Case continued. "But think how the subconscious mind speaks when the reflective mind would say 'watch it.' His subconscious was speaking when he wore a red, white, and blue jacket with the symbol of freedom on the back. That was his subconscious speaking. His subconscious spoke when he told Mrs. Coleman, 'I could be married two or three times over in a year.' How many times did his subconscious speak? Too many to count.

"Did he ever ask anyone what's wrong with my wife, what's the extent of her injuries?" Case said he did not ask because he knew the answer.

"Why did he *hate* her?" Case raised his voice and pounded his fist on the table when he said the word "hate." "The defense wants to talk to you about a madman, someone driven by extreme rage. He may be ridiculous, but he is not a madman."

Case said that the defendant had the nerve to murder her and then tell her sisters and best friends that he did not want to pay for her funeral and that he would soon remarry.

He told the jury that Roger could not divorce Penny because she would get well over half of the wealth the family had amassed. He could not divorce her because so much of his own image depended on her. "Everywhere he goes people look up to him, especially in the faith community. He had nowhere to go. He was not going to divorce this woman. So he just got rid of her."

Bryan Case concluded his presentation by running through the tangible evidence that had been entered by the state, including the incriminating gloves, the steel pipe and carving knife, and the "stolen" jewelry. At one point he picked up the galvanized steel pipe and invited the jurors to try to swing it during their deliberations. He pointed out that it was designed to be a weapon. "You have to have a cap on it, like this, or it would get away from you," he said.

He reviewed the DNA evidence that had obviously befuddled the jury for so many days of the trial. Case insisted the evidence showed that the mystery DNA resulted from contamination and was not a human mix contributed by the victim and an unknown intruder. He directly discredited the defense theory that the trash bag was placed in the Dumpster by the real killer in order to frame the defendant.

"Where are all the people who hated Roger Scaggs enough to kill his wife and frame him?" Case asked.

"Not only did his words in the days after the murder speak for him," Case concluded. "But his actions spoke loudly, too. People who knew Roger and Penny were shocked to find out he used his daughter Sarah's apartment to further the affair. It's a tragedy. Sarah has lost her mother, and now she is going to lose her father. It's too bad that she is going to have to pay for what this defendant has done.

"If it had not been for some sharp detective work, you would never have had to be exposed to this kind of hypocrisy from a church elder, this kind of arrogance that he didn't even think he would be questioned by the police."

Case implored the jury not to send a message to the community that a wealthy man could "buy his way out of murder."

Chapter 25

*R*andy Leavitt opened his side's summation by addressing the physical evidence from the defense perspective. In his first remarks, he also rebutted what he described as the state's "character assassination" of the defendant.

"This is a common prosecution tactic," he told the jury. "They do it because studies show that juries are more likely to convict people they do not like. They have attacked his character in his business dealings, the fact he had an affair with a young lady. They say he is not a good husband because he did not take good care of his wife when she was sick. But all of this has absolutely nothing to do with this case. People remember things differently, and the way they remember things is influenced by their perception of how they think a situation should be resolved.

"Fortunately, the one thing we don't have to depend on people's opinions for is the physical evidence," Leavitt said. "The evidence does not lie. Not one bit of the evidence at that house links Roger Scaggs to this crime."

He described the meticulous work of the Austin Crime

Scene Search team in gathering every "tiny little bit of evidence they could find."

Leavitt walked the jury through the fingerprint evidence that showed about twenty-five locations where fingerprints were taken from the downstairs area of the house. In particular, he pointed to the readable but unidentified prints found low on the piano leg, inches from where Penny's head came to rest during the attack.

"These prints, six inches from the floor, could have been the prints of the killer," Leavitt said. "Do you think the killer might have reached over and grabbed the piano leg for balance when he was taking the jewelry from Penny? They have never identified it."

Other readable but unmatched fingerprints were found in three of the rooms where the killer was that night, including prints on a kitchen counter, the master bathroom sink, and a jewelry box emptied into the bathtub.

Leavitt argued that when the police found the plastic bag in the Dumpster on March 8, they stopped looking at evidence that might lead them in any direction other than toward Roger Scaggs. He said they also never looked for prints on the back door, even though it was found unlocked the night of the murder.

Leavitt reminded the jury that the state's own expert, Donna Stanley, had concluded that DNA taken from three separate places had produced a mixture of human DNA. Tests done on the victim's fingernails, the watery spot of blood on the kitchen countertop, and a small human hair from the carving knife all showed extraneous DNA mixed with Penny's. The weak DNA from the second person, who was as yet unidentified, was described as the type that would possibly be found in saliva rather than blood.

Roger had been eliminated as the contributor of the second DNA in that mystery mix, Leavitt noted. He told the jury that when the crime lab ran these controversial DNA samples a second time, the tests again showed there was a mix of two types of human DNA.

Leavitt concluded that the Austin police had not pursued the evidence that would have led to the real killer in this case, and that the prosecution had simply not made its case that Roger Scaggs was the killer.

Roy Minton took the second part of the defense team's final argument. He described his client as a highly successful businessman and good church member whose career and life had been besmirched unnecessarily by the prosecution. He said that the demands of his job as a chief executive invariably conflicted with his home life, as all executives' jobs did.

"The state has decided that because they do not have sufficient evidence to be able to establish that Roger went home and for some reason out of nowhere murdered his wife in the most brutal manner that you can imagine, they are going to have to make a demon out of Roger Scaggs," Minton told the jury. "And that is what they have spent 90 percent of their time doing. The evidence shows no such thing."

Minton denied there was any divorce under consideration, and said the prosecution had invented the story that Roger would lose 70 to 80 percent of the family's assets if he tried to divorce Penny.

He refuted the testimony of friends and family who said Roger had treated Penny badly while she was sick.

"Where is the evil in what that guy did? Where is the wrong in what Penny did?" Minton asked. He said the prosecution had painted a picture of terrible things Roger had done in the marriage that did not amount to "a hill of beans."

"The one incident of a heated family argument over towels ten years before at the condo in Colorado was the only evidence of Roger ever losing his temper in his entire life!" Minton exclaimed. "They must not have much faith in their evidence if they come out with this on the last day of trial.

"As to motive," he continued, "they have tried to tell you that Penny was an unhappy person. There is no evidence that Penny was unhappy." He pointed out that she had met Roger at home for lunch on March 6, and later that after-noon asked a friend to pray for Roger because he had an important presentation the next day.

He then turned to the topic of the girlfriend.

"The affair is a hard row for Roger and for me," Minton said. "Lots and lots of men have sexual relations with women other than their wives. Even so, some of those mar-riages are sometimes not the worse for wear. Of course, it is a bad idea; but there is no evidence that Penny had snapped to the fact that Roger was taking someone to a hotel. I do not believe in that conduct, but it does not lead us to a cause of murder. There is no evidence that Roger wanted a divorce.

"But in Texas, no matter if your spouse wants it or not, anyone can get a no-fault divorce in sixty days," he pointed out. "They said it would ruin him with his customers. All of this is the imagination of the prosecution, or I should say, they want *you* to imagine it. *Good night nurse!* To say he is going to kill his wife to keep from getting a divorce because if he got divorced he might lose business. That is going so far—it's an incredible stretch.

"They would have you believe that he went home for din-ner and took this pipe and bludgeoned his wife to death and stabbed her eight times after that because he was having stress in his business," Minton argued. He pointed out that the top executives at the company had testified that Roger was doing fine at work.

The defense attorney argued there would have been no financial gain to Roger as a result of the murder.

Minton said the matter of Roger's demeanor after the murder was only the manifestation of a corporate executive handling a crisis the way he had been trained to handle it, with calm and reflection.

"They want to punish him for being a man about his prob-lems," said Minton. "He has conducted himself like a man, and they can't stand it." He argued that on the day of the murder, Roger was doing what he had done dozens of times before. He was completely absorbed in preparing for a very important meeting of the corporate board of directors. He was intently focused on a major presentation.

"Does he have on his mind some fat-bottomed young thing that at times he goes out to a motel with, or wherever?" asked Minton, incredulous. "No he does not! He is getting ready for the board meeting. Is this a marriage falling apart? Is this a man who is sitting around planning to murder his wife?"

Minton went over the timeline with the jurors, pointing out that Roger had been consistent in every statement he ever made about what he did that evening. He said the schedule Roger described to police made sense. It was clear that Detective Carter had urged Roger to try to tell what he thought had happened that night. " 'What do you speculate?' That is what the detective *asked* him to do. Every single thing that Roger has said from the very beginning pans out." He paused for a few seconds.

"Except for the bag that was found in that Dumpster," Minton continued, taking the plastic garbage bag from the evidence table and holding it up. "In it were five gloves. Four of them have fingerprints in them. Those are his prints. Those are his gloves. There is no question in the world about that; those gloves were in this bag out in that garage. The bag was found with leaves and garbage in it, too. There were not two gloves—there were five gloves, and they wound up in this bag.

"I don't know when they got in that bag," Minton said. "And I can't tell you who the killer was. All I can tell you is that finding these gloves in his garbage was not a surprise to us. We have presented testimony that Roger wears these gloves when he does anything. But if you wear these gloves in a vicious attack, and twist and bang a pipe, you would not have the kind of prints that were found in these gloves." He reminded the jury of the expert witness who had testified that after the violent motion necessary to carry out the attack, any prints in the gloves would have been smeared and unreadable.

"So discarded gloves wind up in this Dumpster behind his office," Minton continued, in an effort to minimize the importance of that evidence. "Roger's gloves were found in a garbage bag from Roger's house with other trash from the house. I don't know how the bag got in the Dumpster behind his office. The killer must have been in a panic, grabbed the bag with the gloves and other trash from the garage and thrown the jewelry, the pipe, and knife into the bag. It's all bouncing around in there together. It is no surprise that the gloves would have blood on them, from the blood on these other items coming in contact with them.

"I will never know how the police got on to the bag in the Dumpster, either," Minton said sarcastically. "It is the first time I have seen police confiscate a Dumpster. I do not believe the young officer is lying under oath about it being a hunch and not a tip. But, by golly, it is strange. I have never seen anyone take a crime-scene truck, with all those people and a photographer, to search a Dumpster on a policeman's hunch." He described, with a tone of disbelief, how they had documented every phase of the Dumpster dive and contents with numerous photographs.

"I thought this was crazy—somebody had to be tipping these people [the police] off. But we are stuck with that story," he said. "What we are not stuck with is this: Roger did not have murder on his mind. Are you seriously going to believe that in the middle of everything he was doing that day, that he is going to come home for supper when his wife calls and brutally beat his wife of thirty-five years to death?"

Minton pointed out the conflicting testimony of the state's two medical examiners, Dr. Roberto Bayardo of Travis County and Dr. Vincent DiMaio from Bexar County. Minton gave a somewhat creative interpretation of what the two forensic pathologists said on the stand.

"Bayardo testified that any one of the six blows would have killed her. Every one of those six blows fractured her skull," said Minton. "Bayardo said the other bruises"—the lawyer held up his hands to the jury—"were defense bruises. Then they [the prosecution] go, just like they did with DNA, and get another guy . . . to come up here and take the witness stand without ever having talked to Dr. Bayardo, without having looked at the autopsy. And he tells you, 'Oh no, there weren't but three of those blows that caused a fracture.'

"Why is it that the state puts on their own witness, and then decides they better call in somebody else to clean all that stuff up? Because they wanted somebody to say that she was attacked from the back. I doubt it. I think Penny turned around before anyone got to her, and I think there was some struggle.

"I think that DNA is there [on her hands] and it belongs to somebody else, and by God, it does not belong to that man right there." He pointed to Roger. "Then they hire a high-dollar corporation to send a chemist down here to say that's contaminated and then get on a plane and go home.

"I have thought about it from every viewpoint," Minton concluded. "You have thought about it, too. Did Vanessa do it? Did Sarah do it? No, no, *no!* That stuff is crazy. I do not know who did it. But this evidence does not show that Roger did it. Roger Scaggs is not guilty of murdering Penny."

The defense rested its case.

*A*ssistant District Attorney Buddy Meyer took the prosecution's rebuttal argument to the jury.

"There is nothing on the door of this courtroom that says you must leave your common sense out of the deliberation as you try to reach a verdict 'beyond a reasonable doubt.' The opinions of the defense lawyers are not evidence," said Meyer. "The evidence is what was presented as exhibits in this case and testimony under oath from the witness stand. But when weighing this evidence, you are allowed to use your own common sense."

He went over the key evidence presented by the prosecution during the trial, and then addressed the challenges the defense had raised about some of the state's evidence and testimony.

"It is not unusual that unidentifiable fingerprints will be found at a murder scene in a residence," Meyer explained. "Unidentifiable fingerprints at a scene does not mean that the perpetrator left prints behind."

The previous week Penny had conducted a class of about twenty people in the room where the murder occurred. The Scaggses had a maid who came in once a week to do the vacuuming and dusting. Since she was usually there Thursday mornings, she had not cleaned that room since the last meeting.

"Some of the unidentified prints probably belonged to those who attended that class. We have a responsibility to investigate to the fullest possible extent, to present you the experts and their evidence," he said, "But the police may not be able to answer every question or to identify every fingerprint or fiber left at a scene."

Meyer then addressed the time of death. He said Detective Thompson, who was at the autopsy, had testified that "the contents of Penny's stomach looked like the food in the pot on the kitchen counter, when police arrived that night." Digestion had barely started when she died.

The prosecutor referred to the testimony of the two medical examiners, who had both used food digestion and liver temperature to estimate time of death. "I'm not going to tell you it's an exact science," said Meyer, "because you heard them say it is not.

"The widest range of time that this murder could possibly have taken place was between 5:00 P.M. and 9:00 P.M. The shortest time frame I heard . . . was between five and six o'clock. You have witnesses that he [Roger] left the office at around five-thirty and you have his statement that he ate supper and went back to his office around 7:00 or 7:15 P.M. In the defendant's statement he puts himself in the house during a fraction of the time the experts said this murder occurred. In the narrowest time frame, he is at home."

Responding to Minton's notion that someone else put the murder weapons on top of the garbage at Roger's house, the prosecutor said the garbage had been taken out to the street and picked up the afternoon of the murder. All the trash would have been taken away.

"There would have been no garbage in the trash bag in the garage," said Meyer. He said there was no other trash from the house in the bag containing the weapons, gloves, and jewelry, and that any leaves there must have come from the Dumpster. "Everything in that bag was put in that bag after the defendant killed Penny," he said.

Meyer arranged the damning gloves on the railing in front of the jury box.

"The defendant's fingerprints were found in four of these five gloves," Meyer said. "Both fingerprint experts—the defense witness and the witness for the prosecution—said there is no doubt they are the prints of the defendant. It's probable there were latex gloves in a box in the garage that night—you've seen the photographs."

The prosecutor reminded the jury that on at least one of the gloves (glove number one) Penny's blood was found on both the inside and outside.

"There were bloodstains found inside these gloves. There is no way that the blood from the victim could have gotten inside the gloves except for the defendant to have gotten blood on his hands and then put the gloves on. There is no way the blood could have been transferred to the gloves after the other items were tossed in the bag and rattled around."

Meyer said he wasn't going to talk about the DNA, except to say one thing: "It is real simple. They want the DNA to be a mixture. It is not a mixture. It is contamination, and has nothing to do with who killed Penny Scaggs."

He said that in the spring of 1995, Roger decided he was going to have an affair with a twenty-eight-year-old employee from his company. "That relationship went on up until Penny's death, and even after Penny's death. The defense wants you to believe we are involved in a character assassination to get a conviction. We do not make up the evidence in the case; we bring you the evidence. It is your prerogative to decide what the facts are, and if you do not think it's important, that is your decision.

"The evidence is clear that Penny was sitting at the piano when she was attacked, and there is no way that she was able to resist the attack by Roger Scaggs," Meyer said. "I say Roger Scaggs because he puts himself at the scene in his own statement. After they got through dinner, she put the dishes on the kitchen counter. She thought Roger had gone back to work."

Meyer picked up the pipe and approached the jury box. "Penny went to the piano to play. He wanted Penny to think he had gone back to work, and he did. But the evidence shows that first he went into the garage and got a pipe and went back into the house. He viciously beat her to death with this pipe.

"In the process of that vicious attack the music was knocked from the piano. An earring and her glasses were thrown across the room."

The state's lawyer laid the pipe down and picked up the carving knife.

"After he was finished hitting her with the pipe, he took this knife and began to cut and stab her because he had to make it look like the murder was committed by an angry, vicious person that would not be within his character. When he got through stabbing her, he staged the crime scene, for whatever reason. You saw that he put the music back, but did not realize it was upside down.

"At some time in setting up the crime scene he unlocked the back door. He went into the master bathroom and took the drawers and contents of the jewelry box and threw it into the bathtub to make it look like a burglary. He also went into the kitchen and cleaned off the pipe and knife, and took the jewelry off Penny—the ring, the necklace, and the bracelet, leaving one of the necklaces. At some point he put on and took off gloves. He then placed all this evidence in the bag.

"He left the house with only a very short time frame within which to dispose of the evidence. He had to be able to show he had been at the office at a specific time. He knew the routine in terms of the trash pickup. Because he was short on time and knew the routine, and because the Dumpsters were a safe place, he threw the bag into the Dumpster.

"It makes sense—the time frame, the comfort zone, and knowing the Dumpsters would be picked up," Meyer said. "If the trash pickup had been on time and the Dumpsters hauled away before Detective Carter called to have them secured, we would not be here today. But thank gosh the trains weren't running on time.

"Based on the detective's training and experience, after talking to Roger Scaggs and having his suspicions raised, he had the Dumpsters secured.

"Why would somebody who had been married to someone for thirty-five years, shortly after she had been murdered, say to a number of different people, 'You know I am going to remarry'? Why would Roger say something about remarrying to her sister when she came down here for the memorial service? Why, at the burial of his wife, would he wear a loud jacket with an eagle on the back of it?

"Because he had now been freed, and he could carry on his affair without paying any penalty. This is not a character assassination. This is a crime of greed and lies, and there was no other way to end the marriage," Meyer said.

The prosecutor reminded the jury that the first emergency crews on the scene had not observed any blood on Roger's clothing. All the bleeding was around Penny's head and on the carpet and on her clothing.

"A man who has been married to a woman for thirty-five years . . . tells the detective, 'Penny and I have a wonderful marriage,' goes into the house and finds his wife lying in a pool of blood.

"What would someone do? They would go to their knees and pick the person up to see what was the matter." Meyer dropped to his knees on the floor in front of the jury and went through the motions of tenderly wrapping his arms around a body. "In doing that, they would have blood on them. Roger didn't do that because he knew—because he did it.

"The defendant has some of the best lawyers in the country, the best jury, and a very competent judge," said Meyer. "I want you to be Penny's jury. I don't want you to leave this courthouse and ever think you arrived at the wrong verdict. The correct verdict in this case is that Roger Scaggs is guilty of murdering Penny Scaggs; not because I say it, but because the evidence proves it."

At the end, Meyer stood before the jury holding a large portrait of Penny Scaggs in a vibrant red dress, smiling, her chin propped on one hand.

"I want you to remember Penny the way God made her," he said, "and not what the defendant did to her."

The judge ordered the jury to begin deliberations at 2:30 P.M. They had a late lunch sent in. The first vote they took was eight for guilty and four for not guilty. They asked for a tape player so they could hear Roger's 911 call the night of the murder. The prosecutor had entered the tape into evidence but had not played it. The jurors deliberated until

9:30 P.M. before asking the court to allow them to retire for the evening without reaching a verdict.

A half-dozen newspeople were still sitting in the court-room, talking. As they walked out, one reporter turned to another and said, "I hope Roger's not superstitious. Today is Friday the thirteenth."

Chapter 26

After a night locked up in a downtown hotel under the watchful eye of court bailiffs, the jurors returned to the courtroom at 8:50 Saturday morning to resume deliberations. A short time later they sent a note to the court asking for additional information on three pieces of evidence. The jurors wanted to review testimony by Detective J. W. Thompson about the clothing found in the laundry; Detective Carter's testimony about the time the Dumpsters had been picked up by the trash removal company; and testimony about latex glove number five rendered by fingerprint expert Glenn Unnasch.

At 10:50 A.M. the jury sent Judge Wisser a second note, announcing they had reached a verdict. The courtroom was empty, except for a gaggle of reporters. All the parties to the case had returned to their offices in anticipation of a long wait. Since the jury had deliberated seven hours on the previous day, no one expected a verdict so quickly.

Gradually, the representatives for the defense and prosecution drifted back and took their seats in the courtroom.

Roger and Sarah walked in together. They were sitting at the defense table chatting when Penny's three sisters arrived and took their usual seats at the front of the visitors' section. Tensions were high. The parties barely spoke as they waited. At last Judge Wisser entered, took his seat on the high bench, and told the bailiff to bring in the jury.

A row behind the sisters was filled with spectators who had earlier been identified as friends of Penny Scaggs. Some of these women sat holding hands; two were crying softly. Across the aisle, a small gathering of members of the First Evangelical Free Church sat silently. Several of them were obviously in deep prayer, with their heads bowed, their lips slightly moving. Judge Wisser whispered to the bailiff that he wanted extra deputies sent down to the courtroom from the sheriff's department offices upstairs. When the jurors were seated, the judge asked simply, "Does the jury have a verdict?"

The foreman rose and without hesitation read, "We the jury find the defendant, Roger Thomas Scaggs, guilty of the offense of the murder as alleged in the indictment."

Roger Scaggs looked momentarily stunned. Then the taciturn expression he had worn during most of the trial turned to a grimace as he squeezed his eyes and lips tightly together. Judge Wisser quickly thanked the jury and dismissed the members until 10:00 A.M., Monday, at which time the jury would hear testimony for the sentencing phase of the trial.

As the jurors filed out, Sarah Scaggs came forward from her seat in the audience and went to her father's side at the defense table. She knelt and embraced him. Roger Scaggs began crying silently. He clenched and unclenched his fists in his lap. The lawyers on the defense side looked bewildered by the verdict. The two prosecutors showed no sign of emotion. The sisters, still in their seats, immediately pulled out their cell phones to call others in the family.

As four burly deputies approached Roger, he handed his wallet to his daughter and rose to his feet. A deputy placed his arms behind him and snapped handcuffs on his wrists. With Roger in tow, the officers began making their way through the crowd that had gathered in the courtroom. In the hallway, television camera lights flooded the scene. The officers led Roger down the long corridor to a secured area used to move prisoners through the building. Reporters shouted questions at Roger. His only response to any of them was, "They got the wrong man."

Out on the street, he was led across the plaza, where more TV cameras whirred as he passed, manacled between deputies, to an awaiting paddy wagon for transport to the main county jail. With the verdict in, he was not permitted to remain free before sentencing. He would spend the weekend in the same jail where he had been held after his arrest more than two years earlier.

The defense of Roger Scaggs had been passionate and professional. It was adequately if not liberally funded, with Roger paying approximately $300,000 in legal fees and expenses to the defense team for the effort. The fee was believed to be far less than the going rate for the attorneys who comprised his defense team, especially for legal services of this complexity and duration.

The defense had posited a plausible theory that someone else had murdered Penny Scaggs and framed Roger by planting evidence—including the gloves he routinely wore to clean his private plane—in the Dumpster behind his office.

But the defense case, put on by an expert legal team headed by the renowned Roy Minton, was brought low in the final deliberations by a tiny piece of evidence: traces of fingerprints in blood-splattered, fifteen-cent latex gloves. In expressing his disappointment over the verdict, Minton told Court TV's Clara Tuma, "The physical evidence was compelling. It was my responsibility to get around it, and I didn't get around it."

Although the defendant had been found guilty by a jury, the defense had not lost everything. Roger had enjoyed nearly three years of freedom during the long series of delays between the murder and the trial. And the death penalty, which Texas is so notorious for imposing, had been kept off the table from the beginning. He was going to prison; but would it be for the rest of his life, or with the hope of spending some of his remaining golden years on parole?

Judge Wisser resumed the Scaggs trial at 10:00 A.M., Monday, November 16, for the sentencing phase. In Texas, a convicted defendant can opt to have the sentence set by either the jury or the trial judge. Roger had requested that the jury decide his fate.

Penny's sisters, who had attended every minute of the three-week trial, came together once again for the sentencing phase. As they had throughout the trial, each woman wore a lapel pin made from a shiny 1996 penny, to signify the year she was killed.

In the Scaggs case, the sentencing phase of the trial was extremely important. The jury had wide leeway in the length of prison term it could assess for murder. There was a great deal at stake for Roger in the jury's decision. With a sentence of less than fifteen years, the judge would have discretion to grant an appeal bond, under which Roger could remain free during the lengthy appeals process. A sentence of fifteen years or more required him to begin serving prison time while his appeals were heard.

The prosecution and defense put on only two witnesses each in this phase of the trial.

Marilyn Muecke, one of the twin sisters, was the first witness for the prosecution. She said that for the past two and a half years she had assumed Penny's role as the primary caregiver of the aging parents, both of whom were in nursing homes in the Dallas area at the time of the trial. Prior to her death, Penny, who was the eldest of the four daughters, had the primary role of taking care of the parents, since she did not work and the other sisters had jobs.

"Nothing like this has ever happened in our family," Marilyn said from the stand. "After March of 1996, my parents never recovered. They had some health problems, but were able to do so much for themselves. They have never come back. They were doubled over in pain and they have never been able to stand up again. The loss of their daughter and the hurt that it has caused by their son-in-law has crushed them."

Choking back tears, she said, "My dad has pain and anger in his eyes. Mother's spirit has been crushed."

Mrs. Muecke said that the murder had destroyed her own family's happiness and tranquility forever. "There is a wide, black, dark line across our lives now. Our lives are divided by that line into before Penny and after Penny. I have to go over and over and over again explaining to my children why this happened. I am a person of faith and my faith has been shaken to the ground. If this could happen to Penny, it could happen to me. This is not an intrusion from the outside; it is something from within the family. My faith and trust in everything has been shattered."

The sister said it had also been humiliating because people she meets now question what is wrong with a family in which a husband kills his wife. She said all the years of the family tradition of gathering for Christmas had been destroyed.

Next, the eldest sister, Sharon Fox, took the stand for the second time in the trial. She testified that she had been plagued by nightmares since the murder. The nightmares were that she, too, would be killed and unable to take care of her sisters or parents. Mrs. Fox also said her faith had also been shaken. Shortly after the murder she had sought assistance from grief counseling services.

The defense asked the state to stipulate that Roger Scaggs had never been convicted of any crime, other than a traffic violation, anywhere in the world. The prosecution agreed to the request.

Ken Shifrin, Roger's former boss, took the stand as the

first defense witness. He talked about how well Roger handled pressure on the job during the fourteen years they had worked closely together.

"I have known Roger during some tough periods [for the company], in good times and bad times," the chief executive officer of APS Group testified. "I have never heard him say a negative thing, even when there was a lot of stress. Roger always cared about his employees and did all he could for them. He loved Penny and Sarah and talked about them often.

"I know the jury has made its decision and I still can't imagine that. But when he returns to society, I know he will make a good citizen. I know he will have a tough time finding a job; but when he does, he will do it well."

On cross-examination, ADA Case said, "Is it clear that you, sitting there right now, do not believe that Roger Scaggs is guilty of this offense?"

"Yes it is," Shifrin replied.

Case asked the executive if he was aware that Scaggs had continued the affair with Vanessa after Penny's murder, to which he replied, "I've become aware of it recently."

"Do you have any comprehension of the hurt and pain that this defendant has caused so many members of this community?" Case asked.

"The hurt and pain has been awful for a lot of people. I understand that," Shifrin said.

"Are you aware that the murder of Penny Scaggs has caused hundreds of people in the evangelical church community to have their faith in humanity and in their God called into doubt?" Case pressed.

"Yes, Penny Scaggs was a wonderful person. I don't question that," the executive said.

Then the prosecutor posed a question to the defense witness that summed up the purpose of why they were there.

"Shouldn't a person who killed Penny be put in the penitentiary for a long, long time?"

"Yes," Shrifrin said grimly. When he left the stand, he

went over to Roger and hugged him before walking out of the room.

The only other defense witness in the sentencing phase was Roger and Penny's daughter Sarah. Many people had wanted to hear from her, but she had not testified during the guilt phase of the trial. On the way up to the stand she paused to embrace her father.

Speaking in a small, quiet voice, she told the jury that she was now enrolled as a student at Southwest Texas State University in San Marcos, Texas, with a 4.0 grade average. She was also employed as a part-time health-care worker at a psychiatric clinic in Dripping Springs, Texas.

Under questioning by Minton, she admitted to having gone through some rocky times with her mother during her teen years. "It was rough," she said. But Minton put that in perspective.

"You know, without any doubt, that your mother was a wonderful gal, do you not?" the attorney asked.

"She was," said Sarah.

"And you loved her deeply?" asked Minton.

"Very deeply," she said.

"Has your relationship with your daddy been good?" the lawyer asked.

"Always." Sarah said her father had always been loving, supportive, and caring. "He is . . . he's the most wonderful man I know. My father was always very patient with me, even when I didn't give him a lot of cause to be patient. He was very loving," she said.

Minton asked Sarah how she found out about her mother's death. She described how her father told her.

"He came over to my house and I opened the door, and he said, 'She's dead.' And he broke down and he cried . . . much as he's doing now." She looked over at her father.

Roger, who had been mostly stoic and unemotional throughout, had begun crying when his daughter described her feelings for him. Someone had handed him a large wad of tissues, and he mopped his eyes, one and then the other, repeatedly.

On the night of the murder, Sarah said her father was "very grief stricken." She said before that night, she had only seen him cry once—at his father's funeral. "Since my mother's death I have seen him cry several times."

Roger's eyes, now red and swollen, continued to fill with tears. He dabbed at his eyes and blew his nose.

Sarah explained that the testimony the jury had heard about Roger appearing cavalier at the graveside was false. She said that everyone in the family had agreed to wear casual clothing and that the bright leather jacket was not as outrageous a display as had been described. "My mother loved that jacket," she said.

Then Minton led Sarah through a series of questions, obviously designed to bring home the fact that she had lost a beloved mother to murder and was now in danger of losing her father to incarceration.

"Has your mother's death been a terrible loss to you?" he asked

"More than anyone will ever know," she said.

"And the loss of your daddy, to whatever extent that is . . . will you tell us what that is going to be?"

"It will be very hard," Sarah said haltingly.

When she paused, Minton asked, "Are you going to be all right?"

"I'll be fine," she said.

The state had no questions, and Sarah left the stand. She again embraced her father on her way out of the courtroom.

The prosecution began summation for the sentencing phase, with Bryan Case once more taking the argument to the jury.

The veteran prosecutor told the jury that Roger Scaggs's crime had hurt literally hundreds of people in the community and across the state. He said that what Roger did was worse than the petty crimes of a career criminal. And he said the lack of any evidence of his remorse was obvious in the way he acted after the murder.

"He slapped the face of those women," he said, dramatically pointing to the sisters seated on the front row, "members of his and Penny's church, and fellow employees." He asked the jury to send Roger Scaggs away for a "long, long time" as deterrence. Probation was completely inappropriate in a case like this one.

"What are we, as a community, going to tolerate?" Case asked. Answering his own question, he said, "We cannot tolerate this, especially from a person in a position of leadership and trust. The state asks for a lengthy, severe prison sentence, and I submit that is exactly what the evidence supports."

When Charles Burton rose for the defense, he reminded the jury that the "defense witnesses testifying here were friends of both Roger and Penny, not just Roger. They simply did not believe that Roger Scaggs was the kind of man capable of committing such an act. There are twelve of you here that can consider the wonderful lady Penny was, but also the kind of person Roger has been all his life. Do not return a verdict for the community or the press, but a sentence from your own conscience.

"This is a man who led an exemplary life for fifty-six years," Burton said. "You may feel that something snapped or broke. But consider the kind of person he is now; because at fifty-nine years of age, any sentence you give will affect the rest of his life."

Buddy Meyer argued for the prosecution that anything less than a life sentence for a crime so brutal would be a travesty.

"His age has absolutely nothing to do with your decision. This is a court of justice, not a court of mercy. There is absolutely no mitigation in this case. Can you conceive of any murder case that is worse than what you have heard here in the last three weeks? He very brutally murdered her, and for absolutely no reason at all, knowingly and intentionally. Anything less than a life sentence is a victory for Roger

Scaggs. He has taken everything from this community, from his own family."

At exactly noon the jury retired to deliberate.

In 1998, under Texas sentencing guidelines for a murder conviction, the jury had two main options: life in prison, or a term of years no less than five and no more than ninety-nine. In addition, the jury could add a maximum fine of $10,000 to the sentence. At the time, there was no provision for life without the possibility of parole.

Offenders who commit a crime of "aggravated violence," such as murder, must serve half their sentences in actual time before becoming eligible for parole. If the sentence is sixty years or more, they must serve a minimum of thirty years before parole eligibility.

Parole eligibility is determined by the Texas Board of Pardons and Paroles. Good-conduct time is granted at the discretion of the prison warden. Good-conduct time is necessary to be considered for parole, but cannot shorten the minimum required sentence.

The jury was out for only two and a half hours before notifying the judge it had agreed upon a sentence. The courtroom was packed again when the jurors returned from their deliberations. Behind the last row of seats stood a phalanx of police officers, with a half-dozen deputies in uniform and as many plainclothes detectives.

Judge Wisser asked the foreman to announce the sentencing verdict. The foreman read: "We the jury, having found the defendant guilty of the offense of murder, assess his punishment at confinement in the institutional division at the Texas Department of Criminal Justice for a term of thirty-two years and a fine of $10,000."

The judge imposed the sentence and thanked the jury for its service.

Roger was fifty-nine years old at the time of the verdict. He would have to serve at least half of the thirty-two-year sentence, which meant he would be seventy-five years old before he was eligible for parole.

An appeal was certain in the case.

The sisters expressed disappointment that Roger had not been given a life sentence. Resigned, Carolyn said, "We can at least sleep in peace for the next sixteen years."

For twin Marilyn, there was a finality to it. "Penny would never have divorced Roger, but our family wants a divorce from him. We do not want to ever see or talk to Roger Scaggs again."

Chapter 27

A man who had his every whim catered to by a self-styled subservient wife for almost all his adult life must have found his first prison job as kitchen helper in a sprawling transit and evaluation unit particularly hellish.

Roger's relative wealth, which had bought him more than two years of freedom before his trial, could do little for him where he was headed after his conviction and sentencing for murder.

Roger went straight into the Texas Department of Criminal Justice system at the Holliday Transfer Facility on the outskirts of Huntsville, Texas. He spent his first six months of incarceration at the center, where newly arriving male convicts are diagnosed for physical health and mental condition and evaluated for suitable placement in a permanent prison. Texas operates ninety-six prison units of various types throughout the state.

In recent years much has been written about the Texas penal system being run by the inmates and out of the control of the guards and wardens. While the state's prisons are certainly not the worst in America, the Texas system is over-crowded and understaffed. Texas prison guards, among the lowest paid in the country, are also the lowest paid officers in the state's criminal justice system, earning far less than the average metropolitan police officer, sheriff's deputy, or highway patrolman. Unsatisfactory compensation results in tremendous turnover of personnel at all the prison units and little time to train the replacements. Texas prison funding is considered scandalous, and a low priority for the conservative politicians who assumed almost total control of state government in the early 1990s.

Starvation budgets for the rapidly growing prison population, resulting from stricter sentencing laws, has created what was described as "a fatal environment" by Nate Blakeslee in the *Austin Chronicle*. The investigative reporter, who examined the alarming increase in assaults by inmates on prison personnel, found that security in the state system began to deteriorate rapidly in the late 1990s and early 2000s. More than two thousand Texas prison guards were assaulted by inmates in 1999, Roger Scaggs's first year in prison, compared with only 133 such assaults in 1988. Inmate-on-inmate assaults were also higher during this period. Those who argue that "the inmates are running the institution" may have a good case to make.

The Texas inmate population explosion began in the 1990s, when the public became angered by the revolving door in the state's prisons. The state tried to maintain a manageable prison population by discharging inmates, regardless of their suitability for parole, at approximately the same rate that Texas courts were sending new convicts into the system. When the public demanded that convicts serve longer portions of their sentences, the legislature had to quickly expand capacity and went on a prison-building frenzy. But the lawmakers, either cynically or negligently, did not provide enough new funding to improve management and operations of the system itself.

In 1999, as Roger was adjusting to prison life, Texas temporarily attained the dubious distinction of housing the largest number of convicts of any system in the United States. That year, the prison population soared to 163,190. Texas has since dropped to second place behind California, but its prison population remains consistently high, hovering around 165,000 inmates. The entire federal prison population is only slightly larger than that of the Texas state system.

It has been said that prisons have become the universities for violent gangs. The number of prison gangs affiliated with notorious criminal organizations outside the walls has increased in Texas, as in other systems across the country. In this regard, Roger's advancing age may work to his advantage. The old-timers are of little value or interest to the prison gangs, either inside or outside prison, and if they stay clear of the gangs and mind their own business, they are usually ignored.

For the first time in his life Roger Scaggs's day-to-day existence was completely out of his control, as he faced the harsh reality of a long-term sentence in this system. Just as he had clung to the belief that a jury would find him innocent of the murder of his wife, he now held onto hope that his sentence would be overturned on appeal.

The initial effort to get a new trial was directed at the district court where he had been convicted. Ironically, his former girlfriend, who had become the object of a nationwide search when a material-witness warrant was issued after her disappearance, was once again in the newspaper headlines. The young woman had returned to Austin, providing no public explanation for where she had been before or during the trial.

Defense attorney Randy Leavitt filed a motion with Judge Jon Wisser for a new trial, based on the reappearance of Roger's principal alibi witness. Leavitt maintained that her testimony would have had a material impact on the outcome of the trial, and that a new trial was merited, since this witness was now available.

Vanessa Ferguson was represented by one of Austin's most successful criminal lawyers, Joseph A. (Joe) Turner. He provided the defense lawyers with an affidavit signed by Ferguson that supported Roger's alibi about his whereabouts the night of the murder. The document also denied that the affair had been serious enough to be the motive for murder. In the affidavit, she verified that neither Roger nor the defense team had anything to do with her leaving town, although she did not shed any light on why or where she had gone.

Leavitt's motion for a new trial also made the unusual claim that one of the original jurors for the Scaggs trial was mentally incompetent to serve, due to the effects of childhood encephalitis.

Judge Wisser quickly turned down the motion for a new trial based on the defense effort to have the original verdict thrown out.

While his personal assets had been substantially depleted by the trial, Roger still had the financial means to fund a vigorous appeal. At the end of the murder trial, lawyer Roy Minton had briefly mentioned his client's legal expenses and finances in an interview with Court TV's Clara Tuma. Minton said he believed Roger still had "several hundred thousand dollars," even after paying for his initial defense, which would be more than enough for the appeals process. Minton claimed that, although Penny's will had left everything to Roger, he had "waived it" and given the money to Sarah.

After being turned down for a new trial at the local court level, Roger hired the law firm of Joe Turner—the same attorney representing Vanessa—to take his case to the state appeals courts. Turner, nicknamed "Mad Dog" when he was a prosecuting attorney, because of his aggressive courtroom tactics, headed the largest practice in Austin devoted entirely to criminal law. Since opening his own practice in the late eighties, he had won numerous criminal cases at trial or on appeal. But even he acknowledged that in Texas's hard-nosed, law-and-order environment, the state appellate process was skewed against the convicted. Turner had recently succeeded in getting a highly publicized marijuana possession charge dismissed against Texas music icon Willie Nelson, and successfully represented one of the Waco Branch Davidians against federal conspiracy and murder charges. Both those cases received national media coverage.

While working on the Scaggs appeal, Turner represented another client in a case that drew national publicity. Actor Matthew McConaughey was arrested in October 1999 for playing bongo drums quite late into the night, in his posh West Side neighborhood. Police charged that McConaughey was dancing naked and smoking marijuana when they answered complaints of neighbors, and that he resisted arrest. Turner succeeded in getting the charges reduced to a misdemeanor of disturbing the peace, and the actor paid a fifty dollar fine.

The colorful attorney, whose courtroom tactics included highly animated theatrics more frequently seen in TV crime dramas, was also a vintner. He operated his own winery and vineyards, located behind his home in the Texas Hill Country.

Turner's entry into the case caused another flurry of press coverage. The flamboyant lawyer always made sure his clients' cases got the maximum attention at every stage of the process. He believed that the bright lights of public exposure prevented the innocent and the "little man" from being either lost in the system or steamrolled by the powerful state judicial and law enforcement apparatus.

"The pendulum has swung so far to the right in our appellate courts that a convicted person can hardly get a reversal, even when he's innocent," Turner said. "This case goes to the heart of the system. The appeal is not based on some technicality. Every citizen is entitled to an independent judgment.

"Here we had an unqualified juror, and a defendant is entitled to a full jury of twelve qualified peers. Here you have unidentified DNA in the house and on the victim. Here you have a new witness who can testify that the defendant was focused normally on his work, not behaving like a man who had just killed his wife of thirty-five years. This is how innocent people are sent to prison. Here you have reasonable doubt."

A defense attorney in Turner's office with strong credentials as an appeals specialist was assigned the Scaggs file and began the process. The appeals lawyer was Terrence (Terry) W. Kirk, an honors graduate of the University of Texas Law School. He had amassed an impressive legal record for gaining dismissals and reversals of cases in both pretrial and post-trial proceedings before state and federal courts in Texas.

If Joe Turner was reputed to be a "mad dog" for his aggressiveness in the courtroom, Terry Kirk could be characterized as a "bulldog" for the tenacity he brought to the cases he handled during the laborious appeals process. Roger Scaggs's case would be no exception. Like his colorful law partner, Kirk enjoyed an avocation beyond his law practice. He was a professional actor who had played the enigmatic policeman in the cult movie classic *Slacker,* and frequently pursued other acting roles in Austin's budding movie industry.

When the appeals process began, it was estimated that Roger's appeals would cost an additional $50,000. However, before it was over those estimates had grown to between $75,000 and $100,000.

Kirk petitioned the Texas Court of Appeals to reverse the guilty verdict, claiming six points of error in the trial. The points for reversal argued in the appeal faulted the trial court for:

1. Failure of the state court to hold a hearing on a motion for a new trial

2. Denial of the defense motions for a new trial based on the mental disability of one of the jurors

3. Denial of the defense motions to suppress evidence illegally seized from the Scaggs home

4. Admission of evidence about the state's efforts to locate the missing witness

5. Admission of hearsay evidence about Penny's feelings of hurt and upset that Roger had not taken care of her during a recent illness

6. Permitting the state to withhold evidence that DNA in the case might have been contaminated

In answering the appeal, the District Attorney's Office secured sworn affidavits from jurors in the original trial, attesting to the full participation and competence of the juror the defense had claimed was unfit to serve because of mental disabilities.

Following several appearances that concluded with final oral arguments in December 1999, the Texas Court of Appeals denied Roger Scaggs's pleadings on October 18, 2000.

Kirk next prepared a new appeal to the Texas Court of Criminal Appeals, the highest criminal appellate level in the state court system. While that petition, based on the same grounds as the first appeal, was working its way through the lengthy process, Roger became involved in an unusual federal hearing of an entirely different kind, which had nothing to do with his efforts to gain release from prison.

In November 2003 the Federal Communications Commission issued a show cause order to revoke his Advanced Class amateur radio operator license and a license he held to operate amateur radio station W5EBC in Austin. "Mr. Scaggs's murder conviction raises very serious questions as to whether he possesses the requisite character qualifications to be and to remain a Commission licensee and whether his license should be revoked," the FCC said.

Apparently, few people were aware that Roger Scaggs had a ham radio license or that he operated an amateur radio station. He certainly could not be permitted to operate a radio station from a prison cell. Yet, he had held the licenses since 1954, when he was fifteen years old, and had most recently renewed them in 2000, while serving in prison. The licenses were revoked by the FCC at a hearing in Washington, D.C., on April 22, 2004.

Far more serious for Roger was the late 2004 denial of his motion for a new trial by the highest criminal appeals court in Texas. His attorney was still determined to fight.

Terry Kirk immediately began preparing to take the case to the federal appeals court, based on a claim of ineffective counsel at the main trial. It was a tough sell, since Roger had been represented by one of the best criminal-defense teams in Texas. But Kirk was determined to exhaust every legal avenue available to get him a new trial. The federal phase of the appeals process was finally placed before the United States District Court for the western division of Texas. The court was in Austin, where the entire legal process had begun almost six years before.

Although a criminal appeals process is conducted outside the public limelight, in relative obscurity, the Scaggs case was far from forgotten history in the Austin community, or the country, for that matter. Three nationally televised documentaries about the murder of Penny Scaggs were produced and aired well after the public trial was over.

The first documentary was created for Court TV's _Crime Story_ series by independent producer Richard Kroehling. _Crime Story_ is Court TV's cornerstone series in its expanded prime-time programming. Entitled "Death of an Angel: _Texas_ v. _Scaggs_," the two-hour television special first aired in 1999, the year after the trial, and is rerun regularly.

The documentary featured interviews with members of Penny's family, friends, and fellow church members, as well as attorneys, homicide detectives, and forensic specialists involved in the case. Following the premier of that show, Court TV conducted a live Internet chat on Yahoo with Clara Tuma, who had originally covered the trial for Court TV, and Kayte VanScoy, who had covered the trial for the *Austin Chronicle*.

The national coverage of the Austin murder case gained momentum in 2002 when *Dateline NBC*, in a cooperative effort with Court TV, aired a prime-time documentary introduced by anchor Stone Phillips and investigated and narrated by network reporter Sara James. The documentary, entitled "Dead Reckoning," went beyond a rehashing of the brutal murder to take the audience inside the Texas penal system where Roger Scaggs was imprisoned.

Ms. James was able to secure an interview with the convicted husband—the only media exposure Roger had agreed to, since his conviction. Choking back tears, he maintained his innocence, while insisting to the network reporter that he was unjustly incarcerated.

"I still loved my wife; we still had sex; we still traveled together; we still loved each other," he told James, "I was just too greedy and wanted more . . . I'm innocent."

The third national TV documentary of the case, entitled "The Perfect Wife," was produced by A&E for its prime-time *American Justice* series. The hour-long program, narrated by Bill Kurtis, revisited the case through interviews with the principals from law enforcement, the defense and prosecution teams, and family and friends of both the murder victim and her convicted husband.

On December 9, 2005, after more than a year in the federal appellate process, Roger Scaggs's attorney, Terry Kirk, was notified by the U.S. District Court that the latest appeal had been denied. Kirk remained undaunted. He told his client he was prepared to take the case even higher up the federal appeals channels to the Fifth U.S. Circuit of Appeals.

However, ten days later Roger notified the lawyer that he did not intend to pursue it further. He had been in prison for more than seven years, and still had a minimum of nine years to serve before he would be eligible for parole. Kirk said that with the appeals process concluded, Roger's best hope for a shortened sentence was a special-needs parole based on his advancing age. The lawyer acknowledged this leniency was very rarely offered in a tough law-and-order state like Texas.

As a convicted murderer, Roger Scaggs was permanently assigned to the Alfred T. Hughes unit at Gatesville, Texas, a maximum-security prison.

Gatesville is ninety-one miles north of Austin on a rolling plain of short native grass called the Blackland Prairie. While Austin is characterized by its booming high-tech industry, Gatesville is known for its prison industry. The small town is home to five correctional institutions, including two women's prisons, two men's prisons, and the state's largest juvenile detention center. The Hughes unit where Scaggs is incarcerated has an average inmate population of three thousand, and is one of the more modern prison structures in the state, having been opened in 1990. But it looks like what it is—a prison.

The Hughes unit is built just out of sight of the town on a treeless stretch of table-flat farmland, without even a shrub to break the austere background of white, multistoried block buildings. Sometime in the past the inmate laborers were apparently tasked with an attempt at aesthetic improvement by building a series of low rock walls on the outer perimeter of the grounds. But instead of beautifying the grounds, the rough-hewn structures somehow came off looking like a maze leading into the prison.

Inmates, dressed in white baggy trousers and shirts, are restricted to a life almost entirely inside the prison walls and fences. Because it is a maximum-security facility, the long-term inmates are not taken outside the perimeter of the prison to work in the moneymaking agricultural programs that are found at many of Texas's farm units.

When he arrived at Gatesville, the former corporate executive's first regular job was in the prison's gigantic dining hall and kitchen. In his new life, the formerly pampered husband was now a kitchen helper, feeding three thousand convicted hard-timers and cleaning up after them.

Roger's sleeping accommodations were in even starker contrast to the comfort he had previously enjoyed. He was assigned a bunk, a sink, and a toilet in a large, circular block of cells. The housing facilities for inmates of Texas prisons are not air-conditioned, though the summers often bring weeks of three-digit temperatures with high humidity. The cells face a central guard station, from which inmates in this huge section are under constant surveillance.

Roger's day begins in the middle of the night. He is up at 3:00 A.M. for breakfast at 3:30, and works a twelve-hour day, from 5:00 A.M. to 5:00 P.M. From then until bedtime at nine, inmates can read, write, or study.

His many years as a computer expert ultimately won him a better job. He was assigned as an inventory control specialist in the prison's garment factory. There were no extra benefits attached, except that much of the new job was performed in an air-conditioned prison office. While other inmates swelter through the hellish Texas summer heat both in their living quarters and on the job, Roger can escape during work hours to one of the only cool spots in the place.

Prison life in Texas is spartan. The state allots $38.01 per day to house, feed, clothe, and provide health care for Roger and each of his fellow inmates. Most of that is spent on salary for the guards. The state allots $2.21 a day for food and fourteen cents a day for housing for each prisoner at the Hughes unit.

Roger Scaggs's anguish over his new circumstances was apparent during the interview with Ms. James in the *Dateline NBC* documentary.

He lamented that his thirty-two-year sentence amounted to a life term for him, since he would be seventy-five before he was even eligible for parole. The *Dateline* documentary was made before the appeals were exhausted. In that interview, Roger, choking back tears, told the journalist, "No male in my family has lived to seventy-five. I'll die here if I don't get an appeal and a new trial." His father had passed away at the age of seventy-one.

Roger still has a small, and gradually diminishing, circle of stalwart friends who cling to the belief of his innocence despite the jury's decision. He gets an occasional visitor on a Saturday or Sunday, when inmates are allowed one visitor for a two-hour stay. His visitors are treated politely, but must go through three levels of security searches before being allowed into the restricted area. Then they can only talk with him by phone while looking through reinforced glass windows. No touching is allowed—not even a handshake or an embrace.

His daughter Sarah still comes to see him, but her new career and family have taken her far from Texas, and the trips are now infrequent.

Longtime friend Joe Edwards is one of the few who continued to visit Roger after he was transferred to Gatesville. Edwards, who lives at Georgetown, an hour's drive from the prison, has been greatly saddened by his contacts with his old friend from happier days in Killeen in the late 1960s. While he sees Roger less often now, he still corresponds with him and keeps him supplied with the latest books. Roger makes lists of the titles he wants to read and mails them to Edwards, who purchases the books and has them sent to Roger under the vendor's label. Inmates are not allowed to receive books or merchandise directly from individuals. Money must be deposited to a prisoner's account, rather than given to the prisoner directly.

For several years Joe Edwards's wife, who recently passed away, helped Roger with one of his other new prison pastimes. She arranged to have sent to him, in bulk, copies of literature to hand out at a class he had started inside the walls. The literature was a small religious magazine called *The Upper Room*.

Ironically, Roger conducts a Bible study course in prison. His flock is made up of the most hardened convicted criminals—a far cry from the young women who eagerly followed Penny's biblical teachings on how to make a godly home.

Epilogue

*P*enny's parents lived to see Roger imprisoned for the murder of their daughter. Her father died in May 2000, at the age of eighty-five. Mittie Ehrle was ninety-one when she passed away three years later.

Ten years after the murder of their beloved older sister, Sharon Fox, Carolyn Pittenger, and Marilyn Muecke still join in a telephone conference call at 10:00 P.M. on appointed days to hold a prayer circle. The sessions have helped them cope with this family tragedy and keep Penny's memory alive.

As a direct result of the murder, the oldest sister, Sharon, studied and became a certified grief facilitator through the American Academy of Bereavement. She leads a grief-counseling ministry through her church in a suburban community near Dallas.

Roger and Penny's daughter, Sarah, and Penny's sisters have made every effort to put this sad event behind them and come together as a family. Sarah told a television interviewer that the family had "agreed to disagree" about Roger's role in Penny's murder.

In 1999, a year after the trial, Sarah graduated summa cum laude from Texas State University with a Bachelor of Arts degree in Psychology and a minor in Criminal Justice. She received a juris doctor (J.D.) degree from Temple University's James E. Beasley School of Law in 2004. Her aunts Sharon, Marilyn, and Carolyn attended her graduation.

Sarah practices civil law as an associate with a major East Coast law firm and has done pro bono work through the local defenders association. She is married to the man she was dating at the time of her mother's murder.

Homicide detective Sergeant David Carter, whose systematic investigation led to the first break in the murder case, was promoted through the ranks of the Austin Police Department and named assistant chief in March 2006. In October, Carter and other Austin officials went to Iraq to discuss methods for improving that country's emergency services through coordination of local police, fire, and medical response teams.

As of this writing, Roger Scaggs had served eight years in prison, just half the minimum years required before he could be considered for parole. In correspondence with the author, he has held fast to his assertion of innocence.

"The jury was split, but finally convicted me of a crime I did not commit, and sentenced me to thirty-two years in prison," Roger said. "I was tried and convicted primarily on the basis that my affair provided a motive for murder."

Roger has pragmatically accepted that he faces many more years in prison, and recently said he will put this time and place to the best use possible under the reality of the circumstances.

"I see it as a wonderful opportunity to teach and mentor fellow inmates who have not had the same opportunity," he said. "I am now in a unique position to be a surrogate father and mentor to many men. People who are going to school to better themselves can learn academic facts and vocational skills, which are, of course, important. However, the things that determine success in life are strongly related to attitude, work ethic, and social, personal, financial, and organizational skills. These are the things I am trying to model and teach to those around me. Not only may it have a positive influence on others and give them coping skills for their release, but it also gives me a positive agenda."

Under Texas sentencing laws, Roger will be eligible for parole in the year 2014. Penny's sisters plan to protest any early release.